BLAME THE INTERN

Blame the Intern

ON (NOT) BREAKING INTO THE CREATIVE ECONOMY

ALEXANDRE FRENETTE

PRINCETON UNIVERSITY PRESS
PRINCETON & OXFORD

Published by Princeton University Press
41 William Street, Princeton, New Jersey 08540
99 Banbury Road, Oxford OX2 6JX

press.princeton.edu

GPSR Authorized Representative: Easy Access System Europe - Mustamäe tee 50, 10621 Tallinn, Estonia, gpsr.requests@easproject.com

ISBN 978-0-691-18148-6
ISBN (e-book) 978-0-691-28752-2
ISBN (Web PDF) 978-0-691-28473-6

Library of Congress Control Number 2025949887

British Library Cataloging-in-Publication Data is available

Editorial: Rachael Levay and Tara Dugan
Production Editorial: Jill Harris
Jacket Design: Hunter Brand
Production: Erin Suydam
Publicity: William Pagdatoon
Copyeditor: Leah Caldwell

This book has been composed in Arno

Printed in the United States of America

10 9 8 7 6 5 4 3 2 1

For Simone

CONTENTS

Introduction 1

1 The Education-Industrial Complex 28

2 Dealing with an Ambiguous Role 65

3 The New Mailroom 101

4 Laboring to Earn 129

5 Breaking-In Systems in Transition 166

Methodological Appendix 183

Notes 193

References 219

Acknowledgments 243

Index 247

BLAME THE INTERN

Introduction

In a Lonely Place

Sitting at the only occupied table of a nondescript Chinese restaurant near her office, about two years after she graduated from college, Rita tells me about her career path. She recounts that barely a year into college she found herself thinking, "Oh my god, I need a job lined up before I graduate!" An English major aspiring to establish a career in the publishing industry, Rita attempted to secure an unpaid internship in the field in hopes it would help her land a job after college. She became discouraged, however, after being repeatedly turned down because she lacked experience. In the wake of these rejections, Rita padded her résumé with fictional gigs and exaggerated claims of software proficiency. In her sophomore year, to her surprise and delight, she obtained an unpaid internship at a boutique music magazine in Manhattan. As she reflects on her subsequent internship experience, Rita no longer seems delighted; instead, she voices a complaint common among unpaid interns: "I didn't learn a whole lot of anything at my internship."

An internship is, by definition, a practical educational experience. According to popular conceptions and some academic research, doing work under the guidance of employee supervision allows interns to develop skills, gain relevant experience, and build professional networks. For college students, internships ideally complement classroom learning and help them transition into a career. While historically this type of experience was largely limited to vocational fields (e.g., apprenticeships in the skilled trades) and the professions (e.g., medical residency), the intern economy has expanded dramatically in recent decades and internships are now prevalent in nearly every sector of the economy.[1] Thus, while generations of teens and young adults used to work as lifeguards or camp counselors in the summer sun, college students today are more likely to seek office experience as interns. According to the best estimates, in the last few years, nearly two-thirds of US students graduating with a bachelor's degree held an internship during college, compared to only 17 percent in 1992.[2] In the race to become employable, students perceive securing highly competitive internships as crucial to bolstering their education and launching their careers.[3]

As Rita and dozens of unpaid interns from the cultural industries explain in our interviews, however, these arrangements are problematic introductions to the world of work—they often provide little valuable training and are unlikely to lead directly to a job. In this book, I delve into the complexities of internships as an expanding institution, examining the roles of the three key actors—employers, educators, and interns—and demonstrating who benefits and who suffers, and why, within this changing landscape of work and education.

Rita's story epitomizes many of the pitfalls of the intern economy. She says that on a typical day as an intern she would complete filing duties and write as many as fifteen one-page album reviews, which were published in the magazine without attribution or credit. To make matters worse, her supervisor, who spent most of her time on the phone, rarely acknowledged Rita, let alone offered any guidance. Rita recalls, "I thought she was busy. I didn't want to bother her and ask her to do something else." The social chasm she witnessed between employees and interns led her to feel isolated at the office. This feeling was reinforced by the office layout. Laughing, Rita explains that rather than sitting near her supervisor in the busiest area of the office, she was given an undesirable cubicle far from the action—her desk was at the opposite end of the floor, directly under a vent pushing out uncomfortably cold air, and she sat in relative darkness because of the malfunctioning fluorescent lighting. Feeling lost and hopeless, she often hid in the bathroom, sometimes for an hour at a time, to cope with her monotonous duties and avoid her supervisor, who seemed annoyed at the very sight of her. Once she had replenished her courage, she would head back to her desk.

As the weeks passed and the situation did not improve, Rita found herself with nowhere to turn for advice. Her parents, who worked as a bus driver and home cook, offered little guidance. Neither of them had ever been an intern or held a job in an office environment. Her college, part of the City University of New York (CUNY), did not offer much help either. Rita received course credit for the internship, but her department had canceled the weekly seminar in which students formally reflected on their experience and received feedback, instead pointing students to a web page with tips for interns. When I interviewed the department's internship coordinator, he says he asked to cancel the seminar meetings so his students, who were mostly from working-class backgrounds, could spend more time networking at their internships, which he believes will allow them to better compete with interns from more privileged backgrounds—students enrolled at schools such as Columbia and New York University—if a job becomes available. Eventually, a friend offered Rita some encouragement, suggesting that she just try to stick it out at the internship, in case things improved.

As she chronicles her intern experience, Rita describes a turning point: after working up her courage, she asked her supervisor for more work assignments, sheepishly inquiring, "Hey, sorry, can you, just one second . . . Do you need me to do anything?" As Rita cautiously asserted herself rather than solely passively awaiting assignments, the way a student waits for a professor to outline a clear and detailed curriculum, her supervisor and the other magazine employees slowly began to notice her. She continued to do good work, built trust with the employees, and started receiving better assignments. Eventually, she realized that her supervisor had never disliked her but was just busy and distracted by other responsibilities. For the next year and a half Rita balanced her full-time studies, multiple part-time jobs (including an overnight stint at a pharmacy), and twenty to thirty-five hours of intern duties per week. She was exhausted, had almost no free time, was barely scraping by financially, and at times cut corners at school, but her persistence paid off. When we talk, she is twenty-three years old and has been a paid employee at the same magazine for nearly three years.[4] Indeed, the tables have turned—she now oversees several interns every semester.

Now it is Rita's turn to complain about interns, although she does so with mixed feelings. Like her previous supervisor, she assigns the easiest tasks possible. Yet she still finds supervising interns frustrating, saying, "It takes up time." She describes supervising unserious, untrustworthy interns at the expense of fulfilling the duties of her stressful job. Still, Rita works to ensure her interns have a better experience than she did: "I remember exactly what it was like," she reflects, and "I don't want kids to hide in the bathroom."

Rita tries to connect with her interns more frequently, starting each week by speaking with them casually (mostly sharing their respective weekend experiences) and while she assigns low-level tasks similar to those she completed as an intern, she offers more explicit instructions and clearer timelines and does her best to offer public credit for their work. She laments the way her fellow employees, particularly those several years into their careers, continue to ignore the current interns and treat them as interchangeable. In her opinion, this treatment is problematic because even the best interns are ignored: "I've had interns who are really on their shit [competent], and they still get the same 'I'm not acknowledging you' thing. It kind of upsets me . . . to watch my intern get snubbed." Nevertheless, when Rita talks about Conor, a star intern who eventually landed a paid job at the company, she says she does not call any of her interns by name, explaining:

> RITA: You earn your name. You're "intern!" [*laughs*] Now he's Conor. He was there for a year, and I called him "intern" [*laughs some more*].
>
> AF: No, you didn't!
>
> RITA: I did! I totally did.
>
> AF: You don't call all your interns "intern."
>
> RITA: I do! It's kind of like hazing them because they won't question it. Nobody questions it! I'm waiting for somebody to come up to me and say, "Actually my name is so and so." I'll totally respect it! But they're like, "OK, thanks Rita" and they get back to work. And I'm [thinking], "Why don't they [say anything]?"

My responses were prompted by my disbelief that Rita refuses to call interns by their names, thereby playfully yet explicitly treating them as interchangeable, contrary to her stated goal of improving their experience in the office.[5] Importantly, although interns are technically only one step away from becoming paid employees, the status difference between these two groups is significant and, consistent with a form of hazing, this power dynamic creates fertile ground for employees to tease or make fun of interns without imminent retaliation.[6]

Rita's struggles, triumphs, and transitions encapsulate many of the tensions inherent in the intern economy. How did someone who urgently sensed the need to intern, and felt lucky to secure a position, become disengaged so quickly? Why would someone who initially fumbled in the dark as an intern before making the most of the experience now view interns primarily as a source of annoyance? Further, if internships are now a mainstream component of higher education, why would a school not do more to ensure that students have a constructive experience? More broadly, this book concerns how aspirants break into an industry, and how employers and educators produce and reinforce these pathways. In the coming chapters, I analyze data from participant observation at two music industry companies and over 120 interviews with interns, employees, and educators to answer these questions.

I find that internships are part of a breaking-in system that is rife with ambiguity. This book argues that the three key actors engaged in the intern economy—employers, educators, and interns—have not resolved the fundamental challenges inherent to internships. Notably, employers are neither trained nor greatly rewarded to educate; higher education institutions are ill-equipped to oversee learning in the workplace; and students sink or swim without receiving much guidance. Importantly, students bear the largest burden in navigating the breaking-in system. Because of these challenges, almost every internship begins in a state of ambiguity with all parties working at cross-purposes. There is little consensus about what interns should be doing and what benefits they should get from their experience, which often leads to disappointment and reproduces inequality. This ambiguity is especially pervasive in unpaid internships, which represent nearly half of the internships in the United States.[7]

Making Sense of the Intern Economy

While internships have only recently become a ubiquitous part of college life, work-based learning arrangements are far from new. The apprenticeship, a period dedicated to training and incorporating neophytes into the workforce, has been a part of work life for over three thousand years.[8] The typical internship, shorter and less educationally ambitious than an apprenticeship, takes place in an office, lasts approximately the duration of a school semester, and is part-time (or full-time in the summer). Notably, however, the term "internship" is used to refer to a wide array of experiences and arrangements, in settings ranging from production lines to professional offices. Internships vary significantly in terms of pay, quality of supervision, and assigned tasks.[9] At one extreme, some internships offer close mentorship, substantive professionally relevant work, and reasonable (to high) pay, while at the other extreme, interns receive no pay and little mentorship, do repetitive work, and experience little professional development.

For some students, such as those in business and STEM, the incorporation of newcomers is often more clearly sequenced and planned, with internships more likely to offer a clear pathway to a career.[10] Further, in sectors such as banking, law, and technology, interns are paid well relative to most US employees. For example, interns on Wall Street can earn over $16,000 per month and those at tech firms such as LinkedIn, Amazon, and Meta are frequently paid over $8,000 per month.[11]

At the other end of the spectrum, including but not solely in fields such as the arts and humanities, arrangements are much less formalized and less likely to lead directly to a postcollege job. The example of Rita's internship illustrates how aspirants in the cultural industries might do solely mundane tasks with questionable educational or career benefits. In some cases, low pay, long hours, and monotonous tasks mean internships verge on abusive; because the characteristics of an internship vary so widely within and across fields, such conditions are not limited to cultural industries.[12] For example, for three months, an unpaid intern at a Michelin-star restaurant spent almost all his time assembling beetles made of fruit leather, while reportedly being forbidden from laughing.[13] In 2013, a twenty-one-year-old intern collapsed and died one week before finishing his grueling summer internship at Bank of America, which allegedly involved eight sleepless nights during a two-week period.[14] In China, unpaid engineering "interns" at Foxconn factories spend eleven-hour days assembling Apple, Sony, and other consumer electronic products.[15]

The explosive growth of the intern economy is indicative of transformations in higher education and labor markets; while a bachelor's degree was once enough to secure long-term employment, college students of all stripes must now also demonstrate their employability through practical, hands-on experience. Given the perceived potential of internships to advance the intern's career, many observers praise these placements as valuable opportunities. Lauren Berger, the self-proclaimed "Intern Queen," held fifteen internships within four years and wrote a book celebrating internships as "inarguably, the most valuable experience of today's college student" (2012:5). When *The Chronicle of Higher Education* and American Public Media's *Marketplace* surveyed fifty thousand employers about the role of higher education in career preparation, they reported that when making hiring decisions, employers placed the most emphasis not on factors such as a potential hire's major or GPA, but rather on their experience—most notably, internships.[16]

Until the late 2000s, the internship was overwhelmingly viewed as an unproblematic though rapidly expanding part of the workplace and education system. However, as internships spread to almost every occupation—including unpaid interns tending vegetable gardens, bussing tables at restaurants, and working at doughnut shops—critics emerged.[17] What began as an uncritically celebrated policy (and rhetoric) to facilitate the transition from school to work grew into an unwieldy intern economy. Since the Great Recession started in 2007, the growth of unpaid internships started to outpace paid ones, and employers could more readily replace paid positions with low-paid or unpaid interns.[18] This has prompted growing discontent on the part of frustrated young workers who paradoxically see internships as a barrier, rather than a path, to launching a career.[19] Many commentators have decried internships for exploiting the unpaid labor of overqualified and unprotected young workers often paying tuition to work for free.[20] For example, in his book *The Precariat*, economist Guy Standing (2011:75) portrayed internship programs as a way for employers to obtain "cheap dispensable labor." Shortly before launching her 2016 presidential bid, Hillary Clinton denounced the abuse of unpaid labor by companies, stating, "Businesses have taken advantage of unpaid internships to an extent that it is blocking opportunities for young people to move on into paid employment."[21]

Others have noted explicitly how the intern economy undermines the meritocratic ideals of the education system and US society. In an op-ed, Darren Walker, president of the Ford Foundation, referred to "America's broken internship system" in which opportunity is unequally distributed, concluding, "While many Americans believe fervently and faithfully in expanding opportunity, America's internship-industrial complex does just the opposite."[22] Conversely, Harvard University economist Edward Glaeser suggested the government should offer student loans to unpaid interns, even if they already graduated from college, to provide pathways to employment for aspirants of all economic backgrounds.[23] There is therefore extensive discussion, and disagreement, about who can afford to do internships and who benefits from them.

There is empirical evidence that suggests paid and unpaid internships differ in terms of quality and subsequent career outcomes. According to annual student surveys by the National Association of Colleges and Employers, paid interns are considerably more likely to receive a job offer upon graduation than their unpaid counterparts—in 2021, for example, students graduating from a four-year college who held a paid internship received 1.61 job offers on average, compared to 0.94 offers for unpaid interns and 0.77 offers for students with no internship experience.[24] According to my analysis of data from the Strategic National Arts Alumni Project, a large-scale survey of arts graduates, students who completed a paid internship found jobs rapidly after graduation, but those with unpaid internships had no advantage over students who did not do an internship at all.[25] Therefore, the term "intern economy" obscures significant variation between the benefits accrued by paid and unpaid interns.

With the growth of unpaid internships during and after the Great Recession, the contentiousness of the intern economy gave rise to a new phenomenon: several ex-interns have sued their employers for back pay.[26] Companies, educators, and even the courts became increasingly unclear about how to define and justify a legal unpaid internship. Employers scrambled to catch up with the threat of litigation, with prominent settlement agreements paid by Viacom ($7.2 million), NBCUniversal ($6.4 million), Condé Nast ($5.85 million), and Warner Music Group ($4.2 million).[27] These legal decisions have tightened the link between higher education and unpaid internships, though colleges and universities have struggled to formalize the intern economy and respond to critics who oppose this form of unpaid labor. Simultaneously, some employers have repackaged their internship programs; a few have eliminated them altogether; and others have started paying stipends.

In this book I examine the internship as a rapidly expanding phenomenon within the context of an especially precarious field—the record industry. In glamorous fields such as music, film, and publishing, there is a consistently large oversupply of motivated people enticed by the symbolic rewards of "cool" jobs, driven by the passionate aim to "do what you love."[28] The cultural industries such as music, film, television, publishing, and fashion are widely seen as the worst abusers of intern labor, eagerly exploiting students' efforts and cultural knowledge while offering little training, mentorship, or true career opportunities.[29] Every major record company has been the subject of a lawsuit from former interns demanding back pay.[30] In these workplaces, it is especially likely that an internship neither offers a valuable learning experience nor serves as a stepping stone to a career. While Rita "made it," many interns never transition to paid work in the cultural industries, even if they intern for years (either at the same firm, or as serial interns potentially securing increasingly prestigious or well-suited internships).[31] The reliance on unpaid or low-paid internships in fields such as arts and culture, politics, and not-for-profit organizations creates a barrier to career entry for individuals from marginalized groups, not least those from less privileged socioeconomic backgrounds.[32] Indeed, Rita's triumphant ascent is especially exceptional because first-generation college students are unlikely to intern.[33]

To gather a rich dataset on the intricacies of the intern economy as it plays out within the record industry, I conducted participant observation as an unpaid intern at two music industry firms (which I call "Major Records USA" and "Indie Distribution") in New York City, and I interviewed more than 120 key informants in and around this social world (record label employees, college personnel, and the interns themselves). Using these data, I show how interns, employees, and educators see themselves and each other, manage daily tasks and tensions, and articulate the internship as a path to employment even though very few succeed. To better understand and address these issues within the intern economy, this book centers on the social process of breaking in.

Breaking In as a Social Process

Establishing a career may seem like a purely personal endeavor, at least as experienced by the aspiring worker. In this individualist view, someone becomes interested in an occupation, pursues training to develop relevant skills, and, if talented enough, through hard work and dedication, eventually launches a career.[34] However, I refer to "breaking in" as a process to stress its social character. Breaking in is a social process because it involves the interaction of the aspirant with gatekeeping members of an occupation (and/or organization). Beyond accruing the skills needed for the job, a newcomer attempting to join an occupational community must learn and navigate the taken-for-granted norms and values held by its established members. Breaking in is dualistic in nature in that while the aspirant is trying to shift from outsider to insider, the members of the occupational community are "breaking in" the newcomer by encouraging or disciplining them to shed previous behaviors and attitudes that do not align with those of the community.[35]

Classic symbolic interactionist studies of a newcomer's introduction to an occupation, for example, as a medical student (e.g., Becker et al. 1961) or a police recruit (e.g., Van Maanen 1975), offer a model for understanding the dynamic, proactive ways newcomers learn to adopt a role (or not) in fits and starts.[36] These foundational studies show that newcomers master a new social world by facing a series of "turning points" and "status passages."[37] Because roles are often ambiguous and change over time, and therefore must be improvised, there is great variation in the ways individuals embody roles.[38] I illustrate this ambiguity in the case of music industry interns, who can be understood simultaneously as students, workers, and fans. Further, while internships were once predominantly viewed as an educational endeavor, college graduates in creative fields are now more inclined to view them as related to career development.[39]

The ongoing ambiguity entailed by viewing internships variously as training, work, or an activity done out of passion for music limits cooperation between interns, employees, and higher education personnel, making it especially difficult to standardize this form of breaking in and thus compelling all parties to improvise as they go.[40] While the tradition of studying breaking in as a social process provides a fruitful starting point for this book, these classic studies occurred at a time of relative stability for workers, as I discuss in the next section. Such studies generally assumed the host organization sought to transform the newcomer in some way and invested in the process of doing so, but I find a different scenario in the current labor market: due to the multiple possible motivations of interns, and the increasingly precarious standing of the employees overseeing them, employers are often satisfied with surface-level socialization, with the goal of training interns to unobtrusively respect the basic norms and rules of the workplace.

Scholars in this interactionist tradition, and more recent institutional approaches to organizational life, view an organization's official goals and values with skepticism, arguing that while these matter, they should not be taken at face value.[41] Analyzing the decoupling, or blurry coexistence, of the stated and real (or multiple) goals of organizational policies and practices reveals a variety of official and unofficial aims that contribute to the ambiguity of breaking in. Employers officially host interns to train, sort, and potentially hire their next generation of workers, but unofficially, and at times more prominently, they work with interns to nurture a constant stream of inexpensive labor. Record company employees do not express excessive inner conflict about whether they should act as "teachers" or "managers"—their default is almost always the latter.

Higher education institutions also exhibit a gap between official and unofficial goals, proclaiming that internships offer rich opportunities for connecting classroom learning to the "real world" and facilitate career development, while largely failing to either allocate sufficient resources, or prioritize rigorous pedagogical engagement, for experiential learning. Professors are often not incentivized, do not have time, or do not see it as their job to invest in experiential learning pedagogy, and internship coordination is relegated to administrative or part-time personnel in an academic department or career services. Anthropologist of education David Moore called this the "paradox of experiential learning," noting that schools tout experiential learning (such as internships) yet primarily maintain such programs at the margins of their institutions, as if "real" academics want no part in this endeavor.[42] In brief, colleges promote their internship programs as a selling point for potential students while many professors and some administrators only begrudgingly participate in these low-status endeavors.[43]

Looking closely at shared and at times contentious understandings of breaking in makes visible the culture of educational environments, including the "hidden curriculum," a set of largely unspoken rules and norms that those in power, such as teachers and more privileged students, take for granted as natural.[44] In the classic article "A School Is a Lousy Place to Learn Anything in," sociologist Howard Becker (1972:96) shed light on the hidden curriculum by comparing trade schools and on-the-job training as differently structured opportunities for learning. Becker noted that in the setting of a workplace, students do not necessarily receive the same sort of curricular attention they would in a classroom, concluding, "An ideology common among journeymen suggests that if an apprentice is any good, he will make you teach him; if he does not push, he probably does not have what it takes." Although this ideology is largely unspoken, it leaves learning dependent on the aspirant's initiative, leading Becker to conclude that a "pushy punk learns more than a quiet young man."

Rita's experience is a clear illustration of this dynamic. She eventually came to understand that an intern's supervisor might not provide extensive training or share insights; supervisors are not necessarily charged with—or concerned with—ensuring interns learn a comprehensive curriculum.[45] Therefore, newcomers must learn how to be a bit of a "pushy punk," reaching out to employees to solicit their training and build relationships, if they are to have any chance of staying on for multiple semesters and eventually getting hired. Interns must understand that employees treat them less as students and more as trainees working in the proverbial mailroom, that mythical proving ground where the cream allegedly rises to the top.[46] The intern must actively listen and create their own curriculum. By creating this individualized curriculum, interns learn to accept their uncertain, economically precarious work conditions; at the same time, employees judge interns on their creation of a curriculum (or lack thereof).

Based on the analysis of the experiences of interns, as well as employees and higher education personnel, this book contributes to a burgeoning literature on the social process of breaking in that demystifies the "black box" of higher education, extending this research to the workplace. As Elizabeth Armstrong and Laura Hamilton (2013) argued, although a rich literature uses statistical analyses to assess the returns on college degrees, including differences by type of institution, major, and GPA, these studies miss how the structure of students' social and academic lives shapes social mobility and reproduces inequalities. Recent studies of labor market entry suggest that college graduates are not all on equal footing; they are earning the same credential—a bachelor's degree—but are not all having the same experiences and postcollege outcomes.[47] In particular, the cultural capital, economic resources, and social networks of college students from higher socioeconomic backgrounds result in qualitatively different education experiences and thus subtly reproduce inequalities.[48]

In alignment with these patterns, recent research on parental involvement in college students' postgraduate job outcomes finds that more affluent parents provide connections and funding to help their children obtain and complete internships whereas students with less affluent parents are more likely to graduate without internship experience.[49] To advance their stated aim of "meritocracy," schools may implement what I call "internships-for-all policies" intended to help students and address inequities, such as mandating internships to ensure that all graduates gain on-the-job training during their education or offering scholarships to support low-income students completing unpaid internships. However, because these programs often force students to shoulder additional financial obligations, they may be unproductive or even worsen inequality.[50]

By studying interns, employees, and higher education personnel, the three chief players involved in the production of, and navigation through, the ambiguity of internships, I am studying a "breaking-in system"—the ways higher education institutions and industry create and police pathways by which newcomers can potentially enter occupations. The characteristics of these pathways vary greatly by sector, including how closely educational credentials are tied to occupational skills and identities, the norms and values aspirants are expected to assume, and their openness or selectivity. For individuals in relatively "open" fields with an oversupply of applicants and no clear educational shortcut, aspirants break in by doing what I call "provisional labor"—assuming a conditional role for an indefinite period, usually laboring in a precarious position and for low or no pay.

An internship is one type of provisional labor. Alternatively, in educational settings, an aspirant can take on the role of teaching assistant, whereas in social media production, workers (i.e., hopeful influencers) entrepreneurially do unpaid or low-paid labor with the aspirational goal to establish career footholds.[51] Although the role of "the intern" is low in status, it is aspirational and, as with other roles, it can function as a resource a newcomer can use to claim membership within an occupational community and argue for a promotion to a higher position.[52]

Paradoxically, despite the highly uncertain payoffs of unpaid internships and the low status of interns (who are often labeled "just the intern"), there is widespread agreement among cultural workers that aspirants must complete this type of provisional labor to break in. A few years after I met Rita, she pivoted to a new role at a record company. When I ask her if a student could start a career in music without doing an internship, she shakes her head no, exclaiming, "There's no way." After thinking for a moment, she adds,

> Unless you're already established in the media industry—if you're just trying to break in . . . you're going to have to suck it up and swallow your pride and just work for free. Just for a little while, until you know enough people to not work for free anymore.

While some people I encountered held other roles that served as pathways to breaking in (for example, volunteering at a college radio station, booking shows for bands, or helping local artists), all these paths have one thing in common: aspirants assume the cost of their training as they build their employability.

Importantly, the structure of a breaking-in system is tied to the larger social structure, including the broader employment and education conditions of its historical period. In addition, these systems vary across industries and occupations. In the following sections, I further situate the shifting conditions of career entry for college graduates and contextualize my case study of the music industry.

Making Yourself Employable in the New Economy

In the mid-twentieth century, the dominant breaking-in system for young adults in the United States consisted of workers being hired into stable bureaucratic organizations that offered training and a career ladder—an opportunity structure—allowing movement from an entry-level job upward. The growth of larger, complex organizations in the early part of the century brought the need for employers to nurture a consistent and well-trained supply of labor.[53] The passage of laws protecting workers, including the Fair Labor Standards Act of 1938, which established a minimum wage, and the rise of union membership ushered in institutional protections for workers and helped establish a social contract between industry and labor.[54]

For the three decades following World War II, for the first time in US history, employment was viewed predominantly as a long-term partnership between firms and workers, where loyalty was cultivated and mutually rewarded. Workers received training and opportunities for advancement within the firm, and employers benefited from an increasingly skilled, stable labor force. White-collar workers entered a firm with the expectation of building a lifelong career, incrementally climbing a job ladder.[55] While promotions often proved elusive for blue-collar workers, manufacturing jobs nevertheless offered stability and (by historical standards) good pay for people without a college degree.[56] Because of this new standard employment relationship, as sociologist Everett Hughes (1958:8) noted, "more and more people have assurance, at least on paper, of a smooth and well-marked march by easy stages from the high-school guidance office to a retirement suitable to one's achievements." In this period, workers experienced an unusual level of stability and may have thought this was a permanent new normal.[57] However, recent developments have shown that this arrangement was, in fact, a temporary swing of the precarity pendulum.[58]

Since the late twentieth century, shifts in the economic, political, and social landscapes have led to profound transformations of the employment relationship, prompting a transfer of risk from institutions to individuals.[59] In the 1970s and '80s, global economic integration and competition between companies created noticeable pressure and pathways to outsource work, including to countries with less expensive labor. The decline of unions shifted the relatively equal industry–employee balance of power toward employers. Technological innovations meant firms needed to compete globally but also sped up production and led to faster-changing market trends. Jointly, these developments rendered long-term investments in employees difficult because skills became obsolete rapidly.

At the same time, the United States and much of the Western world saw the rise of knowledge-intensive jobs (for which employers often require postsecondary education) and low-paid service-based jobs, while manufacturing jobs declined precipitously.[60] As a result, firms have become increasingly flexible, and work has become more precarious. "Nonstandard" work arrangements (e.g., part-time, temporary, freelance work) have grown at the expense of the full-time, permanent jobs that were more commonly held by previous generations.[61] Several scholars have argued that the rise of precarious work has led to a more polarized job market in which highly educated workers compete for a shrinking number of well-paying, socially prestigious "good" jobs while fighting to escape the alternatives—often called "bad" jobs because they offer lower pay, even less stability, and few benefits—which have only gotten worse.[62]

These changes in the employment relationship have made careers more chaotic. There is no longer a widespread expectation of long-term affiliation between workers and employers. Today, a career typically involves movement across not only individual employers, but also industries, with US workers holding more than twelve different jobs in their lifetime on average and frequently making dramatic career changes by age forty.[63] The ideal of the tidy, predictable career pathway from graduation to retirement is long gone. Workers must establish and constantly replenish their skills as they manage their own careers under competitive conditions. In 1993, these developments prompted management scholar Peter Drucker to note, “The stepladder is gone, and there’s not even the implied structure of an industry’s rope ladder. It’s more like vines, and you bring your own machete.”[64] Framed by Drucker as a stark transition from depending on firms to “individual responsibility,” workers are now responsible for planning and managing their own careers.[65]

These shifts have important consequences for breaking in. As employers have come to no longer expect long-term commitments from their employees, they have become less prone, and less incentivized, to invest in job training.[66] Left largely on their own, aspiring workers are responsible for developing skills, becoming socialized to a field’s norms and values, and growing a network of relationships to ensure their career entry and stability. In short, workers must build and sustain their employability.[67]

Against this backdrop, Americans have increasingly turned to higher education to escape bad jobs. As of 2013, more than one-third of young adults aged twenty-five to thirty-two in the United States had a college degree, up from an average of one in four in the same age group in previous decades (24 percent in 1979 and 25 percent in 1995). By 2021, nearly 40 percent of the US population over age twenty-five had a college degree.[68] With a highly credentialed population available, employers have raised their standards for applicants for jobs at all skill levels—even entry-level jobs increasingly require work experience.[69]

Unsurprisingly, young workers who lack college degrees are increasingly considered “at risk” in their school-to-work transition. However, amid these long-term and tumultuous shifts in employment, a growing body of research shows that the career pathways of college graduates are often delayed, erratic, and unequal.[70] While in the aggregate college graduates fare better in the job market than individuals without such a degree, the transition from higher education to employment is neither easy nor automatic. The rise of internships has been fueled by the perceived failings of higher education to adjust to this new scenario. According to a Pew Research Center survey, most adults in the United States agree that the higher education system suffers from two problems: tuition costs are too high (according to 84 percent of adults), and students are not graduating with the skills they need in the workplace (65 percent).[71] In the context of a hyper-competitive college admissions market, skyrocketing tuition, and the proliferation of school rankings (including those based on degrees' return on investment), internships have emerged as a way for institutions of higher learning to link a degree to work-ready skills. Increasingly, schools must offer students career training and networking opportunities to stay competitive.[72]

While shifts in the labor market and careers have motivated the implementation of college-for-all policies,[73] higher education institutions have more recently embraced internships-for-all policies. As college graduates face greater career uncertainty at labor market entry, higher education institutions are facing significant pressure from students, their families, and policymakers to improve student labor market outcomes and help students with career preparation.[74] As a result of this pressure, postsecondary curricula are shifting to prepare students for the increasingly uncertain labor markets they will soon confront.[75] In recent decades, this shift has included the incorporation of internships to improve job readiness, facilitate the college-to-career transition,[76] and help students overcome the "career progression paradox"—the catch-22 wherein workers need skills to secure a job, but must first have a job to gain those skills.[77] Importantly, however, the rise of internships has occurred without a consensus about what the experience is supposed to achieve, how it should be managed, and who is responsible for managing it. In other words, structural economic shifts have generated both the growth of internships and exacerbated their ambiguity.

Beyond helping students develop skills, internship experience signals a student's competence and commitment. Employers view internship experience as evidence of prior vetting and a relatively long-standing interest in the field—doing a summer internship rather than holding a more traditional summer job signals "drive."[78] Some workers, even at the start of their career, carefully craft their résumé by building experience at high-status companies; in the music industry, this might include stints at a major record company, an esteemed indie label, or a music-streaming firm such as Spotify. Internships therefore enable college students to build their "personal brand." Career counselors, self-help gurus, journalists, and some parents advise students to develop their personal brand, a coherent professional identity that signals their employability in the labor market.[79] Personal branding has emerged as a solution to a market problem.[80] If career trajectories have changed from a steady climb up a ladder at a single employer to a more chaotic trajectory involving several lateral, downward, or upward moves between firms and industries, having a personal brand—ideally described in three or four words that crystalize a potential employee's "authentic self"—quickly and clearly lends coherence to an applicant's work history in the eyes of potential employers.[81]

The growth of internships as part of higher education has further incorporated building social capital as part of the college experience. As both conventional wisdom and a vast literature attest, "who you know" is often crucial to breaking in.[82] Indeed, according to some music industry employees, who you know is even more important than what you know, although the two are intertwined. Aspirants use their social capital—the resources embedded in their social networks—to gain informational advantages and influence. Similarly, social capital helps employers decide who they consider worthy of investment.

Social capital helps resolve information problems in the job-search process. In his classic study of job searching, *Getting a Job*, Mark Granovetter found that people with more expansive social networks were more likely to learn about work opportunities than job seekers with fewer "weak ties" (e.g., acquaintances) linking them to other social circles. The advent of LinkedIn and other online resources means that the problem for current job seekers is often less knowing about a job and more knowing how to make their application stand out.[83] By interning, as well as by joining clubs and groups, students are doing their best to make their application stand out while building a network of people willing to vouch for them. Because the pathways to jobs in some fields appear so unclear, some hopeful interns resemble the job seekers described by Vicki Smith (2001)—potential employees who believed in a "hidden market" for jobs that are gained through networks, some even hoping they could convince an employer to hire them based on a chance interaction.[84]

Social capital also helps resolve information problems in the hiring process. Employers complain that it is difficult to know how people will truly perform as an employee, even after extensive interviewing, because there can be a mismatch between how people act during interviews (to get hired) and how they act as employees.[85] As I describe further, the ability to present oneself competently in job application materials and in an interview does not necessarily overlap with consistently being a competent intern. The rise of online resources, some of them furnished by higher education institutions, enable some students to thrive at obtaining an internship, even if they view the position as no more than a line on their résumé. For example, career counselors sometimes tell students to express a deep passion for the music field and carefully research a company's artist roster to signal their sincere interest. While employers try to gauge the seriousness of applicants, they have a spotty track record (at best) of weeding out uncommitted interns.

The Site and the Argument

Part of what I have argued thus far is that large structural shifts have created uncertain and unstable conditions for education and work and, in turn, have given rise to internships as a key way for aspirants to break into a variety of fields. The ambiguity inherent in the role of intern is present in all fields, though breaking-in systems vary in their level of ambiguity. This ambiguity becomes more visible by studying differently positioned members of a breaking-in system (interns, employees, and higher education personnel).

An ambiguous phenomenon refers to the coexistence of multiple different interpretations, and this can take many forms: polysemy, vagueness, inconsistency, and instability.[86] Internships as a type of provisional labor take all four of these forms: an intern means a "student" and "worker"; interviewees describe internships as ranging from an aspirant doing high-level work with close expert supervision to the equivalent of "bring your child to work day"; the experiences of aspirants vary greatly across and within companies; and shifts in the legal landscape and through intern labor rights activism have brought instability to what is termed an internship.[87] Importantly, ambiguity is not simply a misunderstanding that can be alleviated with more information—the remedy is for social actors to make sense of the world around them.[88] In this book I focus especially on the commercial record industry, which, like many other cultural industries, features a breaking-in system characterized by an especially high level of ambiguity. For the aspirant, breaking in amounts to an ongoing, ambiguous negotiation for belonging.

While there is variation within the cultural industries, the considerable oversupply of potential workers generally exacerbates the usual challenge of finding one's footing—and, potentially, employment—in the new economy.[89] The allure of cultural industries, in part due to its glamorous performers and bustling events like live performances and parties, helps to explain its considerable excess of aspiring workers. No matter what tasks interns are assigned, occasional but significant brushes with famous people leave them experiencing an odd combination of nearness and remoteness. Interns can feel hope and enthusiasm from their proximity to senior employees and artists, but such contacts are typically occasional and usually do not result in strong ties.[90]

In his work on artistic labor markets, Pierre-Michel Menger (1999) identified two other potential reasons for the oversupply of aspirants and, consequently, the importance of learning by doing. First, a potential worker's suitability for a specific occupation is difficult to discern, both for the worker and for others. Through trial and error, aspirants gain more information about their potential occupation and become better able to gauge whether it matches their abilities and interests. Second, despite the existence of arts- and media-related programs in higher education, many occupations in the field do not require formal training, and therefore education credentials in and of themselves are not sufficient for the selection and screening of talent.[91] Even those creative graduates who receive in-depth training feel like their schooling did not sufficiently prepare them for the professional world.[92] The substantial surplus of aspiring workers prompts some participants to compare attempts to enter the cultural industries to boot camp, rushing a fraternity, or working in the mailroom. While music industry careers are especially chaotic at their onset, they have long been uncertain even as workers gain experience. Standing on uncertain ground, established employees are hardly incentivized to dedicate much time to training aspirants.

Although the record industry has undergone drastic changes since the rise of digital downloads and streaming, the industry has been notoriously unpredictable for decades.[93] In 1959, Goddard Lieberson, the president of Columbia Records, quipped, "This business is like running a gambling house," adding, "You've got to cover yourself in all directions."[94] Lieberson had helped Columbia become the number one company in record album sales at the time by investing in an array of artists and ventures, including the Columbia Record Club. However, his fate illustrates that even giants of the industry can be out of touch. In the mid-1950s, when rock 'n' roll ascended as a cultural form,[95] he believed the genre would be no more than a fad and wanted no part of it—as a result, Columbia rapidly lost ground to their rival RCA, which embraced the trend (notably by purchasing Elvis Presley's contract).

The careers of record company personnel have long been tied to the (unpredictable) success of music recordings. Yet most recordings do not make a profit because, when it comes to cultural products, hits tend to be flukes.[96] Even experts find it difficult to predict which cultural products will be successful, despite strategic and often collaborative efforts to ensure commercial success.[97] This unpredictability is one reason that the careers of cultural workers, including authors, models, songwriters, and visual artists, are especially uncertain.[98]

Careers in the cultural industries are frequently not bound by internal labor markets (i.e., workers rarely build careers through stable long-term employment at the same company). This is most obviously true for individuals doing project-based or freelance work (e.g., songwriters) but also applies to those employed at firms.[99] The commercial record industry is a competitive field organized around a few oligopolistic firms ("major" record companies) and many specialized independent companies ("indies"). The majors tend to frequently reorganize (through mergers or, internally, by combining departments), whereas the indies are inherently small and fragile.[100]

Companies in the cultural industries try to manage risk in part by redistributing it downward, including to artistic and nonartistic laborers in the form of low salaries and temporary work arrangements.[101] To remain attuned to novel trends—for example, to avoid sleeping on the emergence of a new subgenre or being the last company to embrace the next viral TikTok—companies continually welcome an influx of young, culturally savvy newcomers. These new arrivals may make experienced workers feel threatened, and indeed, employees usually do "age out."[102] It is in this competitive, and at times contentious, environment that aspirants in this book seek to break in.

In the following chapters, I further elucidate the sources of ambiguity in this breaking-in system (chapters 1–2) and how key actors—higher education personnel, employees, and interns—attempt to manage or overcome this ambiguity (chapters 3–5).

Chapter 1 considers how the relationship between higher education institutions and employers exacerbates the ambiguity in this breaking-in system. I show how actors within these fields must negotiate between multiple, often contradictory, goals. In particular, in enacting internships-for-all policies, higher education personnel may well be dedicated to educational aims but must also contend with institutional pressures to maximize internship participation numbers while having limited resources to ensure quality learning experiences. Music industry employers, on the other hand, need an influx of inexpensive workers, but the employees who supervise interns often have little time (and are not necessarily rewarded) for acting as "teachers."

The repercussions of an unwieldy intern economy become clearer in chapter 2, which shows how internships-for-all policies accommodate (and drive) a wide assortment of intern motivations. I introduce a threefold typology of music industry interns and their motivations: Students, Enthusiasts, and Job Seekers. Due to this variation, music industry employees operate under the assumption that interns are neither committed nor competent. Rather than aim to transform these newcomers into potential employees, employers invest little by settling for surface-level socialization; therefore, employers generally aim to break in interns just enough to make sure they unobtrusively respect workplace norms and rules.

I further consider the perspective of employers in chapter 3, which analyzes how music industry employees manage ambiguity in this breaking-in system. Tasked ostensibly with educating interns, employees justify their relative neglect of interns by adopting what I call the mailroom model of training. Drawing especially on interviews with employees and participant observation data, I find that music industry employees generally embrace the myth of the mailroom to normalize interns' suffering and position on-the-job learning as the best (or only) way for aspirants to learn. In the process, members of this occupational community legitimate a form of training that puts the burden predominantly or fully on interns to craft a worthwhile experience, thereby shedding the responsibility for employees to act as "teachers."

As a result, interns use a variety of individual strategies to make the most of their experience. In chapter 4, I discuss the strategies job-seeking interns use to overcome their ambiguous standing. Broadly, these aspirants seek to signal their commitment and competence and thus enact what I call the ideal intern norm. To go beyond merely being deemed a "good intern," job-seeking aspirants pursue three key strategies to overcome ambiguities in this breaking-in system: tactful proactiveness, relationship building, and extended investment. However, due to their age, gender, race, and socioeconomic status, some interns are more likely to be evaluated positively as ideal interns and come equipped with dispositions, connections, and financial support that better enable them to break in. Therefore, chapter 4 illuminates how some interns improve their standing, but few can.

In chapter 5, after further unpacking key findings, I conclude the book by considering collective strategies to grapple with ambiguity in breaking-in systems. Notably related to addressing inequities, I ask: Can breaking-in systems change? I outline how intern labor rights activism, lawsuits filed by former interns, and recent policies enacted by higher education institutions and employers offer hope for more equitable, albeit still ambiguous, breaking-in systems.

1

The Education-Industrial Complex

"THE INTEGRATION of rigorous classroom study with real-world experiences, including internships, is a powerful way to learn. Recognizing the value of experiential learning, a growing number of colleges and universities are expanding and integrating internships into their curriculum."[1] So began an April 2010 letter signed by thirteen university presidents including the heads of New York University and the University of California, two key suppliers of unpaid interns for cultural employers in New York City and Los Angeles. The letter, which was addressed to Hilda Solis, then secretary of the US Department of Labor, was a response to "Fact Sheet #71," a statement published by the department's Wage and Hour Division (WHD) that clarified the circumstances under which interns at for-profit organizations are entitled to minimum wage and overtime pay.[2]

With the growth of unpaid internships, which intensified in the early twenty-first century, came the need for clearer legal guidelines. "Fact Sheet #71" updated an earlier six-factor test, which was based on a 1947 Supreme Court decision, by specifying that an unpaid internship must be similar to training that would be provided in an "educational environment" rather than a "vocational school," as the WHD had previously stipulated.[3] The WHD statement clarified this criterion by noting (although in vague terms) that internship programs that are organized more closely around classroom or academic learning, as opposed to an employer's everyday operations, are more likely to be viewed as an educational endeavor rather than employment. The WHD then added that this "often occurs where a college or university exercises oversight over the internship program and provides educational credit."[4]

Although WHD's clarification of the six-factor test did not pose an immediate threat to colleges' and universities' ability to maintain internship programs—in fact, the update better reflected higher education institutions' broad implementation of internships—the thirteen university presidents who penned the response portrayed the Department of Labor's new interpretation as an intrusion on their turf. The letter explicitly marked internships as "educational" territory, stating, "We are troubled by the Department of Labor's apparent recent shift toward the regulation of internships." Further, the letter described internships as an immensely successful, mutually beneficial agreement between students, higher education institutions, and employers. The presidents warned that the department's public statement could discourage employers from offering internships, thus potentially putting the US educational system and labor force at a competitive disadvantage.[5]

While concerns over the erosion of internships proved to be premature, the WHD fact sheet and the presidents' response are indicative of not only the legal ambiguity surrounding interns—who blur the line between worker and student—but also the contentiousness of categorizing internship experiences as educational. In brief, these documents reflect an uneasy partnership between higher education and employers. A college student who interns at a for-profit organization ostensibly does work in exchange for training; however, the specific work responsibilities and training vary tremendously across students and settings. For example, most music industry internships are part-time, but some are full-time (especially in the summer). Some student interns arrive with considerable skills and experience, while others have no such background. Some companies provide highly structured, planned activities and projects but others offer looser, less formal experiences.

Given the wide variation in multiple aspects of internships—including what they entail, their structure, and who completes them—some interns receive strong mentorship and can complete tasks that rely on their creativity and judgment, but many others do not. For example, one former intern described being closely mentored by her supervisor and taking on an expanding set of responsibilities related to her major (music business). In contrast, another reported that she completed only occasional and mundane tasks, had little contact with her supervisor, and ultimately quit her internship after she was sexually harassed by a fellow intern and then was told by her supervisor that all interns would be let go if the issue persisted.[6] Despite the significant shortcomings of her experience, the latter student paid approximately $4,000 in tuition for school credit.

This chapter explores the social production of ambiguity, focusing on how higher education institutions reproduce rather than resolve the ambiguity of internships. Higher education institutions partner with employers even though institutional leadership is aware of the considerable variation in internship quality and the real potential for student mistreatment. The presidents' letter concluded: "While we share your concerns about the potential for exploitation, our institutions take great pains to ensure students are placed in secure and productive environments that further their education. We constantly monitor and reassess placements based on student feedback." The response letter fails to mention that internships are a significant source of income for colleges. Critics have argued that higher education institutions commodify academic credit, earning income from relatively inexpensive internship programs run by low-paid staff or part-time faculty.[7] The stakes, however, go beyond the immediate financial benefits of tuition paid for internship credits. Higher education institutions must cater to the disparate needs of students, employers, and governments, among others, while also supporting their own survival and growth. In implementing internships-for-all policies, higher education institutions are responding to broader societal pressures to create career pathways for students or at least show that they are attempting to do so.

Drawing on interviews with internship coordinators and career services employees at a range of colleges and universities, I show that higher education personnel acknowledge that while internships are ideally educational endeavors, the primary goal of institutions is responding to broader pressures to offer students a "return on investment," without which the schools will likely be at a competitive disadvantage. Although higher education institutions broadly tout the importance of internships, trying to increase student demand for these experiences, personnel describe having a very limited ability to help students secure internships or to oversee the quality and consistency of these opportunities. I also consider how record industry employees describe the reasons for their internship programs. Contrary to public pronouncements that declare companies want to create a pipeline of qualified candidates for jobs, workers on the ground boast that they primarily treat interns as a source of cheap labor. Employees' informal selection of interns based on their availability rather than their specific skills or knowledge further highlights this extractive reason for hosting interns.[8] Finally, although the goals of higher education institutions and employers seem misaligned, I describe two key ways higher education personnel make these differences more palatable without resolving ambiguities: vetting internships, although this practice varies widely, and "reframing work," which lays the ideological groundwork for student exploitation.

Internships for All: Pressure to Build a Practical Path

As he sips tea on a muggy Monday morning, Brian, who is wearing slim blue jeans and sporting long hair with a few stray strands partly tucked into the collar of his button-down shirt, responds to a question about his educational background by saying, "More than anything, I'd always been interested in *the idea* of working in music." At first, I think Brian, now a thirty-six-year-old senior employee at a prestigious indie record company in New York City, is being evasive, but then I realize he is bringing me back in time. He continues, recalling his mother's reaction when at age sixteen he told her what A&R (artists and repertoire) was and that he wanted to work in the field: "She thought I was a little crazy because she couldn't figure out how you went to college for something like that . . . it didn't really seem to have a practical path, which it doesn't [*laughs*]."

Brian shares that while studying English at the University of Texas at Austin, he got a job at what was arguably the coolest record store in town, which led to him getting hired at a music distribution company and leaving school early. He explains, "I did not graduate, because I just started working in music. I got a job that I thought was a good entry point." Eventually, he moved to New York City and worked his way up to increasingly senior positions at a string of indie record companies. Brian describes his formative time at the record store as providing him with "the most valuable education I could have had," unlike the education he would have received "if I continued to be an English major." At the store, he learned how to sell music, but he also deepened his knowledge of music, record companies, and the industry in general as he spent his days surrounded by other people with passions just like his own.

Lacking a clear, practical path to music industry employment through higher education, Brian forged his own way during his college years. I point out that his path did not include doing an internship. He explains that music industry internships were rare in Austin, Texas, in the 1990s, but notes that this was not, and still is not, the case in New York City: "I know kids [today] that have three internships at once, just in the hopes that one leads to something. That's definitely what I would have done had I lived [in New York] when I was twenty-one." With the proliferation of internships, today's college students can more readily find such experiences in Austin, while at the same time aspiring music industry workers navigate slightly clearer practical paths to employment due to shifts in higher education.

Brian's search for a path into the music industry, his dismissal of the importance of higher education, and his mother's concern about how to prepare academically for a career in A&R illustrate the long-standing pressures on higher education institutions to incorporate a more utilitarian emphasis on training for jobs, thereby making degrees "worthwhile." Higher education as a field manages competing, sometimes even contradictory, demands, trying to be both a place for learning "for its own sake" and a training ground for industry. After a period of dominance of liberal arts degrees, in recent decades degrees oriented toward occupational training, such as business, nursing, and education, have become more prevalent.[9] In the case of the music industry, for example, colleges and universities across the country have launched dozens of specialized programs in music business (or "music industry studies").[10] More broadly, in the last three decades colleges and universities have increasingly incorporated internships as part of the curriculum.[11]

The incorporation of internships, which is often discussed under the umbrella of experiential learning, has further complicated this balancing act at some schools. Higher education institutions must balance their liberal-arts educational mission with career development practices and programming, which requires specialized staff to take on career-oriented duties. In the following section I analyze how higher education personnel—mostly internship coordinators/advisors within academic departments and employees in career services departments—perceive and grapple with pressures to prepare students for careers.

Laboring to Learn

The rise of internships-for-all policies in higher education, which aim to have as many students as possible undertake these experiences, stems in part from empirical research suggesting that the activities college students participate in have the greatest impact on their learning and development.[12] Participating in an internship is linked to improved academic performance, leadership abilities, and soft skills such as interpersonal skills and the ability to handle stress.[13] Empirical research also supports the claim that completing an internship leads to better career outcomes, such as finding a job after graduation and earning a higher salary.[14] While these two types of outcomes may seem disparate—the former set focuses on learning while the latter set relates to a career—higher education personnel who work with interns frame internships as educational in a broad sense; for them, "learning" refers to progress toward many types of pedagogical goals, including career readiness.

When asked why students do internships, Scott, a career services employee at a school of art and design, illustrates the pervasively broad and triumphant portrayal of internships as educational, explaining that the experience is about "shaping up younger minds and helping people realize what the workforce is, what responsibilities are, what structure is, what connections are, what networking is, how to be professional." He adds, "I really believe that not every internship is life-changing, but at the same time, they could be, absolutely." Similarly, Mindy, a career services employee at an R2 public university,[15] sees internships as addressing a disconnect between school and work. To illustrate, she reflects on the intensive, monthlong training she undertook (in a "prior life") to become a flight attendant, noting that spending eight hours per day in a flight simulator did not fully prepare her for the realities of the job. Taking on the role of a student, she says, "I have learned from books and professors the nuts and bolts of the things that I need . . . to be knowledgeable in my career field. But putting that into practice are two different things." By gaining experience, students come to "feel more comfortable and feel more prepared" for their lives after graduation. Without practical experience, Mindy concludes, the specter of work after graduation can seem daunting.

As Scott's and Mindy's comments illustrate, one reason that higher education professionals can safely claim that internships are potentially educational is that "educational" can mean many different things: they portray internships as a tool that complements the classroom curriculum, offers students the chance to learn about the "real" world, weakens the distinction between school and work, and introduces students to what it means to be a working adult. Students can also, by extension, determine where they feel more comfortable and what types of employment align with their interests and strengths; for some students, internships provide a reality check about which skills they need to improve or how they should refocus going forward.

Not everyone agrees with this broad, career-oriented view of learning. For example, as Sebastian describes the internship program he runs for a media studies department (working with students interested in music, publishing, film, and television industries), he characterizes internships as "part of this thing that I have mixed feelings about, which is the idea that the point of the university education is to get you a better job." On the face of it, he adds, people with a college degree earn more, on average, than those without one, but he sees his employer (a large public university in New York City) as wanting students "to view the academic pursuit as having real utility for them in terms of their future professional life." The school's promotional materials, speeches by school leaders, and even his department's website tout the career benefits of a college degree. Sebastian portrays higher education as following an increasingly consumerist, career-oriented model rather than what he sees as its prime mission, namely, "thinking critically, thinking analytically, thinking more deeply about things." He adds, "That, to me, is the purpose of higher education. And when I say that I feel old-fashioned." Today, he concludes, a college degree is "supposed to be about an investment in your future earnings. And I still have a hard time accepting that."

Sebastian, who is also a contingent (non-tenure-track) faculty member in his department, tries to treat internships as an opportunity for students to learn, and not just to prepare for the labor market.[16] To do so, however, he must combat the view that the sole goal of completing an internship (and college, for that matter) is getting a job:

> I often say to the students that this [internship] is where you're getting the practical knowledge that supplements your academic knowledge. It's not a replacement. This is not like, "I'm only getting this degree so I can get an internship so I can get a job." These things are supposed to complement one another.

To receive credit for the experience, students in Sebastian's department must write a research paper on the industry in which they interned. He says he is no longer surprised when his students invariably ask, "Why do I have to write a paper?" In response, he explains that they are supposed to reflect on what they learned.[17] Thus, the narrow focus on getting a job, which is prevalent among both students and some higher education professionals, poses an obstacle to the claim that internships are educational.

Another challenge to treating college internships as educational is that this outlook assumes a logical link between the internships and the classroom curriculum that is not always clear and sometimes not even present. Sebastian explains that while an internship can be poorly designed in any field, this is a particularly common problem in media industries. He then contrasts internships in fields like psychology or education, which have a strong tradition of learning by doing, to internships in media industries, which are a more recent development. Referring to the latter, he concludes they are "sort of the same idea" as internships in these other fields, but adds that "it's a little more amorphous in that it's not as [sequenced]: 'OK, now you've learned how to do X, Y, and Z. Now you're taking this out into the world and going to do it.'" A student managing the social media accounts at a record company, for example, is not necessarily applying or extending concepts learned in the classroom.

For many students in creative fields like film, the music business, and publishing, this lack of a clear sequence in which they learn about a certain topic in class and then logically apply it in the working world parallels the frequently untidy career pathways of creative majors.[18] As Bianca, a career advisor at an R1 public university, notes when she discusses graduates from creative fields, "It can be, potentially, a more challenging road to employment. It's not always as clear-cut as, for example, [it is for] an accounting major." Internships-for-all policies in higher education aim to bring more uniformity to the college-to-career transition across fields, even though the curricular fit between classroom material and learning by doing is neither consistently evident nor practically possible in some fields.

Although there is variation and, at times, deep disagreements among administrators, staff, and faculty about the educational goals of college internships, the reasons for the growth of internships-for-all policies become clearer when considering the broader pressures directed at schools. Tellingly, when I ask higher education personnel why their schools have internship programs, their answers tend to focus not on the educational function, but rather on the school's reputation.

School Reputation and Student Employability

While the higher education personnel I interviewed for this study acknowledge that internships are ideally educational endeavors, they tie the importance of these experiential activities to broad, market-driven pressures. In the wake of significant rises in the cost of college, schools increasingly prioritize justifying a degree's "return on investment" (ROI) to students and their families.[19] This career-oriented justification can help maintain or enhance a school's reputation—in a competitive higher education landscape, with schools jockeying for the best students and their tuition dollars, donors, and industry partners, schools that fail to provide a high ROI are at a competitive disadvantage.[20]

In this context, internship programs simultaneously serve multiple functions for higher education institutions: they help schools position themselves as a place where students can earn a worthwhile degree, as an organization worthy of receiving donations (from alumni and others), and as a source of highly qualified, job-ready employees. Therefore, rather than work through the ambiguity of the intern role, the higher education personnel in this study grappled with societal (e.g., parental) and organizational (e.g., their school) pressures to facilitate internships for all, with the goal of preparing students for careers, or at least appearing to do so.[21]

Tania and Rey, two employees at a large private university in New York City, spoke to both the impetus for using internships to prepare students for careers and the emphasis on ROI. Tania, the internship coordinator for a music industry–related academic program, works in this role part-time yet oversaw more than two hundred student interns in the previous academic year, although she admits she does not work with them all that closely. Students submit forms to her, which she almost always approves, and then they take a seminar at the university's career center on, among other things, résumé writing, interviewing, and negotiating. Tania adds, "That's not only preparing them for [the internship], [but also] oftentimes preparing them for their next step. . . . The importance of writing a cover letter and a good résumé all fall in line with just getting them ready to leave the school." Thus, she casts the internship as part of a larger, long-standing effort to equip students with the basics of career preparation.

At the same university, Rey works in career services, specializing in helping students connect with local creative employers. When asked why the school has internship programs, she seems surprised by the question, answering, "It's the way people get jobs now, experiential learning, so you'd be a fool not to do it." Her statement implies both that students would be fools for not interning and schools would be fools for not offering internships. She then expands on the school's perspective, explaining, "People want something for their money, and it's not enough to say that what you're learning in this classroom is worth a quarter of a million dollars. It's not enough." Noting the rising price of tuition,

Rey adds that schools "have to evolve" and offer experiences that could lead to finding a job after graduation "because this is part of their value proposition." Rey reflects slightly and concludes, "From the school perspective, I mean, the story is great, to be a little cynical. We are doing something for you—it's worth the tuition dollars!"

Interviewees consistently stress the importance of preparing students for their future careers via internships; however, they often report lacking sufficient resources to carry out this work. Tania tries to help students who reach out to her, but her role is predominantly to provide administrative support. Rey and other interviewees offer a different assessment, depicting internship programs as serving a performative function—at least in part—by making it *seem* as though higher education institutions help launch students' careers. According to this view, the rise of internships is linked to schools' efforts to symbolically show they are preparing students for careers.

For some schools, the need to justify the value of a degree is especially pressing. Maureen, a senior career services employee, works at a small private university facing such pressure. A few years before my interview with her, a local newspaper published an article using information from a website that ranks colleges based on their ROI (across schools and majors, comparing the financial costs of attending college with graduates' average earnings after graduation). The article reported that despite the school's prestige in creative fields, students were better off not going to college at all than attending Maureen's school.[22] When asked why higher education institutions have internship programs, she does not refer to rankings or the article, but explains, "From the school's perspective, I would say it's a return on investment type of thing." Echoing Sebastian's comment above, she says this approach is relatively recent, noting that decades ago, the primary aim of the school was "learning for the sake of learning . . . [but] times have changed." "Now," she suggests, "it's not just for the sake of learning and bettering yourself as a human being. Yes, you want to do all of those things, but you also need to pay back this money and support yourself after you graduate."

Maureen continues, discussing the school's position given the higher price of tuition and students' demands for a high ROI:

> We're realizing the deficits that we have, and that it's not sustainable for our students to pay this price tag and not get the jobs that they need to be successful and pay the school back. So, it's really making sure that we're providing them the opportunities for professional development, and to be able to do what we're saying [*laughs*] and telling all of the prospective students what we're doing.

Maureen describes her work as aiming "to show that we want to support the students and help them achieve their goals." Signaling an effort to better prepare students for careers (even in the absence of empirical evidence of success) helps fend off increasing scrutiny of alumni career outcomes from the government, ranking organizations, and families.[23] In terms of their day-to-day interactions, higher education personnel primarily report feeling pressure from parents and their institutions.

Shirley, the director of career services at a private university in New York, bluntly notes the importance of internships for her school, saying, "This is what the market's demanding. It's about ROI. Well, at least from the parents' perspective [*laughs*], it's *just* that." She recalls parents explicitly asking about degrees at her institution, "What is the ROI? What is the outcome on the other side of it?" Shirley stresses the importance of internships as a reaction to market demand to ensure the best possible career outcomes given that postsecondary institutions are competing for the best students and their tuition dollars.

Interviewees often describe parents, more so than students, as the strongest advocates of this approach. Brent, a career advisor at a private liberal arts college, notes, "To be blunt, many parents say, 'If I'm paying $65,000 a year, my kid better get a job. And they better get a good job.'" Brent then imitates comments he has heard from parents who embrace the school's liberal arts ideals yet nevertheless expect a return on their investment: "Yeah, yeah, yeah, liberal arts education is great. I want them to get that broad-based education, but I'm paying sixty-five grand." Consequently, "the pressure on the college to demonstrate outcomes is really, really robust." Brent describes the pressure schools face to demonstrate outcomes, including highlighting success stories (recent graduates who found jobs) prominently on his school's website.[24]

In the marketplace of higher education institutions, interviewees often report being pressured by their institution to demonstrate strong internship numbers, a pressure felt more acutely by workers at less prestigious schools. "It's a huge marketing thing," Caty says about the importance of internships for admissions at her university. Telling parents what proportion of the school's student body completes internships helps her recruit students to her moderately prestigious private university.[25] As a career counselor, Caty also mentions that she believes internships lead to better job outcomes, explaining, "We want the best for our students." She adds, "At a higher level they want to be able to tout that we have X number of internships in this many companies, and blah, blah, blah." While she proclaims to be a believer in the value of internships, Caty also describes institutional pressures to boost the number of internships.

Similarly, Mindy, a career services employee at an R2 public university, notes the importance of placing a large proportion of students in internships, saying, "It's going to make us look much better. It's one of the things that attracts students to us." She elaborates further, explaining that widespread internship participation plays a crucial role in attracting potential students:

> This idea—we've got this whole "80 percent of our students are going to graduate with an internship"—well, that's a big deal for a lot of people. And for students, for parents who are helping their student figure out where they want to go, what institution they want to attend, those are the types of things that they want to

> know coming in. And so, institution-wise, they're making sure that we have those statistics and that data [*laughs*], right? To tell our parents, because that way, we of course, from a financial standpoint, you get the students, we get the students coming to our institution. That's better for the institution.

These insights from higher education personnel reveal that market pressures, including prospective students' and parents' concerns about making the best (and most profitable) educational choices, permeate and drive institutional internships-for-all policies.

Strong internship statistics and examples of success stories not only help attract prospective students (and reassure their families), but also extend contact with employers, thus boosting the schools' fundraising efforts and deepening relationships with industry. Interviewees describe how success stories facilitate fundraising and enhance donor relations, with many of these donors being alumni. Cynthia, a senior employee in experiential learning at an R1 university, observes, "Happy alumni are important in our field." In addition to making large donations, happy alumni act as a bridge between schools and industry. Cynthia estimates that "at least 60 to 70 percent of our employer partners have an alum at that firm. In the creative majors, it's just astronomical the number of alumni connections that we have." Some career services personnel, including Lea, who is the director of career services at a school of music, art, and design, express the hope that cultivating relationships with organizations via internships will help future students gain internships and, more broadly, ensure positive career outcomes:

> Those places that have interns from [SCHOOL] that are happy with them will often return to us and say, "Our intern last semester was so great. Can we have another one?" So, it's also helping with the university's relationships in the external world and collaborations and our reputation with external partners. [And] if any company or organization is happy with their intern

from our school, then they're more likely to come to us, not just for interns, but even when they're hiring.

Therefore, through internship coordinators and career services personnel (as well as other staff members and some faculty), higher education institutions act as boosters of internships, with the aim of having as many students as possible complete an internship. Consequently, these higher education personnel see greater internship numbers as a sign of success for the institution.

Building Up the Pipeline

As internships have become more popular and schools have attempted to increase their prevalence, many higher education institutions have used a two-pronged approach to ensure high participation rates that entails kindling demand among the student body and developing an infrastructure for students to secure internships. For the former, the broader culture both within academia and beyond does much of the work of convincing students to intern. Due to internships' current prevalence in academic curricula as well as celebratory narratives in popular media about their power to help students obtain jobs, in recent decades college students have become more likely to report that internships were on their radar. For example, in a survey I designed as part of the Strategic National Arts Alumni Project (SNAAP), which was fielded to over ten thousand arts alumni, I found that alumni who graduated between 2008 and 2017 were significantly less likely than those in earlier cohorts to say they did not intern because they were unaware of such opportunities or because internships were not offered in their field.[26]

Thus, while higher education personnel make concerted efforts to encourage all students to intern, they perceive this as an easy task because many students are already eager for the experience. Most schools typically do not offer course credit for internships until the end of sophomore year, and higher education personnel at times express surprise at some students' strong desire to intern as soon as their first year. For example, Athena, the director of experiential education at an arts school, notes, "The students think that if they don't intern, they'll never get a job. So, they're clamoring for an internship. I have had students in their freshman year say, 'I want an internship this summer!'"

Because incoming students have not yet been fully exposed to the pro-internship narratives at their schools, some interviewees suggested that this enthusiasm is driven by parental influence. Geoff, an internship coordinator at a large private university in New York, offers, "I don't know if it's coming from their parents or them, but [surprisingly] there are freshmen coming in [saying], 'I gotta do an internship!'" This eagerness to intern, however, is not universal. First-generation college students, in particular, are less likely to intern than their more economically privileged peers and are more likely to report not interning because they face difficulties finding time for these experiences in addition to coursework and, frequently, paid jobs.[27]

For students who have not yet caught the internship bug, higher education institutions promote these experiences as essential for career success.[28] Higher education personnel consistently claim that internships are crucial to ensuring a student's employability. Shirley (the director of career services quoted above) tells all students that "there's no such thing as an entry-level job anymore." She considers it a warning, because students "are competing against other students out there . . . who've all done internships." Internships are now required in a large share of degree programs related to arts and media industries, but even when they are not, internship coordinators like Casey, who works for a private university, do their best to persuade students that they must intern to secure a job. She explains, "Internships for our students are not required for any of our majors, but we are point-blank with students right from the day they set foot on campus." Discussing students who aspire to work in the music industry, she adds, "If you do not intern, you will not get a job in this industry." Some higher education personnel frame internships-for-all policies as a way to address inequity in higher education. Elinor, a career counselor at a small arts school, portrays internship programs as "being able to guide all students, regardless of their background, regardless of race, ethnicity, gender. I think it's great to have the opportunity for all."

To ensure students' postgraduation success in an equitable manner—a goal that aligns well with schools' reputational priorities—some higher education institutions go so far as to schedule classroom presentations, so all students are aware of the importance of interning. Amy, the director of career services at a prestigious arts school, reports sending career services staff to classrooms to speak with students no later than their junior year to "make sure people do an internship in the summer between junior and senior year. Because to me that is the essential thing. If you don't do that, they're going to graduate, and their résumé doesn't show that they have that experience." This approach is not uncommon, although at some schools the career services personnel or internship coordinators act even earlier. Near the peak of the COVID-19 pandemic, Lea, the director of career services quoted above, toured classrooms via Zoom to reach sophomores; she recounts, "I went into a lot of Zooms for sophomore seminars to talk about, 'You're going to be eligible starting this summer to do your internship.'" By promoting internships to soon-to-be eligible students, Lea was responding to what she describes as a new school priority to reach out to students earlier, therefore giving them more time to potentially intern.

Find Your Own Internship

While higher education institutions kindle the demand for interning, students are often left to fend for themselves in terms of finding an internship. As Faith, a senior career services employee, notes, "Most internships are found through a connection. So, a family friend or alumni connection. I would love to tell you that most are found at the career center, but it's just not the case and it never will be." Paradoxically, as the prevalence of internships has increased, alumni have become less likely to say they found their internship through school resources. In the SNAAP internship survey, I found that approximately two-thirds of arts alumni who graduated in 2002 or before said they found an internship through school resources, whereas—consistent with Faith's assessment—more recent graduates were significantly more likely to credit their personal networks.[29]

Despite the increasing formalization of internship programs at higher education institutions, which has often included hiring internship coordinators and advisors, these findings about the importance of personal networks are not altogether surprising. The numbers suggest that the rise in internship demand has outpaced the ability of higher education institutions to act as "connectors" between students and organizations. Further, this transition occurred during the proliferation of internet listings for internship opportunities, perhaps reducing the need for higher education personnel to connect students with internships. Nevertheless, for students in need of help, schools do offer some resources.

Music business–related programs build relationships with employers and some programs boast more listings than their students could possibly fill, with one internship coordinator estimating that they had five hundred listings each year. A music business student told me that she and her classmates joked they were paying tens of thousands of dollars in tuition to be on a music internship listserv. Importantly, however, most music industry interns are not enrolled in music business programs, and most programs or schools offer far fewer music industry–related listings for their students. To support students in search of an internship, higher education personnel generally describe offering a "menu of resources," and then students do further work to identify potential internships and decide which ones would be most beneficial to them. Some internship coordinators associated with specific academic programs send out weekly emails listing internship opportunities;

some of the interviewees post a "how to find an internship" guide on their school's website; and others maintain a database (usually via a recruiting platform such as Handshake). Armed with these tools and resources, students are told to find an internship on their own.[30]

Most higher education personnel explain this approach primarily as a philosophical choice to train students to fend for themselves—a "teach them to fish" philosophy that better prepares students for their future as job-seeking workers. Thus, higher education institutions claim to not only enable students to build their employability but also prepare them for the lifelong task of selling themselves in the labor market. Lea, the director of career services who visited classrooms via Zoom during COVID-19, summarizes this approach, explaining that her school maintains both a list of sites where previous students interned and an online job and internship board, and students can make an appointment with her office if they need help. Justifying this approach, she adds,

> Not only don't I have the staff capacity to follow a model where we match students up for internships, but philosophically, that doesn't do them any good in their professional life. And one of the things we always talk about is the idea that the process that we teach them to follow in finding an internship is the process they will use the rest of their life for finding work. So, they need to know how to research and identify the places that interest them and have a top-notch résumé and a kick-ass cover letter. . . . And it's the same in the job search.

In brief, the do-it-yourself approach advocated by higher education personnel offers an ideological justification for a hands-off approach to the internship process; however, at times, these workers also acknowledge they lack the resources that would be required to adopt a more hands-on process.

Higher education personnel also assert that having students find their own internships is a way to set realistic expectations about the job market. For example, James, a career services employee at a large R1 public university, warns against the dangers of "coddling" students by having career services employees reach out to potential employers on their behalf.

> If an institution coddles [students] in a way to where they set unrealistic expectations of what is going to be given to them . . . without putting in the work, that can be a negative, right? And I've seen that happen. There are students that have been given these things and now they feel like life owes them something.

The sense of entitlement perceived by some higher education personnel relates to students' and parents' expectations of a reasonable ROI, especially at schools where tuition is high. Kenton, the director of career services at a prestigious arts and design school, refers to "a quality from students and families sometimes of, 'You better get me a job. I spent all this money.'" While Kenton could spend more time helping students connect with employers, he believes this would prevent them from gaining the ability to push themselves and explore. Instead, in his words, his core responsibility is to "lay out a buffet of resources, and links, and opportunities, and consistently drive students."

Students who approach higher education personnel with the hope of being connected to internships run the risk of being perceived as "coddled" or "entitled." As Leslie, a career services employee at a private R1 university, explains, "People, no joke, thought we were like *Wheel of Fortune*. You'd come in, you'd spin the wheel. Oh, you get this internship here or there; like literally they'd walk in and say, 'Hi, I'm here to select my internship.'" Interviewees describe acting as a gatekeeper when they encounter an entitled student, almost playing the role of an employer (or at least empathizing with employers rather than the student).

Leslie continues, recounting her response to such students, "Oh, OK, well, let's back that up a few steps because I'd first like to know, what is your name? What is your major? What experience do you have? What is it you hope to contribute at this organization?" Similarly, a career counselor from an R2 private university refers to "a whole new generation where they really want that stuff and they often want it handed to them, which we don't do." Some interviewees offer caveats; in exceptional cases where students seem unable to figure things out themselves, employees like Linda, the dean of career development at an arts school, will go above and beyond. She notes, "For those who *really* can't seem to do it, we'll make a phone call or two for them," and continues, "It's really those who feel more lost than not that we end up having to source and handhold more, but we do that as needed." In most cases, however, higher education personnel limit themselves to showing students the tools and helping them gain agency so they can create their own opportunities.

Notably, this "teach them to fish" approach poses two interrelated problems in terms of social inequality, particularly for students in creative fields: not all students have the same resources, and the internship listings offered by schools are often lacking. First, not every student has equally advantageous personal connections, background knowledge, and time. Affluent parents are more likely to act as a "career concierge" for their children, helping them connect with networks to secure internships.[31] SNAAP data on internships in creative fields reflect this pattern, showing important class-based differences in social networks: among arts alumni who found an internship through personal connections (e.g., family members), those with a college-educated parent were more likely to get a paid (and often higher quality) internship than first-generation alumni.[32] Beyond networks, these differences are exacerbated by class-based patterns in cultural capital—first-generation students are less likely than their peers to seek out help from their schools, making it more likely that these students will not intern at all.[33]

Second, in many cases, the lists of internships provided by schools are inadequate. The career services personnel I interviewed who work with students in both arts and non-arts majors noted that Handshake and similar recruitment platforms work relatively well for fields like business and engineering, which feature more formalized college-to-career pathways,[34] but post far fewer listings for arts-related majors. Bianca, a career advisor at an R1 university, observes, "For some reason, those employers do not post on Handshake, and it's hard to even just find postings for them in general. So, students usually have to hunt them down, call them. [The internship listings] may not even be on their website." When schools fail to maintain a consistent, centralized source of internship hosts, students in creative fields not only have to navigate the flooded intern marketplace mostly on their own but also have limited access to information about whether an internship will be "good." These two problems are especially important considering the differences in how employers and higher education institutions view internships, and how the latter attempt to mitigate the built-in ambiguity of this breaking-in system.

Mitigating Ambiguity

The recent rise of internships-for-all policies has created a heightened challenge for higher education institutions as they seek to ensure a baseline of internship quality. Notably, while colleges and universities encourage, and in some cases require, students to participate in internships, ostensibly to complement the curriculum and build students' employability, these goals do not fully align with the aims of industry. Thus, before I explore the ways higher education institutions attempt to mitigate the ambiguity of interns as both "students" and "workers," I review the perspective of the organizations that host internships.

Music industry employees describe hosting interns for multiple reasons: they serve as an inexpensive source of labor; provide an influx of youthful energy, information, and ideas; and allow organizations to train the next generation of record industry professionals, thus creating a pipeline of qualified candidates to music firms.[35] Publicly, firms in most industries focus on training/creating a pipeline as their reason for hosting interns. Specifically, hiring former interns reduces training costs and often results in longer-term retention than "external" hiring.[36] This rationale—identifying and nurturing talent with the possibility of hiring interns as future employees—aligns well with higher education's stated dual emphasis on education and career.[37] However, while this motivation may be plausible at some firms with well-structured, usually paid, internship programs, nearly every music industry employee I interviewed claims that companies host interns to benefit from inexpensive labor. Notably, these claims differ in asserting interns' usefulness: most employees portray interns as facilitators or "extra hands" that benefit the company and, if well managed, can further the supervising employee's career, but some go so far as to describe interns as crucial to company operations.

While institutions of higher education perceive interns as students, music industry employees readily (though privately) describe interns as workers. Employees describe interns as a free-floating resource the company can use to address almost any need, especially tasks that require little training. In an extreme case, a senior music industry employee reports having two unpaid interns film his wedding. Another employee sees no issue with interns fetching his dry cleaning. Other employees disapprove of such menial assignments, and some departments even have interns handle slightly more sensitive, higher-level work such as managing social media accounts and updating a database of promotional outlets. However, almost all descriptions portray interns primarily as a source of cheap labor.

A discussion at Major Records USA that I overheard exemplifies the portrayal of interns as a flexible resource. Marco, the only employee at the Los Angeles office, asks Bill (a senior executive) to sign a travel preapproval form even though the travel has already been completed. Charged with processing the form, Hank (an employee and my internship supervisor) prints out the form and sheepishly hands it over to Bill, who quickly greets it with a look of discontent. Bill tells Hank that signing after travel is unacceptable and blames him for the oversight. Once Bill is out of earshot,

I overhear Hank discussing the incident with an employee (Kendra) who sits nearby:

> HANK: I don't have anything to do with Marco. He's in L.A.
> KENDRA: He doesn't have an assistant.
> HANK: No! He needs to get himself some interns.

In Hank's view, interns are the solution to the Los Angeles employee's lack of administrative support. This exchange typifies the way employees talk about interns as an easily acquired source of labor they can use to tackle almost any staffing issue.

Certainly, several employees I meet say that internships can serve as a training ground and screening device for potential employees, however, they often pair this observation with a skeptical or cynical comment. Nate, a music industry employee, illustrates this skepticism:

> People can sit there and say like, "We're trying to harbor careers" and all that, but the essential reason [music companies host interns] is to get that shit work done, and then hopefully you're going to find that diamond in the rough, ideally; but essentially, it's that reason, it's shit work to get done.

Therefore, while employees do not refute the training/pipeline rationale, many openly question whether it is companies' primary benefit.

The focus on inexpensive labor is further evident in employees' prioritization of a potential intern's availability over other qualifications.[38] Thinking back to his recent HR position at a major record company, an interviewee recalls, "A lot of [employees] just wanted somebody who could do the hours that they needed. I mean, on the form it's required that you list the tasks, but the most important thing for them was the hours." Similarly, Isabel, an employee at a major record company, characterizes the process of choosing interns as a matter of scheduling without mentioning other qualifications: "If we have four kids that want to work only on Wednesdays that's not going to work. We need somebody there on

Monday, Tuesday, Wednesday, Thursday, and Friday." Isabel's department seeks to maximize (and spread out) the labor of their interns, who offer administrative support to the assistants.

Making the Intern Economy Educational

While the pattern is far from uniformly acknowledged, many higher education personnel note the potential mismatch in goals between intern hosts and schools. Higher education employees are aware of the inexpensive labor rationale. As Daniel, an internship coordinator at a large university who works with record industry aspirants, says, "Every place wants an intern. It's free labor." Similarly, when I ask Casey, a career center employee at another university, why companies host interns, she explains, "For the most part it's economics. They hire students for free labor. And then it's my job to help them [the companies] structure it into an educational experience." That host companies view interns as a cheap source of labor is not contested but rather perceived as a complication to be addressed.

As Don, the dean of an arts and media school specializing in film, television, and music industries, diplomatically explains, "As an education institution, we have certain kinds of objectives for an internship experience for our students. The employers have certain kinds of objectives that they try to meet through internships." He continues, "There's not a hundred percent alignment between us and the employer. Right? They have certain kinds of needs and expectations that don't necessarily align with what it is that we believe is important for the students."

Don notes that employers typically bring in student interns to do low-level work, making it difficult for them to gain much experience or mentorship. His school's solution has been to develop deeper partnerships with a select few intern hosts: "We're working on projects together as opposed to simply supplying students to perform certain kinds of labor that the employer needs or wants." School staff and the employer jointly designed the project, which carefully combines having students complete work for a local media company and giving them closer access to employees, opportunities to see how creative decisions are made, and chances to further unpack these experiences in the classroom. In this program, students sign up for an internship course built around launching a new initiative at the company. Importantly, however, partnerships like this one are time-intensive and represent a small minority of internships; as Don puts it, most of the school's students do "normal" internships.

Over time, especially since dozens of former interns began filing lawsuits for back pay in 2013, higher education institutions (and some employers) have increasingly tried to limit the most blatant abuses of cheap labor. College and university personnel, in conjunction with industry partners, have worked to design better experiences for interns. Some schools have even begun to require a training plan for interns, or at least a clear set of tasks and learning objectives agreed upon by all parties. Similarly, to protect themselves from lawsuits, employers (sometimes called "hosts," "partners," or "sponsors" by schools) increasingly require signed documents from school personnel stating that students are receiving school credit for an unpaid internship.[39] Nevertheless, higher education personnel, who have limited access to resources and are tasked with running internship programs rather than rigorously overseeing the experiences of individual interns, report that most attempts to regulate internships are modest in scope.

The aims of higher education institutions and music industry employees are not fully aligned, and in practice, the ambiguity of the distinction between "work" and "education" persists. As a result, higher education personnel use two key practices to make these arrangements more palatable: vetting internship hosts, including oversight during and after these experiences, and reframing work. The former excludes what schools consider the most illegitimate internships, while the latter provides an ideological basis for interns to be treated like exploited workers.

Vetting

In effect, higher education institutions work to control what constitutes a legitimate and valuable internship. Vetting is a proactive attempt to prevent predictable problems. In practice, vetting entails a dual focus on protecting students from exploitation and protecting schools by providing an infrastructure for determining which internships are understood as educational opportunities.

While all higher education interviewees describe using some type of vetting criteria when considering internship postings, these criteria vary widely, and most set a low bar. Vetting criteria for new internship hosts fall into two general categories: baseline acceptability and interpretive criteria. Those in the first category are most common and include official guidelines and basic red flags interviewees have devised, such as requiring that the host have a company email (e.g., no Gmail addresses allowed) and company website; have been in business for at least one year; have an office (no home offices, although this rule was relaxed during the pandemic); and provide interns with a designated computer and workspace (the intern cannot be asked to use their personal laptop). This group of criteria is paired with baseline criteria for students, such as whether they meet the school's minimum GPA requirements and have accrued enough credits to be eligible for an internship to ensure that students are ready for the experience and to prevent an unprepared intern from tarnishing the school's reputation. Schools also have clear rules about translating interning hours into academic credits (e.g., forty-five to fifty hours of interning is equivalent to one academic credit).

The interpretive vetting criteria take more effort to implement and are unevenly enforced across institutions. These requirements include, for example, that interns must be assigned an experienced supervisor; most of an intern's duties must be career relevant; and the host must define relevant learning objectives. When possible, this vetting work is transferred to the students themselves, who are asked to identify which competencies a proposed internship will help them develop—therefore, students help schools decide whether an internship is worthy of academic credit.[40]

Higher education personnel describe trying to maintain lists of "good" hosts but note that these rapidly become obsolete due to high turnover rates in the cultural industries. For example, an intern can have a great experience in a department only for the manager to leave by the next semester. Due to limited resources and rapidly changing hosts, higher education personnel encourage interns to be partners in deciding whether an internship is appropriate or beneficial. As Casey, an internship coordinator, reports, "We really emphasize to students the importance of researching companies and asking questions during the interview process to learn what that experience might be like." There is broad recognition that resources for vetting are limited and, while a specific internship might allow a student to earn academic credit, the responsibility for vetting the opportunity prominently falls on the student.

Vetting potential internships based on interpretive criteria demands resources (especially time), which higher education interviewees lack. Therefore, interviewees address only the most blatant red flags. For example, Carina, a career services employee, says she is mindful of listings that use the word "assistant" rather than "intern." She explains, "We are very careful about anything that says 'assistant' . . . because those are often scams, you know?" Jane, an internship coordinator for a music business program at an R1 university, shares that she turns down internship listings that include custodial tasks, adding, "Our students are not janitors. We don't allow them to do custodial tasks, but we do have some flexibility."

For some creative majors, the match between the type of employer and a student's major is more important. For example, one interviewee recalls rejecting a dance major's proposed internship at a music venue. The student's proposed learning objectives centered around learning how to run the restaurant at the venue, and the school decided "this student was not going to be able to earn credit for a summer job at a restaurant, which it clearly was." However, had the student been a music business major and indicated they were learning how to book or promote acts, "that would be approved." Similarly, a music business student seeking an internship at a comedy television show like *Saturday Night Live* is expected to intern in the music department rather than another department.

Some schools go further in the vetting process by considering the credentials and experience of the on-site mentor. In these cases, higher education personnel try to ensure a student is being supervised by an expert. Michelle, for example, notes that supervisors "have to essentially have more experience than the student." A few other interviewees emphasize that the intern must not be the sole expert in their role. Christina, who runs an internship program, notes, "We're very strict with our participating organizations that this is an internship experience. This is not a freebie job." Thus, an intern could not earn credit for managing social media at a record company if the firm does not already have a social media employee. She adds, imitating a fictional employer, "Oh, I can't hire a social media manager, so I'll get an intern to do it." However, even when schools enforce such supervisor requirements, hosts may find loopholes. In recent years, HR departments at larger record companies frequently ask that manager-level (or higher) employees officially oversee interns, but in practice day-to-day supervision duties are frequently carried out by junior-level staff (e.g., assistants). Without visiting these sites, if the student does not report any problems, higher education personnel cannot enforce these rules.

Because colleges and universities do not invest significant time and resources in either site visits for new and existing internship hosts or in-depth oversight of individual internship experiences, hosts and interns can often easily sidestep rules. Very few interviewees report visiting intern sites or having substantive follow-up conversations with hosts/partners. Instead, higher education personnel might simply instruct the employer to make the experience as educational as possible without following up. Mindy mentions that she asks hosts: "Are you having weekly conversations with your intern regarding what they're learning and what their goal is?

And they have to have a goal, right? There has to be an actual goal, [*laughs*] right?" Tony, who works at a small, elite university is an exception to this pattern in that he reaches out to internship hosts midway through the semester/summer. He explains, "In the middle, we have a conversation. That conversation really is about the student's goals. And like, 'Are you helping the student meet their goals?'" Tony is an exception not only because he works at an elite university, but also because he oversees a small yet expensive master's-level program—he has more resources than most other interviewees but also more visibility with students in this relatively small program.[41] Generally, however, higher education personnel only report scrutinizing internships before they begin and possibly after the fact (if at all).

Higher education interviewees report that they rely on student feedback to identify problematic experiences. As one interviewee notes, "We do rely on our students to relate to us when, and if, we've missed the mark." Another interviewee offers a similar perspective: "We have had students come in and say, 'You know, I worked for this person. I did get paid, but it was really bad.' And then we'll get two sides of the story, and we have cut people off [from] our posting list." Interviewees estimate that by using these practices—setting a low bar when vetting hosting sites and waiting for negative feedback rather than being proactive—they "cut off" at most two or three intern hosts per year out of hundreds. Given that higher education personnel lack detailed knowledge about their interns' experiences, the policies and practices at colleges and universities enable the coexistence of internships that range widely in quality.[42]

Reframing Work

While higher education personnel use vetting to limit the ambiguity of internships—and in doing so, curb exploitation—they also deny and normalize this ambiguity through "reframing work." Higher education personnel take two steps to help students reframe their internship experience: they socialize students to accept, or even embrace, their exploitation as workers, and they act as apologists for the intern economy, especially when students complain about negative experiences. As a result, higher education personnel prompt interns to think of themselves as workers while also marking these experiences—no matter how exploitative—as educational.

As previously noted, more career-oriented staff members at higher education institutions help "sell" internships as a crucial career opportunity. For example, Elinor, a career counselor at a small private college, describes instructing soon-to-be interns to embrace the role: "I tell students to take that internship and run with it . . . [to] put their best foot forward because they never know if it can turn into a full-time position." She continues, "Even if it doesn't turn into a full-time position, it's a great opportunity for them to learn." Thus, in Elinor's view, embracing an internship means a student accepts its uncertain outcomes but also reframes it—in case they have any doubt—as a can't-lose scenario.

Some interviewees, especially those at larger, more prestigious public and private universities, urge students to go beyond expectations and create their own opportunities. James, who works in career services at a top public university, tells students to be "go-getters" at their internships: "What I coach is creating opportunities for yourself. . . . Nobody's going to hand anything to you. You've got to fight for yourself to be seen." James also warns students that success may not be immediate, but enduring suffering will pay off when they least expect it, advising them that "one great opportunity comes out of all those things that maybe you felt were a waste of time." Working hard to be a great intern, enduring suffering, and accepting uncertain or delayed rewards prepares students for the mailroom model of training that employers embrace, as I describe in chapter 3.

Some interviewees go further in socializing students to not only embrace internships, but also to view themselves as workers. In doing so, higher education personnel reduce the ambiguity of the intern role; they tell students that as interns, they should see themselves more as workers than as students. Leslie, who works in career services at an R1 private university, encourages interns to empathize with the internship host, suggesting that they work extra hours or at least offer to do so. She tells students that if they finish their assigned work they should "at least say, 'What else can I do?'" and recommends that they "think more strategically about their value at the organization." Leslie explains that students often seem surprised by this advice because they have "tunnel vision," and she then describes instructing them to empathize with employees:

> [*IMITATING A STUDENT*] "I'm here for six hours and I'm just going to go in and get it done and move on." And it's like, you have to understand on the employer side, they're there sometimes twelve-, fourteen-hour days, gosh, and working from home sometimes sixteen-hour days. And so, if you can even give them just a couple more hours of your time or at least inquire about it, that's going to show that you're that much more interested in this opportunity in the long-term.

Some interviewees stress that interns, as students, sometimes treat the internship as a class and the employees as teachers, and thus think in terms of doing what is needed to "pass" or "get an A" and go no further. In the workplace, however, overtaxed workers do not share this general understanding.

By encouraging students to do more, higher education personnel help socialize interns to embrace their exploitation as unpaid or low-paid workers. Because it is difficult to enforce rules and policies concerning intern hours, some interviewees explicitly instruct students to sidestep official work-hour limits.[43] An internship coordinator for a music business program at a large private university shares that students often work extra hours (i.e., go beyond their official internship hours). The coordinator notes that although a student registers for either one course credit (fifty hours at the internship) or two credits (one hundred hours), they sometimes intentionally turn a blind eye if the student goes beyond these limits:

> What often happens is that even though a student signs up for one credit or two credits, they often spend many more hours at the [company]. And that's OK . . . most of them if they sign up for two credits and they're supposed to be there for 100 hours, if they really like it, often they'll be there 200–250 hours. Whatever fits into their schedule.

In this person's only meeting with students before they start an internship, they stress the importance of going above and beyond expectations. Notably, interviewees who advocate this approach never mention that not all students can afford to work additional hours.

Another way higher education personnel do reframing work is by acting as apologists for the intern economy. Higher education personnel at times reframe students' experiences as less exploitative or at least as educational, especially when students share complaints about an internship's poor quality—for example, saying they are overworked, only doing low-level tasks, or receiving little mentorship. The apologists sometimes side with the employer or simply try to reinforce the status quo and, given the difference in power between students and school personnel, this practice can resemble gaslighting.[44] More often, however, school staff members focus on helping students build themselves back up after (or during) a bad experience, thus functioning as a maintenance crew for the intern economy. The latter approach is partly in response to students' concerns; as one educator put it, students who experience professional conflicts at an internship are concerned that if their school gets involved (e.g., reach out to a problematic supervisor) the intern is "going to then be completely ostracized from an industry."

While some career services professionals try to end relationships with extremely exploitative internship hosts, others advise students to endure negative experiences, reframing them as "learning opportunities" and a necessary part of paying your dues. Scott, a career services employee at an R1 private university, seems disappointed that some people and companies treat interns as cheap labor, lamenting, "Unfortunately there are still individuals who would say that all internships are just running and getting coffee and being that free labor to companies." Despite his disapproval, he adds that even in those cases, the student is putting their "foot in the door" and may learn important lessons about the world of work. He describes advising students to "bear" a disappointing internship experience:

> A student might come in and say, "I didn't expect that [I] would have to take garbage out." Sometimes you have to explain that not every internship [involves becoming] a CEO of the company and running their operation, their businesses, and sometimes it is a sort of manual labor, and you will have to go through this.

Scott reframes exploitative experiences as educational, normalizes low-status tasks (e.g., he says that getting coffee or taking out the trash is still educational), and implies that students who complain about starting at the bottom are entitled. This type of reframing is self-serving for both higher education personnel and educational institutions, which are poorly equipped (in terms of time and resources) to ensure the quality of internship experiences.

Although Scott offers an extreme example, many interviewees claim there is no such thing as a truly "bad" internship. Leslie and her colleagues, for example, tell students, "It doesn't matter necessarily where you're at. Anywhere you go [intern], you're going to gain some great experience; you're going to learn really quickly about the industry and what you can do." Leslie continues, using this apologist reframing to support the rise of internships-for-all policies:

> Even from a negative experience, whether it was because of the type of work you were doing or the supervisor, or just the overall office environment, you're going to learn something. And I think that that's really helped to even the field and recognize that regardless of where you're at, as long as you can gain some insight, it can then be applied for future opportunities.

Importantly, because students from less privileged backgrounds have fewer resources they can use to connect to the highest quality internships, the perspective that any internship is a good internship does the opposite of making the playing field "even"—rather, this view obscures the struggles of first-generation students and students from other minority or minoritized groups, and the rise of internships-for-all policies further drives students to do bad internships.

Finally, some apologists acknowledge students' negative experiences but nevertheless encourage interns to interpret their difficulties in a more positive light. For example, Faith uses the term "reframing" to describe how she helps students reinterpret negative experiences as worthwhile learning experiences. As if addressing a student, she explains:

> You're not having a great experience, but what could come from this? So, some good things can come from this. You know you don't want to do that again. And this is just a short-term experience. That's what an internship is for, to figure out if you like something or not. So, that's just kind of reframing the situation. Does it suck right now? It sounds like it, but what transferable skills are we going to talk about in interviews next year? How could you frame this as an answer to a question about risk-taking, or overcoming adversity?

By helping students interpret a bad internship as a learning experience and a challenge that can have some redeeming value on the job market, apologists help smooth over the intern economy's ambiguous and exploitative edges.

Conclusion

Higher education institutions exacerbate rather than diminish the ambiguity of the intern economy. An internship, broadly described as a form of experiential learning, can mean many things to educators, and these understandings frequently do not align with the interests of industry. As internships have become more common in recent decades, higher education institutions have increasingly formalized their policies and practices in hopes their students will have worthwhile experiences; however, these changes are often geared toward the goal of internships for all. In essence, schools prioritize the reputational gains that come from being able to boast about strong returns on investment for graduates rather than running these programs in a rigorous manner. The next chapter explores how opening the floodgates for college students to enter workplaces that are primarily interested in exploiting their labor has created further challenges as interns seek to break in.

2

Dealing with an Ambiguous Role

SWEATING AND SLEEPLESS, lying on his bed shortly before the sun rises, Ryan ponders his future with a newfound sense of exhilaration. As a twenty-year-old starting his sophomore year of college while living in his parents' home in New Jersey, Ryan is struggling academically and, until this moment, had no clear sense of what career he wanted to pursue after graduation. A committed night owl, he stumbled upon a 3 a.m. television show portraying a day in the life of an A&R (artists and repertoire) person. People who work in A&R scout new musical talent and shepherd the artistic development of a label's signed artists. This was not Ryan's first glimpse into the music industry. In his late teens he routinely hung out with a local hip-hop group that was under contract with a major record label, accompanying them in the studio and acting as their informal assistant. The show, which featured an interview with Tina Davis, an A&R representative who worked with big acts such as Jay-Z, sparked a thought: "Man, the music industry, maybe *there's* something I can do."

Six years later, as Ryan and I sit in a major record company's lavish conference room designed to double as an intimate music venue for its staff, Ryan has been employed in A&R for two years and points to that sleepless night as a turning point in his life. He recalls staying awake, thinking, "I figured out what I want to do for the rest of my life and now I have to figure out how to do it." Ryan quickly decided that the best path into the music industry was an internship, a decision he based on the experiences of Sean Combs (aka Puff Daddy, P. Diddy, Puffy), who ascended from intern to industry executive: "Puff Daddy was a lowly intern when he started. . . . He's a legend now. You look at those stories, and you're like, 'Wow, that's what I could be.'" In that moment of imagining his future self, Ryan began his career with what sociologist Robert Faulkner (1974:157) called a period of "illusionment"—a time when young adults are attempting to establish a foothold and success seems possible. Over time, however, aspirations are replaced by "new mobility outlooks and motivations,"[1] which depend on what the worker achieves and the conditions they encounter. As the internship has become, over recent decades, a key pathway for breaking into various occupations, there remains a large gap between the formulation of job-seeking aspirations and securing a career in the record industry, leading most interns to move on to other pursuits.

Ryan faced some hurdles as he sought an internship. He explains that he did not meet his university's GPA requirement to take part in an internship program, so he did everything he could to improve his academic performance, recounting, "I busted my ass; went to school year-round; literally took classes in the summer, winter, spring, fall. If there was another season, I would have taken a class [then] and turned my grades around." Ryan's hard work paid off. He improved his GPA considerably, even earning a 4.0 GPA one semester.

Next, Ryan had to find an internship. His university's career center did not have contacts at any record companies, so he searched online for internship contacts and made some cold calls. Eventually, he landed an interview for an internship at a major record company's A&R department, the most in-demand and therefore challenging type of internship to secure at a record company. On the day of the interview, after getting off the train in New York City, Ryan ran toward the record company's office building to ensure he arrived well before the appointed time. Recalling his sense of desperation, Ryan reenacts the moment, gesturing with his arms as if he were running, and turning his head from side to side, repeating, "Where's [this street]? Where's [that street]?" He explains that he was so anxious about time he eventually hopped into a cab, saying, "It was a two-minute walk, but I had to get in a cab . . . I can't miss this interview." He describes the interview as a casual conversation with two of the three employees in the department:

> They're on their computers looking at me, still typing away, asking me random questions . . . I told [the main interviewer] flat out, "This is where I want to be. Please take me as an intern. You can do whatever you want to me, but just promise me that you're going to teach me. Just any small thing, I'm willing to do it." They're like, "*Fine,* come on board."

The interviewers' disinterest in response to Ryan's sincere passion is indicative of how the next steps in his internship experience would play out. His early days as an intern were difficult: "It was an absolute struggle because the reality is you're an intern. The reality is you're not getting paid." Frustration quickly set in, he adds, because he was paying tuition and transportation costs to do unpaid work yet was assigned only a few intermittent tasks. He continued,

> You can come in here and spend six hours and do nothing and sometimes that would become frustrating because sometimes there's no work for you to do. You're just there, you copy something, you staple something, and sometimes you just sit there and [think]: "*Damn,* I spent X amount of dollars to get these credits and I'm not doing anything." You know, that was kind of my first week here. I was thinking about quitting. I'm like, "I'm coming in here and doing nothing."

Interns sometimes go to great lengths to secure an internship and bring considerable excitement to the position, yet, as Ryan's case illustrates, being an intern often entails a mix of humility, pride, accomplishment, and doubt. In his plea to the interviewers, Ryan seemed willing to do whatever it took to break in, but he did not yet fully understand the conditions under which this would occur—namely, that he would have to navigate through the ambiguity of the intern's role as he tried to learn the ropes.

In this chapter, I describe how internships are infused with ambiguity, leaving room for multiple aims and interpretations among both interns and employers, which makes it difficult for aspirants to break into a full-time job. While Ryan viewed his internship as a pathway to employment in the industry, not every intern shares this "employment" type of motivation. The interns and established employees I spoke with also described two other types of motivation: education and fandom. I show that many interns are not seeking immediate employment; further, employees may not believe or support an intern's professional aspirations because employees often presume interns are uncommitted and incompetent. Moreover, record industry internships, by design, involve modest investment from host firms, which only increases the ambiguity—internships demand relatively superficial change from newcomers, in a process of surface-level socialization.

A Motley Assemblage of Types

There is a long tradition of sociological studies of the social process of breaking in, often called the period of initiation of newcomers, and a key assumption in such studies is that newcomers want to become insiders.[2] In the case of the music industry, however, interns are not necessarily trying to gain immediate employment. Music industry interns are a largely homogeneous group—while they vary by age and background, most are approximately eighteen to twenty-one years old and enrolled in college[3]—but in terms of their motivation, they are a motley assemblage.[4] When interns and employees discussed why someone would complete a record industry internship, they suggested dozens of potential reasons, although these centered around three main themes: to learn about the world of work and more specifically the record industry; to experience meaningful involvement with the music world, potentially as an extension of fandom; and to take a first step toward eventual record industry employment. These three motivations drive three types of interns, which I call[5] the Student, the Enthusiast, and the Job Seeker, as illustrated by Amanda, Paula, and Ryan.

The Student

While all interns in the Student mold are motivated by a desire to learn, the learning they pursue takes on multiple forms, including learning about an industry, clarifying career goals, developing skills, extending classroom learning, and simply figuring out how to become a working adult.[6] Amanda, who attended New York University (NYU), is an example of an intern who just wanted to learn how to survive, and maybe thrive, in the work world.

Growing up in upstate New York, Amanda spent her teenage years attending shows in the punk and hardcore scene, although she also enjoyed jazz, rock 'n' roll, and classical music performances. When deciding where to attend college, she opted for a school in New York so she would be close to the city's rich and eclectic music scene: "I wanted to go to lots of shows all the time." As she started her junior year at NYU, studying English and philosophy, Amanda entertained vague notions of wanting to work in the music industry after graduation but did not know what role to pursue or what type of company to work at. Through friends, she first secured an internship at a prestigious music magazine and then, in her senior year, interned at a music marketing firm. She chose these two very different internships to, as she put it, "be better rounded" in her education concerning the world of music business.

Through her two internship experiences, Amanda learned that despite its mystique, the music magazine was struggling in the digital age, and she did not quite fit in with—nor could she financially keep up with—the fashionable interns and employees who wore expensive clothes and lived in the trendiest neighborhoods. At the music marketing firm, however, Amanda found that she fit in much better, enjoyed working with the smaller team and taking on tasks that included reaching out to blogs and interacting with musicians and employees from record labels she respected. The second internship also allowed her to improve her computer literacy—"I got to know a lot of programs a lot better than I would have otherwise"—when she spent time building and maintaining a database of promotional outlets.

The Student views interning as an opportunity to apply, extend, and possibly replace classroom learning. Amanda explains that she took one music business course and enjoyed it, but she thinks internships are the best way to further probe the subject. "College isn't real at all," she adds. Despite her longtime passion for music, her plan was to take only one course about the industry to obtain general background information and then intern at different places and "figure it out from there, because I think you learn so much more by *being there*." She credits college for making her a sharper thinker and helping her grow up but notes that it was only through internships that she learned how to interact in a professional setting. At her internships, she learned whether you could swear in the office (sometimes), how people react when their boss yells at them (stay quiet and try not to engage), and how employees casually interact with one another (while bringing up a reading by French philosopher Jacques Derrida worked with her classmates, the topic was not deemed conventional workplace banter). Amanda also took note of how employees used certain specialized language and crafted sales pitches, thereby picking up some occupational vocabulary and tricks of the music marketing trade.

Although many people I spoke with, including Amanda, seemed terrified of making mistakes while they interned, when they did, they realized—at least, in hindsight—that the consequences for missteps were minimal. Becoming a working adult involves making mistakes along the way, and, as Amanda says, "If you act kind of weird or you don't know how to act [at] the job, [an internship] is a really good way to figure that stuff out." For the

Student, an internship offers a safe way to ease into becoming an adult with minor consequences when things go mildly wrong.[7]

Now that Amanda has graduated from college and is working in another industry, she looks back positively on how her internships helped her through what she calls the "weird transition" between being a student and being a working adult.[8] She elaborated, "When you're a student, you are kind of an adult, but you're not really yet." In sum, Student interns are motivated by the desire to find their footing in the world, and while their learning takes a variety of forms, it is oriented less toward gaining employment and more toward personal growth.

The Enthusiast

Paula's description of her early experiences in the music industry exemplifies the motivations that drive the Enthusiast intern. As she puts it, her first internship was done "more from a fan type of perspective than '*I want this to become my job eventually*'" perspective. Paula recalls becoming a fan of punk rock at the age of nine, after the rise of Nirvana in the early 1990s filled radio airwaves and MTV with indie rock and punk-influenced music. By the time she attended middle school, she was deeply invested in "punk and indie stuff," and most of her favorite music was recorded and produced locally, in the San Francisco area, where she grew up and later attended college. As a nineteen-year-old student at the University of California, Berkeley, with college graduation still two years away, Paula interned at a venerable punk label more as a pursuit of her personal passion than for educational or career purposes. She describes her motivation as follows: "When I decided to intern there it was mostly [out of] fandom and [the] romantic intrigue of helping out a label that had so many bands that I loved when I was younger." Behind the mythical name, the record company that helped launch many of her favorite bands was a scrappy, cash-strapped small business with few employees that entrusted a rotating cast of half a dozen unpaid interns with low-level tasks.

The esteemed record company, Paula quickly learned, tasked interns with "super basic intern stuff" such as putting together packages with CDs, vinyl, and posters. The interns powered the "mailroom," even though they did not have their own room. Paula adds, "The most dreaded and most common intern task was cutting triangles." As a cost-saving measure, the company routinely asked interns to break down FedEx boxes and use these to construct "tubes" for mailing posters. She laughs slightly as she explains:

> They were so low budget. [The interns] would take FedEx boxes and turn them inside out and then roll them up to make poster tubes. But because they were made out of boxes, the ends of the tubes would always be triangles instead of circles. So then we would have to take other cardboard and cut triangles to [cover the ends of] the tubes.

Such work assignments did not diminish Paula's enjoyment. Despite the "actual tasks," she had fun because "everyone there was great." The Enthusiast intern, who takes a position primarily out of enthusiasm for music, without clear educational or career aspirations, cares less about work responsibilities and more about access to the source of their passion. While Paula received tangible "free stuff" including music, T-shirts, and entry to shows, as she describes her experience, she stresses the intangible benefits of being involved in a field that was meaningful to her.[9]

The motivation of the Enthusiast intern suggests an immediate, short-term orientation and therefore often corresponds with a brief intern career. These newcomers relish their experience yet are likely to become disenchanted or broke or develop new interests they want to pursue via other ventures (although their zest for the experience may linger or return years or even decades after the internship). Some Enthusiasts eventually see the work they do as interns as a potential career and change their orientation. After spending the summer at the record company, Paula declared a business major at the beginning of her junior year in college but quickly felt she did not truly fit in with the accounting and finance students around her. She soon became excited by the possibility of a career that paired her business skills with the atmosphere she enjoyed at the record company. She recalls, "It occurred to me that music is a business, and I can *potentially* apply these textbook concepts to something creative," adding, "I wanted to stay in that atmosphere." Paula continued to intern at the company intermittently for two years, first transitioning to a Student motivation and then finally to a Job Seeker motivation.

The Job Seeker

Some interns are motivated primarily by the opportunity to advance their employability. Like the Student, the Job Seeker wants to learn about the music business, develop skills, and clarify[10] their career path; however, the Job Seeker does so with an explicit goal: landing a job. This motivation can be oriented toward either the short-term or the longer-term. In the former category, students who are about to graduate are usually seeking immediate employment, while in the latter category, students like Ryan, the intern introduced at the beginning of this chapter who was still two years from graduation, see the path to a music career as a longer-term pursuit.

Job Seeker interns aim to establish a career foothold, which involves doing unpaid or low-paid work for a period to gain experience deemed relevant by the occupational community they seek to join.[11] Focusing on future employment involves developing relevant skills and experience, adopting the attitudes held by established employees, and growing professional networks of mentors and potential referrals, but it also involves decoding and accepting how hiring works within the industry.[12] Ryan was open to the mailroom model of training, meaning he would do any small task with enthusiasm and even go above and beyond the typical expectations of interns. By centering future employment opportunities, Ryan relegated schooling to a secondary priority. He recalls, "I would schedule all my classes around the internship.

So, I'd take an 8 a.m. class, hop on the bus, come to my internship." He would then return home to work an evening shift at a retail job. On days he did not have classes, he spent six or seven hours at the internship, leaving him little time to study.

Toward the end of Ryan's first semester as an intern, during the record industry's tumultuous transition from primarily selling CDs to focusing on digital revenue streams, an employee in his department told him, "The music industry is sinking and there are zero jobs as an A&R." Ryan quickly reframed this bleak warning as a helpful insight, and he began to view the task of building his employability as requiring an entrepreneurial approach to proving his worth to the company. He says, "I knew just by being there [*knocks on the coffee table in front of him*] for two years doesn't mean I'm going to get a job; doesn't mean I *deserve* a job." He continues, "I knew that I had to create a demand for myself." Ryan describes having tunnel vision and focusing on proving his worth by throwing himself into every task with gusto. One particularly onerous duty for interns in his department was to organize and catalog thousands of demo CDs. Ryan viewed this burdensome task as a chance to stand out:

> I used to come in there and literally, for seven hours straight, there were days I racked CDs alphabetically. And I enjoyed every minute of it because I knew that if the [demos] were in alphabetical order and the president of the company would come down and go, "Do we have so and so's demo?" And we went down there, and he found it in a matter of seven seconds as opposed to ten minutes, I knew that it would look good on my supervisors in my department and that would kind of trickle down onto me.

Ryan's initial disappointment over being assigned few or no tasks was replaced by a focus on forging a stellar reputation. By doing every task with zeal and taking efforts to make his work reflect positively on his supervisors, Ryan built stronger relationships and eventually earned more responsibilities.

By making an aspirational claim to record industry employment, Job Seeker interns enter a state of limbo, living in the conditional tense for an indeterminate period—it is unclear how long they will have to do unpaid or low-paid work before they can establish a career foothold, or even whether they will break in at all. Both Student and Job Seeker motivations imply that an internship is a future-oriented investment in the self, but for Job Seekers this investment explicitly involves taking a risk.[13] Job Seekers often question their choices, albeit internally, and their confidence in their future routinely wavers. Ryan illustrates this persistent sense of precariousness when he says, "There's not one day that passed where I didn't think about interning, and what the future holds, and if it's the right thing. . . . When you invest so much time and money into it, that burden plays a factor." He acknowledges that his internship experience was rocky, noting that there are "the good days where you'd go out and see shows and get a beer with the supervisor. And there's days where it's like, 'Damn, I may need to quit, because I'm not going to get a job here.'" Job Seekers vary between those serial interns who complete internships at a variety of companies and those interns who invest more time at one employer (e.g., interning for several semesters at one firm). Ryan falls in the latter category, staying on as an intern at the same major record company, in the same department, for two years. He spent thousands of dollars on tuition for the experience and eventually achieved his goal, moving from Job Seeker intern to paid employee with the firm shortly after graduation.

What Kind of Intern Are You?

While each of the interns I met reported that at least one of these three motivations drove them to seek an internship, it is important to reiterate that these are ideal types—Student, Enthusiast, and Job Seeker are abstractions of the motivations distilled into their purest form. Most of the interns I talked with experienced some combination of these motivations. An Enthusiast might seek out an internship as an extension of fandom while simultaneously wanting to test out this career path (a Student motivation). Further, an intern's motivations, and their respective importance, often fluctuated over time. Some interns claimed to start with Job Seeker aspirations but eventually lost interest in the record industry, or a particular part of the industry (e.g., a public relations department intern realized they did not like public relations and moved on to intern in the marketing department), or—sensing they had little chance of finding employment—later emphasized a different motivation. The existence of an array of publicly acknowledged motivations for interning enables dejected Job Seeker interns to reframe their loss of interest or rejection as a learning experience.

One motivation missing from the prior discussion is meeting people. Most of the interns and employees mentioned meeting people, but because interns do not network for its own sake (but rather in pursuit of another goal), it does not constitute a distinct type of motivation. Rather, "meeting people," whether it be a contact, a mentor, or a champion who helps them secure a paid position, takes on various meanings that align with the three motivations described previously: the Student looks to meet people who will directly or indirectly teach them about the world of work and the music industry; the Enthusiast is interested in interacting with those involved in the creation of music (company personnel and musicians/artists); and the Job Seeker develops relationships to increase the chances of future employment.

This distinction between the ways differently positioned (or motivated) interns view meeting people shows how, by claiming to intern for a particular reason, aspirants justify their activity to themselves and to the outside world; their justifications imply a certain type of impression management.[14] For example, an intern aiming to secure employment attempts to present themselves as competent and committed. Record industry employees recognize and sometimes suggest these motivations to interns, but they also occasionally contest interns' accounts of their own aspirations. In other words, employees do not necessarily share interns' interpretations of their reasons for undertaking an internship. Paid employees may interpret interns' motivations in a more critical light, often because they perceive an intern as lacking dedication or commitment to organizational goals. These contested motivations affect the negotiation between interns and employees concerning the intern's occupational identity (the answers to "who am I?" and "why am I here?").

Employee Assumptions about Interns

The emergence of internships-for-all policies in higher education has created a motley assemblage of interns with diverse needs and motivations who aim to meet their respective education, consumption, and career goals.[15] While employees recognize the various potential motivations of aspirants, the built-in ambiguity about what interns aim to accomplish fuels uncertainty among employees about how to manage these temporary team members.

Job Seeker interns are more common in professional fields such as medicine, law, and consulting—elite professions in which more rigorous vetting occurs via the education system before an internship starts. In contrast, I find that Student and Enthusiast interns are more common in cultural industries (and probably politics and nonprofits), which often have lower educational barriers for entry and a certain allure or socially meaningful attraction. Therefore, as a breaking-in system, the music industry's intern economy is designed to accommodate the motley assemblage. The presence of Students and Enthusiasts makes employers take the earnestness of the Job Seeker less seriously. However, the dynamic is not so straightforward—in addition, the staff, who are precariously employed themselves, do not (or cannot) necessarily trust even the seemingly most dedicated interns, at least at first.

As new interns arrive every semester, each intrigued by different aspects of the industry experience, employees quickly conclude that the interns possess various levels of commitment and competence. The cautious approach, on the part of employees, is to presume that all interns have low levels of commitment and competence unless proven otherwise, and even then, employees continue to be cautious when delegating work because they know that if anything goes wrong, responsibility ultimately falls on the supervising employee.

Presumed Uncommitted

An important and common perception among employees is that interns have a weak commitment to their internship. This criticism acknowledges learning, passion, and career building as reasons someone would intern but questions the typical intern's investment in these pursuits. Commitment is distinct from eagerness or excitement—interns may come off as happy to be there and embody a kind of wide-eyed eagerness, but employees voice concerns that interns are frequently credential-seeking dabblers who invest little in the experience beyond simply showing up, are more interested in consumptive pursuits than doing work, and often have unrealistic expectations about the industry or role.

As a temporary role, an internship provides the opportunity to test out an identity—to explore what it would be like to take part in an industry or, more specifically, to work in a particular department or type of company within an industry. As one employee concludes, "I think a lot of people go into the internships being like, 'Let me try this out for a while.' They try this hat on." Employees, to varying extents, attempt to gauge the type and strength of interns' motivations, and this matters because, if an employee perceives an intern as more committed, they might invest more time and energy in educating or otherwise supporting that intern.[16] Conversely, employees report investing little to no time on interns they perceive as uncommitted. Employees view most interns as dabblers, but they predominantly treat the least committed ones more harshly, no matter which motivation or goal the intern claims.[17]

Employees generally say that learning about the industry is the best reason to intern but criticize interns who treat this experience as just another course. Speaking of interns as students, but not necessarily very dedicated ones, Max, a music industry marketing professional, comments, "Most see it as, 'Oh, I have to do this. Everybody's required to do an internship.'" The rise of internships-for-all policies in higher education nurtures, or creates, students' urge to seek out these experiences, and the rise of internship requirements, whether formal (for an academic program) or informal (because it feels like something students must do), contributes to Max's perception. Max claims that because many people view an internship as something of a requirement, interns go through the motions rather than seizing the opportunity to learn: "It makes me so sad when I see interns who don't realize they're in a place where so much creativity [happens]. There are so many opportunities." Because interns in his department are typically assigned low-level tasks, at least at first, Max frames students' motivation as either to simply tolerate the experience or to use the opportunity to obtain a unique education and possibly land a job.

> [The internship] could be, basically, doing shitty tasks for no money for your résumé. Which to me is, you know . . . no wonder a lot of them are not really happy. Or you can be like, "Oh, wow, I can learn so much here that I can't learn in school from professors that maybe haven't been in the business for ten years or twenty years when it was totally different." And literally, they have to bust their ass and get jobs out of [it].

Max suggests that students who invest more in their internship could gain unique knowledge that is not available to them in the classroom, but also, through hard work, they might even secure a paid position. But instead, he explains, most interns "blow it off" and view it as "just a line on your résumé." In an era of internship inflation, his suggestion that students view internships solely as a credential, whether in the form of school credits or a line on their résumé, offers a less charitable understanding of the Student and Job Seeker motivations.

Other employees offer variations on Max's description of uncommitted student interns. Nate criticizes college students who think an internship in the music industry will be an "easy, fun gig," akin to an elective course ("or gym class"), that entails easier and less frequent tasks than a more demanding internship. He goes further than Max by describing a subgroup of interns who, because the industry is glamorous and seemingly laid back, "figure this will be an easy internship as opposed to . . . a hard internship. . . . That kind of person, I'm worried for their future." Another music industry employee says students view internships as "time that they're not doing [term] papers." The employee adds, "When people are in college, a lot of times . . . their parents are paying for college. It's an extension of high school for them," meaning that these student interns are committed to neither their intern host organization's goals nor educational goals.

According to certain employees, some interns do not want to do much work; these interns appear to embrace the idea that they are "just the intern" too dearly, expecting to do little. Nancy, an A&R employee at a major record company, recalls interns making a plea for less work: "I've definitely had some kids that come in and they just sort of want to phone it in and are half-assed about things. And then when I actually push them to work really hard, they're sort of like, 'Uuugh, this is an internship!'" The employees I talked to say some interns expect easy credits, display a distaste for the work, or decide the internship is not for them and cut their losses.

Ben, a junior employee in Nancy's department who supervises a group of interns, describes working with a range of interns, including some who showed little interest in doing work. He concludes, "There's a lot of people you can tell just . . . don't want to work in the music business. They have no interest in it." Shortly thereafter, he adds:

> And I think this internship is totally what you make of it. We've had people who come in here and sit here and watch videos on YouTube. If that's your prerogative, awesome, do your thing, I'm not going to stop you.

The uncommitted intern who shows no interest in working in the industry, nor any real inclination to learn about the industry, may be tolerated but ignored by employees. Paid employees frame an intern's commitment as an ongoing choice, not an accomplished fact.

Max also frames interning as an entrepreneurial endeavor, explaining, "I really do feel that as an intern, you have the choice. You can get whatever you want out of it." However, he adds, "a lot of kids don't even realize [it]. . . . They have no idea." His statements suggest that newcomers are unaware that this experience is *what you make of it*—commitment drives an intern's bundle of tasks and ultimate accomplishments.

Sometimes employees have a positive initial impression of an intern until an incident makes them question the intern's commitment. For example, Max recalls that after developing rapport with an intern who carefully and competently completed several tasks for him, he invited this person to a promotional shoot, which he describes as the best opportunity for an intern to see what his job entails. The caveat, however, is that these shoots—which may involve filming videos with artists and others on set—usually start very early in the morning (5 or 6 a.m.) and end well into the evening (7 or 8 p.m.). The intern responded that they could only attend between 10 a.m. and 6 p.m., a response Max interpreted as signaling a lack of commitment. He jokes with me, pretending to address the intern, "Guess what? You just signed your *I don't give a shit* card," indicating that Max labeled the intern (or the intern inadvertently labeled themselves) as lacking commitment. He continues, asking rhetorically, "[Why] waste my time on teaching you anything, like my pool of knowledge or whatever that I've learned through the years, if you don't even want to get up early and show up?" After some probing, though, Max confirms that he did not ask whether the intern had any other obligations—a job, class, or care responsibilities.

While committed, hard-working interns might eventually receive more and more enviable assignments, interns perceived as uncommitted are less fortunate. One senior A&R employee refers to uncommitted "bad" interns who arrive fifteen minutes late, skip every other week, and leave early; he concludes, "OK, they're just looking for college credit and then they're going to move on to something else. Which is totally fine. They have to find their path, you know?" In such instances, he adds, he assigns the intern only low-level tasks: "gofer things, stupid things: running errands, running something down to a different floor, you know, stuff like that." The bar for commitment is low for many internships, with employees tolerating some of the behaviors mentioned previously (like showing up erratically) but in such cases assigning only mundane tasks.

Another type of intern that employees criticize for a lack of commitment is an intern who acts more like a fan than a worker. Employees view most interns as being at least somewhat motivated by an enthusiasm for music because otherwise they would not be willing to do unpaid or low-paid music industry work.[18] When I ask Nancy, an A&R representative at a major record company, why she thinks people want to intern in the music industry, she immediately responds in a playful tone, "*Because it's cool, man!*" After encouraging her to unpack what she means by "cool," she portrays the record company as the backstage where the magic happens, a place of mystique and curiosity.

> Because you're going to be around artists, and you're going to see the creation of things that you've consumed your whole life as a kid, you know? Where do music videos come from, where do records come from, where does the imagery I see on the internet and I see on TV, and I see on posters, like, where does it come from? Where does it start?

In this view, some interns seek a better understanding of the music industry as an extension of fandom rather than as a learning opportunity. Entering the music industry as an intern is, Nancy continues, "like seeing behind the curtain of something." By extension, music industry personnel are key players in the creation of the music and the imagery, working at the center of the artistic enterprise.[19]

While employees expect interns to demonstrate some passion for music, they believe newcomers must also exhibit a certain level of commitment to organizational goals.[20] If interns are dedicated solely to their consumption of artistic products, acting only as fans and not also as productive members of the workplace, they will draw the disdain of employees. Employees reserve harsh criticism for interns who are interested only in the superficial rewards of the music industry—for example, students who do an internship to gain favorable social status among friends, family, and peers, and do little or no work, or who only want a closer affiliation with the musical artists. As Bela, a twenty-nine-year-old music industry employee, observes, there are "annoying interns that basically want to party with the band and be friends with rock stars or who think they are rock stars in their head." Such interns, she adds, might not view working in the music industry as a viable long-term option, but rather might be thinking, "'Oh, I'll do it in college for an experience.'" Interning as an extension of fandom becomes framed as a problem when interns do not fulfill their duties. Describing an intern she met at a small independent record company, Bela complains that the intern wanted to hang out with a band after their performance rather than sit at the merch table selling records and T-shirts: "And I was like, 'Dude, you have to help out with the merch.'" Instead, the intern kept disappearing to go backstage and Bela thought to herself, "She's fired," and the internship ended abruptly.[21]

Like students seeking easy credits, career-minded interns who seek no more than a line on their résumé are also subject to the criticism of employees. While this credential attests to a workplace experience, an intern whose only goal is to pad a résumé, and therefore is not committed to organizational goals, is not perceived as a valuable addition to the workplace. In the competitive race to employability among college students, Job Seeker interns include those whose goal is to add the name of a large record company or a cutting-edge boutique firm to help them boost their résumé even though they are not yet committed to the music industry.

Even interns who passionately proclaim that they hope to secure a job in the music industry might not be taken seriously if employees doubt the seriousness of their career pursuits, particularly if this is their first music industry experience. Employees report that some interns are "spooked" when they realize a record industry job can be a corporate office gig like any other. These interns become disillusioned after a few weeks of observing employees work long hours and complete mundane tasks and after getting a sense of the industry's relatively low pay compared to other fields. One such account is provided by Nate, at Indie Distribution, whose job involves managing YouTube content for various record companies. When discussing previous interns, he tells me most were not truly interested in music industry careers even though "most of them *thought* they were." He explains, "A lot of people *think* they're interested in music, and they want to do this," but he adds that newcomers with little experience of the industry do not have realistic expectations of what such a career entails.

> They think it's all glamorous, but it's not a very glamorous job, working in music. You're the back end. You're the shit end of the stick. You're doing all the work that you know you never get credit for. No one gives a fuck what I do on YouTube, really. But [record companies] need that. They don't have their videos on YouTube right now, it's nothing, but is your average fan going to thank me? No. They don't give you a second thought.

The thankless, often mundane duties of music industry personnel are one aspect of the field that Job Seeker interns may not expect. In addition, many employees mentioned that interns often have unrealistic views of the industry based on previous, more lucrative eras. Nate adds: "It's not the '90s anymore where every release party is going to be stocked with champagne and cocaine." Therefore, he concludes, "you're only going to be in it if you really want to do it and you have passion for it."

In sum, the motley assemblage of interns brings a wide variety of motivations, or combinations of motivations, to their internships. Employees acknowledge this variation in motives, and this awareness, when paired with their general sense that interns often lack commitment, leads them to interpret interns' motivations in a more critical or negative light.

Presumed Incompetent

The problem of lack of commitment overlaps with what employees describe as the intern's presumed incompetence. In popular culture, a running joke ties "the intern" to incompetence.[22] When something goes wrong, for example, like when a company's social media account features an offensive post or a glaring error, people often joke that employees will or should *blame the intern*.[23] In the context of the workplace, employees share stories of incompetent interns with one another, some with a tinge of humor and others more explicitly warning newer colleagues not to trust interns. Among the pool of interns, there are varying levels of competence. As Patrick, an employee at Indie Distribution, observes jokingly, "A good intern knows where to put a stamp on an envelope. A bad intern, I'd say, wouldn't." Employees and many interns know stories about "bad" interns who did little or no work, were fired, quit, or simply stopped showing up. Consequently, employees often do not trust interns enough to delegate much work. After all, the work delegated to an intern is ultimately the responsibility of the employee above them; if an intern makes a mistake, the consequences fall on the shoulders of the employee.

Kendra is a twenty-two-year-old temp worker who is just a few weeks into her job at Major Records USA. As an intern, I sit about ten feet from Kendra, whose cubicle is next to Hank's and across from the publicity department's intern station. On a quiet morning, while Hank is away, Kendra tells me she interned at this company for a year, and, a year later, when there just happened to be an opening in the publicity department, she ran into her former boss at a nearby Starbucks and secured an interview for the position. During our conversation Kendra mentions that she does not work with the publicity interns who sit only a few feet away. Slightly surprised, I tell her I thought they were "her" interns. She responds that they are the department's interns and are utilized more by the people "over there" (she points to her right, where other people from the department sit). She goes on to explain that she could delegate tasks to them but does not want to be blamed for any mistakes they make. "I'm pretty self-sufficient," she adds, and says that if a mistake is made, she wants it to be made by her.

Later that morning, I hear a woman call Kendra's name from a nearby office of a senior publicity employee. Kendra says, "Yes?" but there is no answer. She gets up from her desk and walks into the office. The woman says something to Kendra, inaudible to me. Kendra responds, "Alright, I'll put it back the other way. I'm new here, I didn't know I had to put it that way." The person answers loudly, "Everybody puts it back that way but *you. That's how I knew it was you*!" Kendra walks sheepishly back toward her desk, says, "OK, I'll make a note of it," and sits down without saying another word. I think back to our morning chat. Kendra told me she aims to move up in the company, at least to a more stable and slightly better-paid job; for now, she makes ends meet by living with her mom. For a newer, especially precarious employee such as Kendra, taking the time to determine whether she can trust an intern is a luxury she does not feel she can afford.

The status of interns can change with time, but employees, even ones in more stable positions, tend to play it safe upon meeting interns by assuming they are relatively incompetent. Larry, a senior-level employee at Major Records USA, depicts this cautious approach when I interview him:

> You come in not as somebody I know who you are now, but you come in as another intern. . . . Intern A comes in, Intern B comes in, one of them is good, one of them is bad, and you don't know what they're capable of doing. So automatically you just generalize and say, "OK, it's an intern."

To protect themselves from the risk of a mistake-prone intern, several employees describe delegating tasks based on a sliding scale of importance. The most unproven interns are given low-level tasks such as running errands. An intern that employees deem incompetent will complete only the most basic tasks. The prevailing wisdom among employees is that if interns are ever to be assigned higher-level tasks, they must first demonstrate their ability to do mundane work. Some interns commit such memorable displays of incompetence that they leave a lasting, unfavorable impression. As Nate recalls, one intern he oversaw had difficulty changing a light bulb, which then precluded assigning him anything but the easiest tasks.

> There's a three-light-bulb set in the women's bathroom. "Could you change one of the light bulbs in there for us?" And one of them is out. We only had two light bulbs going for some reason because we're ghetto like that [*pause*]. He changed the one that was working [*laughs*]. That was the end for him! From that day on he only cleaned the storage room, pretty much . . . [*laughs out loud*] and organized promos. That was the end of his life as an intern.

By describing the inability of an intern to successfully complete a task as simple as changing a light bulb, Nate vividly illustrates why some employees are reticent to work closely with interns, even those who exhibit high commitment.

As I talk with Bela, she highlights the relationship between the two main characteristics that employees view as problematic in interns—their presumed incompetence and lack of commitment. Employee distrust of interns, she suggests, comes "from past experiences with interns that may not have been that competent [or] dedicated." Bela tells me about an intern who somehow "blew up the copy room." When the intern left the copy room, ink from the photocopier was everywhere. Instead of letting employees know about the accident, the intern, Bela recounts, hurried to her supervisor and said, "'Uh, I have to go. I forgot I have an emergency.' She left that day and never came back!" Bela laughs as she finishes the story, but then takes a more serious tone as she adds:

> I think there's an underlying assumption that because that person's not a permanent employee and they're not getting paid, that they don't have the same dedication as an employee that is getting paid. You know, so I think part of it is a question of competency and another part of it is a question of somebody's dedication.

Because employees tend to assume interns are neither very competent nor very committed, interns must distinguish themselves as more than "just the intern" if they hope to be trusted with higher-level work. The need to prove themselves may be frustrating for the more committed interns who want to receive more training and be trusted with high-level tasks—the Job Seeker intern hoping to eventually land a paid job in the music industry finds that their intern career is affected by other interns' incompetence and lack of commitment.[24] In this way, "unserious" interns pollute the pool of interns. The problem of lack of commitment and competence of some interns is dealt with, organizationally, by assuming in practice that all interns possess a low level of commitment and competence, and therefore not trusting interns with much responsibility and setting minimal goals for the breaking-in process.

Surface-Level Socialization

Returning to the case of Ryan, the Job Seeker intern who worked doggedly to improve his GPA so he could secure an internship and who rushed down the block to ensure he was on time for the interview, he was surprised that his enthusiasm and investment in terms of time, tuition money, and transportation costs were met with lukewarm employee responses. His original reaction of disappointment can be described as a "reality shock."[25] Newcomers arrive equipped with a sense of what being an intern means, including the tasks they will carry out, how they will fit into the office environment, and where this experience will lead them. Because the intern's preconceptions are likely to be at least somewhat different than the reality they encounter, they must refine their conceptions during the early stages of the internship.[26] In Ryan's case, while he perceived an internship as a way to learn the ropes and break into the music industry, he was not fully aware that most employees dedicate little time or effort to guiding interns through this transition. More broadly, internships such as his are designed to allow for a wide range of motivations and results. This ambiguity creates a challenging situation—it is difficult to break in when members of the occupational community are not focused on breaking in newcomers.

As organizational ethnographer John Van Maanen (1976, 1978) pointed out decades ago, incorporating newcomers, which he called "people processing," helps ensure an organization's stability, although the strategies used to do so vary greatly by context and circumstance. In some instances, such as in the military, recruits undergo a harsh and extensive introduction to an organization's culture. Newcomers are asked to break from their prior affiliations and are cut off from the rest of society in terms of both location (e.g., living in barracks) and appearance (e.g., wearing a uniform), with the goal (the recruit's and/or the organization's) of utterly transforming recruits so they accept and adopt the norms, values, and behaviors expected of them. This extreme, all-encompassing form of socialization occurs in organizations that have the power to control, at least temporarily, every aspect of the newcomer's day-to-day life. Sociologist Erving Goffman (1961a) called such organizations "total institutions." In *The Mint,* T. E. Lawrence (1955) described his own transition into the Royal Air Force, beginning with the words "God, this is awful." His opening statement foreshadows the repetitive, painful, and at times crushing and humiliating process of becoming "minted," or molded to fit the air force's norms and ideals.

While these extreme settings for socialization—such as bootcamps, monasteries, and prisons—are relatively rare, Van Maanen (1976) suggested the usefulness of analyzing how all organizations, to varying extents, operate as total institutions. In this perspective, organizations fall on a continuum in terms of the *means* and *goals* of socialization, in other words, the extent to which they can exercise control over members and seek homogeneity. At one extreme of this continuum, a total institution such as the military carefully designs people-processing strategies to ensure almost complete conformity; new recruits either come in line with organizational demands or are eventually discharged. At the other end, organizations have a more limited reach, and their less intense people-processing strategies lead to no more than superficial change in recruits; in these cases, organizations must accept more heterogeneity. This type of diversity is reflected in internships, with organizations across fields maintaining widely different means and goals for their internship programs. On the more intensive side, some finance and tech newcomers, for example, are required to work long hours and are subject to more sophisticated indoctrination programs designed to "marry them" to their company.[27] Music companies tend to fall at the other end of the continuum. Because music industry employees view interns as cheap laborers not necessarily seeking imminent employment, internship programs typically have relatively modest goals and companies invest few resources into training these newcomers. Thus, employees are not concerned with achieving a profound level of socialization but rather seek to instill "surface-level" changes in newcomers via basic onboarding and policing the ways interns look and sound to ensure they "fit" with the music industry.

Onboarding

Several interns told me they felt scared, intimidated, and humbled at the start of their internships. Emily, who has had five internships, still describes the disorientation of the first day, "because you don't know what's going on. But it's something you have to learn." She continues, "I don't know anybody who has come back from their first day at an internship that [says], 'I kick ass.' Everyone [says], 'I'm a terrible intern!'" The process of onboarding—initial training related to the workplace and the intern's role—helps interns better understand the activities, personalities, and expectations around them.

The process of onboarding new interns varies across and within companies, but the most common approach involves having supervising employees or senior interns (returning from a previous semester) teach newcomers the basics. Many interns report going on "the walk" on their first day—their supervisor gives them a tour of the office, showing them key areas and introducing them to the colleagues with whom they will likely interact. Some interns are not given a tour and instead are simply instructed how to complete ongoing tasks and perhaps offered background information on the company and their department; further instructions come only when needed. Companies and individual departments often develop internship guides meant to welcome newcomers that might include orienting information about their internship program goals, a brief overview of the company's history, a list of key employees, a description of what various people or departments do, and, crucially, step-by-step instructions on how to complete certain tasks. This early training usually includes basic tips on office etiquette: show up reasonably on time, do not act disruptively, and other basic guidelines.

Music industry interns often report receiving little supervision, even at the start of their internship.[28] Danielle recounts receiving only a brief training at her internship in music marketing, where, as she explains, "you were just *in*. . . . One day I wasn't there and one day I was there, and I was supposed to all of a sudden always have been there." At a previous internship in music publishing, Danielle was immediately trained on how to fill out her department's paperwork, but in her music marketing position no one had an hour to spare for training. Here, when she was given a task, for example, an employee would say something like: "'You know PowerPoint, right? You know this, right?' And you do but you don't know how *they* do it. How they want to format it. You kind of just pick it up." Training becomes a process of trial and error—the intern seeks models for their work and looks for clues about their performance. As a result of this lack of early supervised training, on their first days, most interns feel like they are not performing very well. It is normal for new interns to feel bewildered in this unfamiliar environment—resolving the anxieties that emerge from new surroundings, responsibilities, and interactions is a key motivator for them to conform to expectations of their role—but while socialization into other work roles comes with relatively high expectations, the bar for the intern is often low. If an intern does not perform a task correctly, an employee might correct them, but if the employee does not need the intern to do the task regularly, they may opt to move on without offering feedback.

The lack of training for new interns can confirm their presumed incompetence, in the eyes of both employees and the interns themselves. A key task that makes many interns uneasy is answering the phone for a supervisor. Some of this unease may be due to a generational divide—younger people are much more likely to communicate via messaging than phone calls—but the challenge is intensified by a lack of onboarding. On one day at Major Records USA, Agatha, an intern in the publicity department who sits a few feet away from me, is charged with answering a junior employee's (Kendra's) phone while she attends a departmental meeting. The phone rings, but the call is on another employee's line, not Kendra's. As Agatha's hand slowly moves toward the phone, she asks my supervisor, Hank, if he thinks she should pick it up. Hank says, "Only pick up Kendra's line," but Agatha has already answered, saying only, "Hello?" as she puts the receiver to her ear (rather than offering a professional greeting or saying, "publicity department"). Hank looks at me, dumbfounded, and blurts out flatly, "She answered it" and then laughs slightly. Agatha takes a message for a senior employee in the department and after she hangs up Hank instructs her to only answer calls from Kendra's line.

When I catch up with Agatha later, I start to ask her what it was like to cover the phone and before I have a chance to finish the question, she exclaims, "Oh my god, that was scary!" She adds that people kept calling and she did not know who they were: "[Artist X's] manager called, and he said, 'Nouveau Rich is calling.' And I said, 'Who's Rich? Rich from where?' He said, '[Artist X's] manager.' And I was like, 'Oh! Sorry about that!'" Agatha is embarrassed because Nouveau Rich manages one of the company's most prominent artists. As we talk, she concludes that she is unsure she has the skills to be an assistant at the company. However, if Agatha had been trained on how to answer the phone and received a directory of key contacts, her experience, and her (and Hank's) opinion of her abilities, could have been much different.

While offering little initial training and support for interns saves employers time, interns who feel more fully integrated into the organization have a more positive experience in terms of both mentorship and getting assigned higher-level tasks. The onboarding process and the company's decisions about the conditions under which interns work—for example, whether interns receive a personalized email address (name@company.com) or a generic one (intern@company.com) and whether they have their own workspace and computer or use shared spaces with no assigned computer—set the tone for the extent of incorporation. These decisions are often embedded within a company's culture; however, a sympathetic or organizationally savvy manager can make exceptions—one A&R employee tells me he had business cards made for his unpaid interns in their first week so they would feel emboldened to do work and help him find cutting-edge talent.

Employees, particularly those who were interns themselves, know that new interns would benefit from more training and support, especially early in their time with the company. For example, Shane, who is now employed at the indie record company where he once interned, characterizes the typical early disorientation of newcomers and identifies some of its sources:

> It's very difficult to be an intern, I think. And I'm sure it is in every industry. You come into a place, you don't know anybody—at a small business, at a label, there's no HR [human resources department]—there's very little structure to begin with, so you're coming into a situation where you know nothing; you're not really sure what you're supposed to be doing; the people around you aren't really good at telling you what to do. So, you come in and you're kind of lost.

However, as I discuss in detail in the next chapter, employees view the lack of onboarding and close supervision as a test. Shane adds, "A good intern just makes their way; they find a way to be valuable." Shane recalls feeling slightly neglected as an intern but says, "Now I don't see [myself as a neglectful supervisor]; I just see myself as busy . . . I do try to take the extra moment with the intern to try to provide a little bit more structure, training, or whatever, but it's difficult." Employees, at times somewhat sheepishly, describe themselves as being resigned to focusing on their own precarious job rather than wasting resources on interns.

Although there is some variation in socialization across companies and individual departments, in general, employers in the music industry accommodate the motley assemblage of interns by setting low expectations for their socialization—they do not aim to profoundly transform these newcomers. Rather, interns are expected to follow basic rules of office etiquette and to learn, often with very limited training, how to perform their assigned tasks. Such shallow investment allows workers to spend almost all their time on their everyday work responsibilities.

Learning to Look and Sound the Part

Beyond undergoing the limited onboarding that provides a basic understanding of duties and office etiquette, interns are rapidly pushed to make superficial changes to their self-presentation based on the demands of their environment. Newcomers must learn to fashion their behavior (including presentation style) according to a code of conduct I call "industry cool."[29] Although the local culture is largely implicit, like other forms of professional socialization, interns learn to understand and respect these norms and customs through a moral education that generally leads to conformity.[30] Industry cool includes forms of dress, etiquette for interacting with coworkers, and a professionally appropriate enthusiastic-yet-detached relationship to music.

As much as appropriate clothing lends itself to an appearance of competence, dressing inappropriately challenges (intentionally or not) the social order of the organization. Employees describe a newcomer dressing too formally as a physical manifestation of cluelessness. Ryan, looking back on his years as an intern, recalls wearing a suit during his interview and his early weeks at the internship. After recounting his gaffe, he describes his (white-collar worker) father's surprise at the office's relaxed dress code:

> And I look back at it now; it's the silliest thing. *No one* here, including executives, really wears suits. This is very informal. I remember when I first started, I was at home, and I was leaving one day to go to work.[31] I had my jeans on, sneakers, and a T-shirt and my father goes, "What the hell are you wearing to work?" I'm like, "If I go in a suit, I get laughed at." I literally came in here one time in khakis, a dress shirt, and shoes when I was working here, and I was made fun of the whole day.

Another music industry worker shares a similar recollection of interviewing for his internship at an indie record label in inappropriate attire. He showed up wearing "a blazer and a button down, suit pants, and [the employees] were like, 'What are you doing?' . . .

They made fun of me because I came all dressed up." Despite his inappropriately formal attire, he was granted the internship on the spot. He continues, "The next day I come back in my normal outfit, and they were like, 'Thank god.' I'm in a hat, jeans, and T-shirt." Several interns and employees observed that they can tell it is an intern's first day if they are overdressed. In contrast, a hip but casual outfit might earn an intern high praise—I witnessed many interns and employees receiving compliments for expressive, stylish, and usually informal clothing. Thus, employees enforce the dress code informally by giving clueless interns a hard time and praising those who dress the part.

There are certain exceptions to the "don't overdress" rule. For instance, Hank, my internship supervisor, consistently wears suits to the office and often receives compliments on his style. He sports designer clothing and a meticulously groomed look. Once, when someone told him his suit looked nice, he replied in a comically loud voice, "It better be, it's *Tom Ford*!" (a brand whose suits usually retail for several thousand dollars). The formality of Hank's appearance is not inappropriate, arguably because he has over ten years of experience in the industry and his form of dress is interpreted as culturally aware and expressive rather than "clueless" and discrediting.[32] In sum, overdressing as a form of expression is acceptable, but blind formality is not.

Ryan not only learned to dress a certain way early on, he also quickly came to understand the "correct" way to address people—once again, employee feedback schooled him on the informal workplace culture. He reveals, "I called everyone Mr. and Mrs., which offended *everyone*. . . . My first two days I called my supervisors *Mister* Shaw and *Mister* Smith." He relates that his bosses did not seem pleased and responded: "'Dude, just stop. Don't ever do that again.' So, I was like, OK, note to self, don't do that." Ryan explains that despite being an intern, many employees were his peers in terms of age, perhaps only four or five years older. People call one another by their first names, or nicknames, a pattern that extends even to most executives, who do not want to be called "Mr." or "Mrs."

because it makes them feel old. Now in his mid-twenties, Ryan tells me he already feels old when an intern calls him "Mister."

Discussing why he initially overdressed and addressed employees too formally, Ryan points to his family background, specifically having a father who worked in a more typical office environment, but also the guidance he received from career services personnel at his university.

> When you go into these career counselors, they prep you on how to interview; they prep you on what to wear, and how to sit, and how to stand, and somehow you kind of stick that in the back of your head. Alright, I'm going on an interview, let me apply this stuff. So, I wore a suit. I called everyone Mr. and Mrs.

Because he majored in business rather than an artistic field, Ryan received professional training from his university that did not match the music industry's code of conduct. He notes, "They prep you on how to prepare for the professional world, but not how to prepare for an industry like [music]." Once interns arrive in the office, surface-level socialization pushes them to adjust to this specific organizational culture.

As well as dressing the part and addressing people in the correct ways, interns must embrace an enthusiastic yet detached relationship to music. If an intern shows little passion for music, employees may begin to question their level of interest. However, interns must not act merely as fans. They must convey excitement but, at critical moments, display the correct level of detachment. Brandon, a recent college graduate and temporary employee at Indie Distribution, tells me about his recent internship at a major record company. He recalls meeting artists as one of the perks of the internship. When I ask about these experiences, using a show as an example, he specifies a certain code of conduct:

> AF: So, you would chat with the artists?
> BRANDON: Yeah, you could go over and talk to them. Usually, I stayed with the people I knew from work, but we went

over and said hi to the artist. We didn't *hang out* with them, like, be all over them.

AF: Why not?

BRANDON: Because that's weird and you'd probably get fired for that?

AF: Oh really?

BRANDON: Yeah. I mean, if you become one of the crazed fans that starts screaming, that's not really professional. So, I guess they could probably let you go.

Although neither of us had heard of an intern getting fired for being a "crazed fan" per se, Brandon pinpointed another key aspect of the culture of industry cool: personnel must both appreciate the distinctiveness of (sometimes famous) artists and act "normally" in their presence. Brandon continues, specifying how an intern should not act:

> When you look on TV and you see the crazy fans, like the little girls, they scream for the [boy band], they go crazy for that stuff. If you worked in a record label and you screamed like those girls when somebody famous comes in, they will not keep you around because you wouldn't scream for any reason in the workplace, but especially because you don't want the artist to feel uncomfortable also, like this person can't handle working with somebody famous.

Music industry workers must handle their proximity to artists with moderately detached professionalism.[33] Brandon claims he was never starstruck in the office during his internship, although he describes a time some of the interns became excited when they saw a prominent male artist in the office and ran over to fellow interns saying, "Oh my god it's *Artist X*! It's *Artist X*!" Because the artist was not within earshot, their excitement was deemed acceptable or even appropriate behavior. If the artist was in the immediate vicinity, however, the expected script would be different. Brandon concludes, "But you would never run up to him and say that. Like, if he walked by you, you would just say, 'Hi' or 'How are you?' or something like that. You wouldn't go screaming and asking for an autograph." One of the key takeaways of interns' accounts of coming into contact with artists is that artists should feel comfortable at the record company, which is a site of business.

Nonetheless, workers in the music industry are allowed to break from their professional, detached demeanor under the appropriate circumstances. A junior employee from a record company describes an especially notable moment when Kanye West (aka Ye), at the time one of the most popular musical artists in the world, came to the office to unveil his newly recorded album to the head of the publicity department. No one in the office had heard the finished record, so while employees maintained a cool composure outwardly, behind the scenes they excitedly messaged one another (e.g., "Kanye's here!") and attempted to listen as the record played on the publicist's stereo. The employee recounts that West seemed to understand the buzz in the office:

> [Kanye West] comes out of the office and screams in the hallway to no one in particular, "Don't act like I'm not playing my new shit! Come listen to it!" So, he just calls whoever happened to be there and like ten people listened to his brand-new album. And then he goes, "Alright, I'm going to do this" and he . . . put in just the instrumental [recording] and he actually performed it for us in the office.

The employee adds that events like this one illustrate the excitement, distinctiveness, and pleasure of music industry work; that Kanye West rapping live in the office is the sort of symbolic event that draws people into such workplaces: "People think that stuff like that happens all the time, so they want to do it." However, music industry personnel must conform to and appropriately partake in the local culture. If Kanye West had not issued a broad invitation to the staff, the employee continues, "No one would have gone. And that's kind of the unwritten rule that everybody knows." The employee notes that on a different day, the superstar singer

Rihanna came into the office and "some intern went up [to her] and she said, 'I'm a huge fan.'" A senior publicity employee later tersely told the intern, "Never speak to an artist like that unless you're told!" Therefore, as citizens of the workplace, interns face few demands and low expectations; however, to avoid disrupting the everyday culture, they must learn how to present themselves, address others, and demonstrate a passion for music in professionally appropriate ways.

Conclusion

This chapter introduces a threefold typology of interns and their motivations: Students, Enthusiasts, and Job Seekers each approach an internship with a unique goal in mind. At the same time, employees have difficulty discerning the motivations of individual interns, at least initially. The variety and contestation of motivations contribute to a tolerated ambiguity that characterizes the process of breaking in. This ambiguity originally stems from the key parties interpreting the internship in distinct ways and is sustained by a system whereby the occupational community mildly "breaks in" newcomers, actively influencing interns, but only at the surface level. The precariousness of employees' jobs, paired with their presumptions that interns lack both commitment and competence, further contribute to the challenging conditions of the breaking in process. In this environment, it is the intern's responsibility to make the most of their experience and go beyond surface-level socialization. As the next chapter demonstrates, employees frame it as the intern's responsibility to ensure their own training and demonstrate their worth if they want to ascend beyond the most basic work responsibilities and superficial integration in the company culture.

3

The New Mailroom

A FEW HOURS into my first day as an intern at a major record company, I head to the human resources department to fill out forms that, among other things, testify to my status as a student. As I sit in silence with three other interns who are also filling out forms, I notice that the long tables we are sitting at are arranged in classroom-like rows, although there is no teacher standing at the front of the room. The tables, which are surrounded by tall filing cabinets, face the entrance to a small office occupied by Aurora, an HR professional who oversees the internship program. Every semester, hundreds of interns circulate through this room, fill out these forms, and receive brief guidance from Aurora before returning to their respective departments. The office space is unusual in that no music is playing in the background, and I jump slightly when I hear "Next!" and realize it is my turn to meet with Aurora.

After I hand her my forms, Aurora reciprocates by offering me a thick booklet with the words "Unpaid Internship Paperwork" on the cover. The document mostly comprises a code of conduct that applies to all workers at the firm, but the packet also includes a single page with tips for interns. Aurora sits down, swivels her chair until her back is turned, and proceeds to offer a few words of guidance as she simultaneously enters the data from my forms into her computer. She says some students see this internship as a source of easy school credits, but if I work hard and make myself visible, the internship might lead to a job ("We do hire our interns"). If I am interested in getting hired, she adds, I should know these decisions are "all about relationships. . . . People need to know your work ethic." Glancing down at the name I entered as my supervisor (Hank), she praises him and offers a bit of insight into working with him, saying, "Hank has high expectations. A lot of people are more lenient. Hank will tell you if you're not doing well—some people won't bother." Our conversation lasts less than five minutes.

After walking back to my department, I take a moment to read the page of the booklet with tips for interns, which describes the internship program as an introduction to the world of entertainment and "an invaluable experience" designed to enhance my studies. The page also offers basic advice on how to leave a lasting positive impression as an intern, instructing the reader to be punctual, detail oriented, and cooperative; communicate absences with their supervisor in advance; avoid using the phone for excessive personal phone calls; and refrain from bringing friends or family to the office. Beyond providing these behavioral guidelines for this work environment, the document also instructs interns to express interest in their daily duties; be positive and enthusiastic; and show initiative (volunteer to do more).

Shortly after I finish reading through the tips, Carlos—an enthusiastic go-getter who was described to me as the department's "afternoon intern"—arrives and eagerly walks me through some of our daily intern duties. We circulate through a series of offices to check whether refrigerators holding water bottles and cans of soda need replenishing. He walks me through sending a package using the UPS website. We briefly look through the shared email inbox (a generic email address for the department's interns), and he shows me the storage room where I will occasionally fetch or store promotional records. Earlier that day, Hank described some of these duties to me and added, "One thing that is important is . . . it's not just about the work that you're doing. What you learn most from is from paying attention to what's going on around you. Listen, pay attention to what's happening, what people are saying." Once the tour is complete, Carlos asks Hank if he has anything for us to do, and Hank responds, "No." Carlos and I then sit at opposite ends of the intern station, which is a makeshift desk (i.e., a table in the hallway) near Hank's cubicle and the office of the vice president of sales and marketing. As we await further work assignments, Carlos and I just sit there, occasionally glancing at each other, a phone, or a computer screen, and listen to the background buzz of the office.

A common criticism of internship programs, particularly those with unpaid or low-paid positions, is that they are exploitative—neither explicitly educational nor a clear-cut opportunity for gainful employment. With the emergence of internships-for-all policies in higher education, interns experience the uneasy, and at times contradictory, coexistence of educational and career-oriented goals for internships as a vague promise—in the workplace, interns are viewed and view themselves sometimes as students, other times as workers, and yet other times as neither or both.[1] As described in chapter 2, interns have a range of motivations; they may seek easy credits, a job, or a way to fulfill their fandom. Further, the extent to which employees supervise or monitor interns varies widely, particularly since, to music industry employers, creating a pipeline of trained potential employees is secondary to extracting interns' inexpensive labor. This chapter examines how key players merge these disparate views and sustain a tolerated ambiguity.

My brief and only interlude at the HR department and my early interactions with Carlos and Hank offered me glimpses into how these processes play out, which I call the "mailroom model" of training. I found that employees in the music industry commonly use this framing to situate and justify the standing of interns. According to this model, even if an intern's tasks are mundane, if they work hard, make themselves visible, and meet people, the internship might lead to a job—although, as Aurora and others note, getting a job is never guaranteed. Similarly, if interns pay close attention to what happens around them, they can make their time at the company an educational experience. Therefore, by instructing interns to be proactive, work hard, and take responsibility for their own training, the mailroom model of training places the burden predominantly (if not fully) on the interns to create a worthwhile experience, whether that means obtaining important skills and knowledge or gaining full-time, paid employment. Even though internships are purportedly an educational experience, employees advocate for what I call "osmosis pedagogy," which enables them to fulfill their basic responsibilities as "teachers" while still focusing almost fully on their own (and often precarious) jobs. Employers can thereby wash their hands of responsibility for training or educating interns beyond providing a small space, delegating mundane tasks, and occasionally offering a bit of guidance.

The mailroom model of training reinforces the provisional nature of interns' labor by allowing employees to treat interns in a way that distances them and keeps them provisional indefinitely unless they somehow prove themselves worthy of inclusion. This chapter examines how the occupational community (companies, their employees, and the broader music industry) recognizes and produces legitimate narratives[2] that enable aspirants to make sense of their experiences as a transition, albeit an open-ended one, to employability and possibly employment even though their internships may involve earning little or no money, doing mundane work, and receiving little direct instruction.

In particular, this chapter scrutinizes the perspectives of employers, explaining how they frame the intern economy as a breaking-in system that draws on the myth of the mailroom. By adopting this framing, music industry employees normalize interns' suffering as an ennobling rite of passage, portray on-the-job experience as the best way for an aspirant to learn, and shift the responsibility for training onto interns.

The Myth of the Mailroom

The pull-yourself-up-by-your-bootstraps ethos is an age-old American belief, famously promulgated by Horatio Alger Jr. in his popular coming-of-age novels published in the nineteenth century.

Every field has myths and scripts about breaking in that relate to this ethos.[3] For the business side of the cultural industries, the mailroom is a powerful symbol of humble beginnings, low pay, and repetitious work, but also a potential route for ascending the ranks—a place where the cream seemingly rises to the top through any means necessary. There is a real-life basis for this model: the mailroom was the starting point for several media moguls, including David Geffen (Asylum Records; Geffen Records; DreamWorks), Barry Diller (Paramount Pictures; Fox Inc.), and Michael Ovitz (Creative Artists Agency; Walt Disney Company).

In *The Mailroom: Hollywood History from the Bottom Up*, writer David Rensin (2004) presents the oral history of the mailroom as a stepping stone for entertainment industry employees, particularly talent agents in Hollywood. Referring to the people in the mailroom as both employees and trainees, Rensin describes the mailroom as a launching pad, a type of apprenticeship program at companies such as the William Morris Agency and Creative Artists Agency. In these places, mailroom trainees work for low pay (about $37 per week in 1937; up to $400 six decades later) in "a high-pressure crapshoot that weeds out the weaklings."[4] While there are other routes to success in the cultural industries, few are as romanticized as starting at the bottom in a place like the mailroom and working one's way up.[5]

Since the late 1930s, talent agency mailroom trainees have done everything possible to be taken seriously and move upward, including getting up at 5 a.m. to buy groceries for a morning staff meeting, washing the boss's car, and dropping off their supervisor's stool sample at the hospital (Rensin 2004). Indeed, those who aspire to work in the cultural industries are allegedly so desperate for a chance to prove themselves that they will tolerate whatever task is thrown at them—some employees have described the process as a test of will—all while accepting that this industry must be learned from the bottom up. Lacking the guidance of a clear curriculum, mailroom trainees attempt to learn about the company by purposefully overhearing conversations, reading people's mail, and schmoozing their way into parties in hopes of maneuvering their way into better standing. These stories about the thrilling, but frequently ugly, path to success are inscribed in the mythical history of these industries.

These days, however, the mailroom is not the main path to establishing a career in the cultural industries.[6] While mailroom programs still exist at talent agencies,[7] and similar training programs have emerged in other industries,[8] in most fields, internship programs have become the closest and most common formal equivalent to the classic mailroom experience. A 2006 op-ed in *The New York Times* heralded the rise of internships, announcing, "Instead of starting out in the mailroom for a pittance, this generation reports for business upstairs [as an intern] without pay."[9] Anticipating this point a few years earlier, a journalist for the cultural criticism journal *The Baffler* wrote, "Tomorrow's Mike Ovitzes, David Geffens, and Barry Dillers won't have started in the mailroom at William Morris, they will have been interns there."[10]

A key difference between the classic mailroom and modern internship programs is that internships are explicitly (and increasingly closely) connected to higher education, rather than being fully contained within the host firm. Aside from this locational difference, however, the parallels are striking. Mailroom and internship programs both offer aspirants the chance to do work hosted by an employer and, in the process, potentially learn the ropes and maybe even secure an entry-level job. Mailroom trainees and current interns start near the bottom of the ladder and are expected to learn primarily on their own. For both roles, entrants complete many of the least desirable tasks and, if they choose to continue, aim to work their way up. Mailroom and internship programs are also similar from an organizational perspective: both demand a low level of investment from the firm and entail relatively low-risk work assignments (at least at the beginning) to accommodate varying levels of commitment and ability on the part of aspirants. The mailroom and an internship both serve as a point of entry, an initiation into the industry where vetting occurs on-site. Within the mailroom model of training, aspirants learn and pay their dues, and although they are low in status, the experience is *what they make of it.*

A more recent analogue to the classic mailroom success stories is the case of Kevin Liles, who started as an unpaid intern at Def Jam in 1991, and by 1998 had risen to president of the record label. In his part-memoir, part-self-help book *Make It Happen,* Liles states that achieving success in music boils down to finding "the will, focus and drive to achieve" (2005:1). Liles supports his narrative of fierce individualism with a dazzling array of success stories. For example, he praises twenty-three-year-old Walter Randolph as an exemplar from the "armies of kids" who were willing to prove themselves through unpaid internships at Def Jam. Liles emphasizes Randolph's humble beginnings: he interned without having a place to call home, often sleeping on the subway or on a bench and developing an ulcer from his poor diet. In the book, Liles pairs the details of the harrowing hardships Randolph overcame with implicit instructions for how to act: "No matter how tough it got, he never complained" (2005:19). In short, in the face of adversity, interns must remain persistent, humble, and hardworking. Liles also portrays the record label as a site for learning (2005:19) and notes that Randolph was an astute observer:

> Every day, he'd sit at the workstation outside my office taking in everything around him. When I dropped knowledge, he was there to catch it. He'd listen in on meetings and study the major players as they walked and talked through the halls. He was one of Def Jam University's best students.

Liles recounts that even in earlier years, when the record industry was more robust economically, most interns left the company before getting hired as employees because, unlike Randolph, "they got tired of doing the stuff that nobody else wanted to do and eventually realized that making it in the music industry was just too much of a challenge for them" (2005:19). According to this perspective, failure is due to an individual's lack of commitment.

Despite facing considerable adversity, Randolph the intern worked longer hours than most paid employees at the company and became indispensable. Eventually, when Liles got a job at the Warner Music Group, he hired Randolph as a paid employee.

Liles's book is an updated version of the Horatio Alger Jr. narrative that offers a moral script for an intern's behaviors and values. Aspirants must not only work hard, be persistent, and likely overcome challenging conditions, but also demonstrate a positive attitude throughout the process. In this narrative, interns control their destiny. Mirroring the mailroom model of training, Liles's account proclaims that an internship is what you make of it.

I often saw music industry employees reproduce these beliefs during my fieldwork. As I stocked the refrigerator in the office of an executive at Major Records USA, he told me, "I've seen a million interns here get jobs in marketing and whatever and I think that it's what you put into it." The executive, Larry, knew I was conducting research and referenced Liles's book, focusing on the "what you make of it" trope:

> [As an intern, Liles] used to get bagels and lox for this guy every morning, and coffee, and there were a ton of interns that thought that was beneath them. Not only did he not think it was beneath him; he made sure that he got him the best bagel and the *best* coffee and got it to him hot . . . and that was his attitude. And he would do anything.

While Larry's retelling takes liberties with the story's details—Liles's ascent did not involve fetching coffee, although when I worked as Larry's intern, I routinely picked up his coffee—he summarizes Liles's basic point that an intern should work hard and not be overly proud. Larry concludes, "[Liles] writes about how he set out to be the best intern in the world compared to the people that thought it was beneath them, and [he] knew that he would be noticed that way, which he was." According to Liles, interns who follow this script will almost certainly find success. He writes, "To get noticed, all I had to do was play my position and serve my boss to the best of my ability. If you do that, you'll shine no matter where you're at in the food chain" (2005:118). In sum, music industry employees describe internships as producing varied results depending on what the intern "makes of it," and therefore as meritocratic rites of passage.[11] Importantly, however, success is not guaranteed—it involves paying your dues.

Normalizing Suffering

Within the context of the mailroom model, employees expect the most dedicated and serious interns to prove themselves and pay their dues. But how do employees make sense of the challenging and at times humiliating ways they treat their interns? In other words, how do they reproduce the mailroom model for the intern economy? To normalize the suffering of interns, employees frame internships as a trial period during which aspirants must assume a low status—most visible in the mundane character of the work, location in the office, teasing by employees, and pain (including the pain of being broke)—for an indefinite length of time. Employees frame these practices as a rite of passage, however, there is no clear end point to paying one's dues, which at times becomes less about proving oneself and more about humiliation for its own sake.

After a day of work at the indie music distribution company, Patrick and I sit down for dinner and talk about his experience working with interns at his previous employer, an esteemed independent record company. He says, "From my understanding, everybody pretty much views interning as rushing for a huge fraternity. You know, it's *hell*." Drawing on his experience at a large public university in the Midwest where Greek life is pervasive, Patrick recalls the "trial period where [fraternity members] just torture you psychologically, probably light physical torture, and humiliate you. . . . Once you've gotten through that, then you're good, you're golden. I think that's how a lot of people view interning." According to Patrick's perspective, as interns attempt to transition from aspirant to employee in the record industry, they are at a threshold—they are in what anthropologist Arnold van Gennep (1960) called the "liminal phase" of rites of passage. Of course, as described in chapter 2, not every intern aims to launch a career in the industry, but even those with other motivations persistently face a baseline of suffering and humiliation. Patrick describes the low status and pain of interning as most evident in the types of tasks assigned and the physical conditions of the work.

As we continue our conversation, Patrick argues that companies host interns to do low-level "crap work" that no employee "really wants to do." He continues, "I always feel bad for interns because most of the time that's exactly what they're going to get." To make matters worse, at this company interns were physically segregated from employees, with many of them stuck "in the worst possible place you could possibly fit them because, 'Who cares? They're interns.'" This company did not provide interns with designated seats; instead, they worked in whichever cubicle happened to be available that day or "a lot of times they'd be up front in the lounge area stuffing mailings." Patrick compares the company's interns, who are shuffled from one less-than-ideal space to another, to Milton, a character in the 1999 movie *Office Space* whose employer moves him from one undesirable cubicle to another until he ultimately sits in the building's cockroach-infested basement.

When I offer Patrick a counterexample, mentioning that at our current company I have a dedicated cubicle located immediately next to his own workspace, he responds by noting that light torture can take various, more subtle forms. To illustrate his point, Patrick flashes a knowing smile and asks if my chair disappeared around the time a new employee was hired, implying that on one of my days off the employee went chair shopping in my cubicle. Indeed, my chair had mysteriously disappeared a few weeks into my internship.

The unglamorous intern life Patrick portrays is consistent with the way Isabel, an executive at a major record company, describes interacting with interns. Reflecting on her twelve years of experience in the music industry, she admits to "either lumping [interns] together as 'the interns,' like, a group of people . . . or kind of not really directly focusing attention on them as much as I should be." She offers two reasons for her approach: "Part of it is I might be too busy and part of that is just, 'Ah well, it's the interns.'" While Isabel's bluntness regarding her neglect of interns may seem surprising, like Patrick, she characterizes the plight of interns as a common rite of passage:

> You know, but the thing is that anybody, like ninety-some percent I'm guessing, of the people who are saying ["Ah well, it's the interns"] were an intern and they [understand] you go through that. Everybody's pretty much gone through it, and you know what it's like to have to go to Starbucks and get coffee and be like, "What am I learning? Nothing. I'm learning how to order a mochaccino."

Employees may justify their low level of investment in training interns based on their own experiences facing similar challenges in the past. In this context, many employees construe it as normal for interns to be ignored or treated with a lack of respect.

The power of the mailroom model is perhaps most evident when considering the experiences of interns who later become employees. Some of these employees told me they actively attempt to limit certain aspects of this hazing ritual while, perhaps inadvertently, continuing to reproduce others. For example, as described in the introduction, Rita said she was upset by employee neglect of interns and claimed she actively tries to treat interns better, but later noted she calls them "intern" rather than by name.

Other employees, like Danielle, seem to erase their negative experiences as an intern or perceive them as an undeserved aberration. When I first met Danielle, she was graduating from college with a degree in music business but no job. She lamented the strongly hierarchical structure at her final internship, with a company that did not offer her a long-term position. She described the company's culture by imitating an employee she encountered—"'Oh, I am the VP, and you are the intern, so don't talk to me,'"—and then concluded, "There was that separation." As an intern, she tried to speak with employees despite this separation, but felt she was being "humored."

Five years later, when I catch up with Danielle to ask about her transition to working as an employee at a major record company, she proclaims, "Interns should be seen and not heard, and they should be available always." Having read the transcript from our first interview earlier that day, I am surprised by her words and pause as I try to articulate a response. Danielle fills the gap by clarifying, "Interns should not try to make friends with people. They should be sitting at their post, ready to answer the phone. . . . When you need someone, you don't want them to be chatting with somebody like they've *earned* that." Employees who withstand normalized suffering and eventually break in might then reproduce the mailroom model with surprising force.

Other employees echo Rita, insisting they try to treat interns with respect. For example, Nora explains that she aims to make the experience feel more worthwhile than the internships she and her business partner endured before they started their own small music public relations firm. Nevertheless, she notes that, "to most people it's like a joke" to work with interns. She explains that supervising interns allows often low-paid employees to feel that they are in a position of power and boss people around and it is "something to brag about . . . because it means you're in a position of management and power." She concludes, "People love to humiliate. It's like hazing," and adds that her colleagues often say things like, "Guess what I made my interns do?" thus reproducing some of the difficult conditions they faced as interns.

Nora offers the example of an incident captured on the television show *Making the Band*. In the episode, artist and executive Sean Combs (aka P. Diddy, an ex-intern himself) makes a group of young musicians on the show walk more than twelve miles from Midtown Manhattan to Brooklyn to fetch him cheesecake. She recalls, "It was the talk of the town for like a week. People were like, 'Oh my god, Puffy made the interns [walk] to Junior's.'"[12]

Although she describes this incident as an extreme case, she nonetheless concludes that interns are commonly subjected to humiliation in less intense forms.

Nora also recounts a less extreme example involving a colleague who interned under an executive at a record company and was asked to miss a school function because his boss needed him for a special assignment. After staying late at the office, the intern realized he was asked to stay late to carry a bag of dog food from a car into the office. Nora says that this incident is "insulting" and unacceptable but that it is the type of humiliating episode that employees would later describe as paying one's dues. Too often, Nora explains, employers believe aspirants need to do anything that is thrown at them and call the experience training.

Discussions among Nora's peers about the cheesecake incident suggest that the normalization of suffering has its limits. The mistreatment of interns can result in employees being reprimanded or interns quitting, or both. A supervisor or the HR department might warn an employee not to send interns on personal errands, particularly if an intern complains about such tasks.[13] One interviewee recounted quitting an internship after helping an employee move three pieces of furniture out of the office—the affront was not the task itself as much as the employee complaining to the intern that she was taking too long and calling her intellectually slow (using an offensive term). The intern recalls standing up for herself, saying she had done everything the employee had asked and more, to which the employee responded, "Don't speak to me. You're an intern, so don't you dare speak to me" and then turned his back and left. After other employees told the intern not to take their colleague too seriously, not to worry, and acknowledged, "He's a bit strange sometimes," the intern decided to leave because she viewed this treatment as too extreme.[14]

Job seekers aiming to break in to the industry are incentivized to pay their dues by "playing nice" and accepting their low-level role, even if some employees mistreat them. By demonstrating their willingness to complete low-level tasks (no matter how insignificant) and by withstanding other challenging conditions, aspirants may eventually "earn" improvements in their circumstances, including closer mentorship. For example, during the cheesecake incident mentioned above, Sean Combs defends the assignment as a way to test the seriousness of these aspirants prior to investing in them. He claims, "It's not about me trying to do a mean-spirited initiation hazing act," adding, "Somebody's going to quit. Somebody ain't got the heart, the stamina . . . the passion, the drive, the intensity to want it. Somebody's mental capacity breaks at a certain point. I need to see it now!" With a seemingly never-ending supply of potential workers vying for positions, employees do not hesitate to make sure an intern is worth their limited time and resources before investing in them.

Nate—who was an intern at an independent record label for over two years, was then hired as a full-time paid employee and has now supervised interns for more than five years—mirrors Sean Combs's framing of success in that he emphasizes the importance of an intern proving themself before employees invest in them. In addition, his description is typical in that, in hindsight, successful former interns often frame their experience as a heroic feat. As he recalls his own internship experience, he says he started to pay his dues immediately. When he was asked to stuff envelopes for promotional mailings, he embraced the assignment, even though one of his arms was in a cast.

> I'd go through mailings [really quickly], so I was taking, whatever, five-hundred-piece mailers to the post office, no problem, with a cast on. And I wasn't complaining—it was dead in the middle of summer. So, they're like, "OK, this kid works hard." So [an employee] took me under his wing.

In addition to enduring difficult conditions, interns must demonstrate enthusiasm about their position and maintain a positive attitude. Nate describes one intern who came in with considerable experience and seemed smart but who also "did everything I ever told him to without a word, without a peep, with a smile on his face. I trusted him, so I took him under my wing, so did a lot of my coworkers."

While employees might tolerate interns they do not perceive as worthy of investment because of a seeming lack of competence, enthusiasm, or a positive attitude, they do not see these interns as paying their dues. Nate comments, "If you're not willing to pay your dues, you can stick around and just stuff envelopes and waste your time. We're not going to hire you, but we will use you for the [crap work]." He laughs slightly and then explains that the intern economy, as a "system," is a highly efficient way of using aspirants for their cheap labor for extended periods of time, concluding, "It weeds out the hungry kids; it filters out [the others] and you're left with the hunger. And you want those hungry kids."

A final form of normalized suffering is enduring the slow, financially costly path to a career. Jerry, a senior executive in A&R at a major record company, suggests that aspirants should get involved in the industry through an internship or whatever other experience they can find. When I respond that unpaid work can represent a financial burden for interns, he agrees yet describes shouldering this cost as a test of will: "It's a test. How bad do you want it? Remember that awful Don Henley song, 'How Bad Do You Want It ?'—I mean, it's a test." He then adds, "If you don't want it, a thousand people do." Jerry points to the extremely competitive process of gaining music industry employment as an excuse for enforcing economically precarious conditions—as such, being broke is its own rite of passage.

Some employees construe those who cannot afford to intern as insufficiently committed. A junior employee, Ben, tells me about a promising intern from the previous semester who had to leave:

> He was *awesome* and everyone loved him, and he ended up going. . . . You know, "My parents are cutting me off; they're not going to pay for me anymore." You know, "I owe money to my credit cards" and whatever. "I owe money from being in this band," and . . . we said to him, "Look, if this is what you want to

do, you're not going to just get miraculously hired. There aren't a ton of jobs open in this industry." . . . And it's like, "Yeah, but I can't afford [to]." No, you *can* afford to. You just can't afford to do that and, you know, have the lifestyle to which you're accustomed. I know a ton of people who, you know, leave here and then go work elsewhere and, you know, work on Saturdays and Sundays and do it . . . and then hustle, do anything you can because this is where they want to be. So, I think it is possible, it just doesn't make it easy.

Therefore, while employees construct internships as a process of weeding out uncommitted job seekers, the process advantages those with economic resources. If an aspirant cannot afford to remain an unpaid or low-paid intern, employees view their choice to leave as inconsistent with the entrepreneurial, pay-your-dues ethos.

Devaluing Formal Education

While assuming a low status, completing mundane tasks, and enduring pain might not seem like ideal conditions for an educational experience, employees frame an internship as the best way to learn their job. Employees describe formal education—and specifically music business programs—as an insufficient or even counterproductive route to gaining employment. Music industry personnel describe classroom curriculum as obsolete and instead privilege on-site experience; however, they take little responsibility for ensuring that learning occurs once interns are in the office.

As I sit in an East Village bar with Abby, we discuss her path to employment in the music industry. She interned at a small indie-oriented firm in New York City that promotes records to college and community radio stations; when a junior employee was let go shortly before Abby graduated with a bachelor's degree, her internship experience led to a paid position at the company. At the time of our interview, she has worked in the music industry for approximately five years. (She later became my internship supervisor at Indie Distribution.)

When I inquire about other paths into the industry, Abby stresses the importance of her internship. I ask if she has heard of people studying music business at college. "Yes, I have," she answers as she grimaces slightly, adding that she met various music business majors while studying at NYU. She clarifies that NYU features both a music business program and a recorded music program—she describes the latter program in a positive light because she believes it helps students gain technical skills needed to become a studio employee (for example, an audio engineer), which is something "you could go to school for." However, she does not portray the former program as positively, explaining, "Most of the people I know in the music industry totally think it's *ridiculous* to be a music business major."

Abby questions the wisdom of narrowly specializing in music business given that the field has offered fewer and fewer jobs with the decline of compact discs, yet music business programs have grown since the early 1990s.[15] As we discuss music business majors, she asks rhetorically, "Are they not reading the papers?" To support her point, she asks me to imagine a scenario where the library field was similarly failing, with brick-and-mortar facilities being replaced by online repositories: "What's going to happen? And instead, we have an entire school dedicated to library science and all of these people graduating with library science degrees!"[16] Switching back to the record industry, Abby continues, "I don't know if [music business students are] getting the message we're putting out. We don't know what's going to happen." Her criticism of the growth in music business programs stems in part from the disconnect between a flailing industry with an uncertain future and an expanding body of academic programs.

Abby also questions the relevance of music business curricula, a criticism that is also expressed by other music industry employees and even some music business majors. I suggest that an industry in transformation might gain from people studying it in depth, to which she responds, "I don't know if people going to music business school are really trying to innovate so much as just join." Using the example of NYU, she suggests that in such programs, the curriculum is geared toward understanding historical figures, such as "the guy who found Michael Jackson," and she questions whether this type of knowledge is relevant in the current (and next) iteration of the music industry.[17] The music business curriculum, according to Abby, looks backward and never catches up to an industry that is constantly uncertain about its future.

Bela, another NYU graduate who became a music industry employee, echoes Abby's point by questioning, in her own way, the "out of touch" curriculum. Bela took "a few" courses in the music business program and summarized them as "kind of bullshit." Based on her own experience, she advocates taking one or two such classes to provide background but says that the music industry is changing too rapidly for academic curriculum to keep pace: "Right now it's changing *so much,* like even people that I worked with at [a cutting-edge digital music firm], they don't know what they're doing. They're making it up as they go." She goes on, suggesting that because the record industry functions as a chain of innovation through imitation there simply are no clear fundamentals to teach.

> And people at the majors [key music companies], they don't know what they're doing, they're doing whatever the indies are doing. The indies are just kind of making it up as they go too. And, in fact, [Apple] is pretty much doing the same thing. Everybody at this point is just making it up as they go.

The employees I met almost universally noted a disconnect between music business curriculum and the fast-changing industry.[18]

A related employee criticism of music business programs stresses the chasm between schooling and the "real world" of work. During the summer between his junior and senior years at a Midwest college, Shane, who was working toward a bachelor's degree in business, interned in New York City at his favorite indie record label. Shortly after his graduation, the company hired him as a full-time employee. When I ask Shane if the record company promotes its internship program at colleges, including music business departments, he answers no to both and then adds, "Those music business programs, I think we all kind of smirk at . . . because we all know that our education played a minimal role." While he does not dismiss formal education altogether, he explains that "to a certain extent the industry could do with people who are more trained in certain technical aspects, you know, certain understandings of budgets and things; but you know a lot of that is [learned] on the job." Shane expresses some appreciation for those who gain "technical" business skills as he did, but he ultimately privileges on-the-job learning (or, to use a term that includes unpaid interns, "on-site" learning).

Music industry employees consistently claim that their jobs cannot be learned from a book. Ryan, who has been employed in A&R for about two years after spending more than two years as an unpaid intern at that same major record company, stresses the importance of learning through involvement: "You'll never know this industry unless you're in it. There's no book, there's no test, there's no equation that can teach you how to survive in this industry." He recalls meeting "a lot" of interns from music business programs and describes an overall mismatch between book learning and work in the music industry. Ryan portrays an intern's reliance or focus on applying classroom concepts to the work environment as a recipe for failure:

> It's a very cutthroat business and we get a lot of interns who come in and come from that background who try to bring their workbook into the work environment and somehow, you know, articulate what they learn in class to what's going on here. If you come here thinking you can apply [music business classes] to this work environment, you'll [only] survive a day here. You know, not to discredit any of those programs, but I just feel as if there's more to it.

From Ryan's perspective, students, whether in a music business program or another field, can learn the vocabulary of the music industry, but are missing crucial context.

As further clarification, Ryan describes showing interns a contract between the company and an artist to illustrate the workings of A&R: "I sometimes say to my interns, 'Here's a deal on the table. This is how it's broken down. This is what they're saying. This is what the language reads.'" Ryan continues enacting the imagined exchange, describing an intern's response when they recognize a word in the materials: "Oh yeah, I know that word, my professor said it and we learned about that" or "I took a contract course. I kind of get what they're saying" or "Oh yeah, I understand what that paragraph is." He pauses. Although there are no interns in the room, Ryan wears what I perceive as a look of slight annoyance as he continues:

> That's great but unless you're *here* and you actually can sit down and break down how *this* contract [*points downward*] applies to this record company—that to me makes more of an impact than just kind of being like, "Oh yeah, I saw it on page 36 of my book, and I remember my professor mentioned it to me. Oh yeah, the words you said, that's what it means."

According to Ryan, this example illustrates the limits of book learning relative to the situated knowledge of a workplace and industry. He later adds, "Just because you've seen it in a book, and you read about it doesn't mean you can articulate it and go out and make a business decision." Ryan stresses the gap between theory and practice, or school and the "real world." The "page 36" comment, seemingly an exaggeration used as a form of mockery, evokes a key difference between the perspectives of a student and a worker. Students must read a book on contracts and report on its contents; workers will not pass or fail a test based on knowing terms from books, instead, their standing at a company, their career, and the success of all parties concerned are intricately tied to the workers' complex, situated understanding of contracts as well as their ability to make sound business decisions.

Ryan's reaction to a student connecting a classroom concept to situated experience runs counter to the goal of internships as educational. Certainly, Ryan's point—that to truly become a professional worker one must learn to master bodies of knowledge and interpret information—is consistent with scholarship on expertise.[19] As organizational scholar Beth Bechky (2021:9) noted, expertise extends "beyond formal knowledge to skills that are both tacit and embodied" and "is a form of visceral knowing." However, Ryan expresses palpable annoyance at an intern simply making an explicit connection between the classroom and his work. He is willing to take a moment to show interns a contract but sheds his temporary role as teacher when an intern acts *too much* like a student by connecting a concept learned in a reading, a behavior that would be celebrated in the classroom.

Overall, music personnel endorse a strong "learning by doing" orientation, relatively divorced from schooling, which is consistent with the pay-your-dues ethos of the mailroom model. Aspirants who are perceived as trying to skip paying their dues, for example, by earning an educational credential, face adversity, as Nate colorfully demonstrates when he mocks interns who study music business.

> I hate the kids that come in with this like, "I study music business at Berklee College of Music" or whatever. I don't care, dude; you don't know what it's like in the trenches. You ain't even interned before; you need to be in the trenches. You need to know what it's really like. You need to have ran [*sic*] a master to a fucking engineering studio at three in the afternoon in August heat by foot and subway and felt that pain and brought back boxes of promos. . . . You have to *feel* that to really understand what it's like to work in the music industry and appreciate it.[20]

While music industry employees see some value in higher education—after all, with few exceptions, interns must be enrolled at a postsecondary institution, and almost all new hires have a college degree—they prioritize on-the-job experience over classroom learning. Notably, this pattern of employees describing the classroom curriculum as obsolete or far from complete while privileging learning through on-site involvement, including internships, is somewhat paradoxical as internships are often part of a formal education curriculum.

Osmosis Pedagogy: Learning by Being in the Room

While music industry personnel largely dismiss classroom learning as less valuable than on-site experience, internships are an informal and uneven type of training. Even though some college students complete an internship as part of a college course, paid employees do not necessarily design a clear training plan or detailed curriculum for interns.[21] According to employees, learning occurs mainly via the intern's active involvement in the workplace. Once again, consistent with the mailroom tradition, this model of training frames "intern" as an entrepreneurial role (it is "what you make of it"), which limits the organization's responsibility for educating aspirants beyond granting them access to the workplace. Interns must create their own curriculum, with some leveraging their presence in this environment more than others. Ultimately, as one employee summarizes it: "It's sort of like learning by osmosis." I use the term osmosis pedagogy to emphasize how employees justify their mostly hands-off instruction as educational; inasmuch as some employees might struggle with the ambiguity in being "teachers" and "managers," the idea of osmosis pedagogy allows them to shed the former by delegating the teaching to the environment and the construction of knowledge to the intern.[22]

I got to know Bill, a self-proclaimed self-taught employee who worked his way up from the bottom, while interning at a major record company. He got a job at a record company's warehouse during high school and continued to pack and ship boxes, load and unload trucks, and mail records for the company throughout his college years. Since that time, he has worked in music sales and distribution for over thirty years, eventually becoming a senior executive and working at several major record companies. He stresses the importance of learning through doing, noting, "No one's going to teach you how to sell a record."

Bill emphasizes the value of firsthand experience for learning how to manage human relationships, for example, like learning how to handle "a buyer at Target and the guy's a prick or the guy's a real nice guy." He continues, "No one's going to teach you what he likes and doesn't like. Right? No one's going to teach you what's important to him. You have to figure that out for yourself." Bill focuses on the personal, self-directed process of managing relationships, something that may be learned (or "figured out") but cannot be taught. He describes studying music business in college as potentially "helpful" for aspirants, but he concludes that, "amongst others, this is one of the businesses where experience, being in the environment, there's no better teacher." Most employees and interns mention that "being in the room" is essential to learning about the music business, although they focus on a variety of potential educational benefits interns can glean from this type of experience.

Many respondents use making a phone call (e.g., to a buyer or writer) to illustrate what someone can learn indirectly during an internship. Isabel, for example, emphasizes overhearing—or observing—as a key part of learning how to work in the music industry. She interned at a music PR firm before becoming a publicist at that company and later working for a major record company. She stresses the importance of her physical proximity to paid employees during her time as an intern at the PR firm, saying, "We were all in one room and I learned a lot" and "It's a lot of observing." She recalls not even knowing what publicity was before starting her internship but figuring it out as an intern. Isabel asserts that overhearing employees was a more valuable learning experience than the tasks she carried out as an intern: "Even if I was sitting there just doing a mailing, I was still [aware] of what the publicists were doing and how they did it and how they pitched people on the phone." For example, she overheard "how they managed to get somebody to come review a show" and "how they would offer people tickets" or "send them [merch]." Based on her own experience, she describes interns' training as their meaningful understanding of the surrounding activities more than completing any workplace task.

Isabel relates her experience as an intern in the late 1990s to the current situation for interns at her job. She claims to have an open-door policy: "I have an office with a door. I rarely close it." Interns come into her office and "they'll be doing stuff in my office and, you know, ask what I'm doing." Isabel explicitly contends that while interns may do mundane work, their experience is educational due to their proximity: "Even though their task might not be, you know, something that's so beneficial to learning . . . they're just immersed in being with us, so they learn a lot." By being immersed in an environment, interns have an opportunity to construct what is happening around them, ask questions, and derive practical lessons. Isabel describes learning as an active process for the observer, but not for employees, who do not necessarily direct interns' learning—instead, interns as observers must assume responsibility for inferring valuable industry knowledge from their daily experience at a firm.

Similarly, Nate also describes learning how to make a phone call by observing employees. He recalls sitting next to the person responsible for radio promotion during his internship at an indie music label. The radio promo person was "on the phone constantly just trying to sell records, trying to get 'adds' at radio stations."[23] Wheeling and dealing with a record store buyer, writer, radio station music or program director, or other promotional outlets involves finesse, tact, and savvy—some tricks of the trade, it seems, that can be picked up by overhearing.[24]

> You listen to someone wheel and deal a lot who's very good at doing what they do—luckily, he was also very good at doing what he did—you kind of learn ways of how to get people wheeling and dealing, when you should nudge a joke in, when you should try to go to a casual conversation.

In his job at Indie Distribution, Nate still consistently makes promotional phone calls and builds rapport with digital vendors. He describes his early internship experience as more important than his classroom education: "You can learn a lot of terms in school, but I feel like I learned a lot more from my internship than I ever did from school anyway." Nate recalls spending more time at his internship than at school, partly because he could maintain reasonably good grades even without attending certain classes: "I'd get away with B's and C's without going to class, easily, so I was like, 'You know what, I'm really not learning much there so I'll just intern more.'" He recounts interning four or five days a week and taking many evening classes, explaining, "That helped too. I could intern all day until six and then go to class if I had to." To Nate, the benefits of being in the room outweighed the benefits of attending his college classes.

Given their belief in the importance of overhearing and observation, employees such as Nate and Isabel define an internship as an educational experience no matter what tasks an intern completes. Nate further illustrates this point at the end of a busy day at Indie Distribution (his employer and my internship host). The day had been especially stressful because the department head was unusually demanding, pushing the digital sales team to produce a considerable amount of work. As an intern, I was charged with gathering information from multiple sources, including Nate, to produce "marketing plans"[25] for twenty-four upcoming releases during the last two hours of my day. On a typical day I usually complete a few such marketing plans, among other interspersed tasks. The process essentially entails copying and pasting content I receive via email from various members of the digital team. I format the information into uniform Word documents (one for each release) and occasionally follow up with staff members if I need additional details. Thus, the task involves going through several emails and looking up information in the company database, which tests my eye for detail under pressure. As I write my fieldnotes I realize that this late-hour crunch could provide a less experienced office worker with a disciplining and helpful foray into the regime of office work (i.e., an educational experience).

Just a few hours after leaving the office, Nate and I reminisce about the day with beverages in hand. Nate expresses his fatigue from the late sprint due to the boss's fury (and my requests to fill in the marketing plan blanks). He seems somewhat surprised that I completed twenty-four marketing plans in such a brief period and interprets my intense burst of tedious work positively.

> Jesus. But, going through that repetition, seeing all those marketing plans, seeing what's important, what's highlightable-worthy, what's pitch-worthy and what not, and what people are doing, it's going to just get ingrained in your brain as you do it. The most worthless exercise can be helpful in the end.

Although both Nate and Isabel stress the benefits of learning through overhearing, Nate has a slightly different take; in his view, repetitive, administrative tasks *in and of themselves*, even a "worthless exercise," can be helpful for the aspirant—interns learn, although incidentally or indirectly, about the music industry while completing such tasks.

Moreover, in addition to seeing value in observing and completing tasks, employees stress that interns can learn by asking questions. Looking back on his internship at a small but prestigious indie rock label, Shane recalls completing many mundane tasks, including stuffing envelopes, running errands, bringing postcards to record stores, and handing out postcards at shows. He explains that no matter what task he was working on while at the office, he spent a lot of time listening.

> Just sitting in the room, this open office, you hear people talk on the phone, you hear people have conversations. People don't hide what they're saying in the office. They say what they need to say, so I just listened.

However, his next comments show that Shane was not completely passive, he did not *just* listen. He recalls trying to help the employees whenever he could and, when possible, start conversations with them. He says that these conversations, sometimes seemingly very casual, provided much of his music industry education.

> To me, now, I guess that was the most important thing about the internship. It wasn't any specific task that I did as an intern, which I think was ultimately beneficial about it. It was sort of those off moments when you're making packages maybe and then you get into a conversation with one of the [employees] about the industry or records or record producers or how did this tour happen.

Thus, in addition to observing day-to-day events at a host company and learning from doing, interns can initiate or extend conversations with employees. Further discussing the "off moments" with employees, Shane adds, "That's when I think you learn a lot from the music industry, those times, because it's unlikely you're going to be given anything *really* meaningful [to do] as an intern." In sum, paid employees stress that interns can learn through overhearing, completing seemingly menial tasks, and engaging in conversation with employees. In all three cases, however, the burden of constructing knowledge rests on the intern.[26]

Conclusion

From the classic stories of the mailroom to today's intern economy, breaking in to a highly competitive cultural industry involves enduring humbling conditions as a rite of passage, or so employees argue. As interns step into the role, they are often told this experience will be what they make of it, though they do not necessarily realize the extent to which this is true. According to the mailroom model of training, for an intern to forge an educational experience that will potentially lead to employment in the music industry, they must pay their dues, proactively construct their curriculum, and—as I discuss further in chapter 4—have sufficient economic means to remain in this transitional stage indefinitely. Employees are primarily workers and are rarely explicitly teachers, assuming that interns will learn by being in the room. The narrative of the mailroom model brings legitimacy to what would otherwise seem purely exploitative. As such, this chapter presents a cultural mechanism surrounded by ambiguity: this mechanism helps create the "ambiguity by neglect" often experienced by interns in the cultural industries, and in addition it emerges from and reproduces the ambiguous boundary between "work" and "education" that is inherent to the social process of breaking in.

By laying out the mailroom model, I have suggested that provisional labor is a state of becoming for the intern and a labor supply opportunity for the employer, who can portray paying one's dues as an educational experience. Employers view the mailroom model as a way to test commitment (when interns adhere to it) and sift out uncommitted aspirants.

Notably, the intern's role, particularly as captured by the mailroom model, prepares students for failure. That is, their low expectations of landing a long-term position help them save face—because they are unlikely to make that transition, they are somewhat protected from failure. And yet interns feel this failure in many cases, sometimes quite intensely. In the next chapter, I explore how interns understand, come to believe in, and eventually either accept or reject this model—in effect, how interns attempt to use individual strategies to overcome the ambiguities of their role.

4

Laboring to Earn

IT'S ALMOST LUNCHTIME at Major Records USA when I hear a phone ring and see Hank (an employee and my internship supervisor) pick it up and then promptly hang up while swiftly getting to his feet. He moves away from his desk and hustles down the hall as he blurts out, "Food on the fourth floor. Be right back!" During his absence I stand up and start talking to Mara, a new mid-level sales employee who occupies a nearby office. Larry, a senior employee in the department, walks by shortly thereafter and also announces the news of free food—leftovers from an employee meeting—two stories below. "Cuban food," he adds as an apparent incentive. I thank him, and Mara asks whether I am going down. Larry chimes in again, suggesting we should hurry up, "Before all the interns run down there." As an intern myself, I am covering the phones for Hank, so I tell Mara I should wait until he returns in case someone calls the head of sales. Mara offers to wait as well.

After Hank returns with an overflowing plate in hand, which he later tells me will be enough food for two meals, Mara and I head to the elevators. In the fourth-floor conference room we find large, mostly full trays of food on long tables lining two of the walls, with eight people queued up. Glancing at the line for meat, beans, plantains, salad, and desserts, I see there are only two interns. One of the interns, Elise, is an outgoing twenty-two-year-old woman who often chats with sales and publicity employees when she walks down the hall; later she tells me she hopes Major Records USA will hire her as an employee. Elise is one of the most personable interns I have met, but today she is unusually quiet as she stands in line with her immediate supervisor (a paid employee). Eventually, I hear Elise say to her supervisor, "I'm so tired." As if rehearsing a previously agreed upon script, the supervisor corrects her: "No, you feel great and you're happy to be here." Suddenly smiling, Elise loudly voices her agreement, "Oh, yes! That's right!" as she shifts her posture from a slight hunch to a straightened back.

As this brief episode suggests, the eager, smiling, helpful intern who is happy to be in the office is not just a stereotype—it is a role that employees and some fellow interns construct and reinforce daily. Playing the role of an ideal intern is surprisingly difficult, requiring considerable work and careful presentation of self. Being an intern involves a mixture of nearness and remoteness—interns are ideally in physical proximity to employees, and they are technically members of the organization, but their integration to the workplace is weak compared to most employees and they are stigmatized by their low status (in part due to their association with mundane duties).[1] As sociologist Erving Goffman (1959:38) suggested, playing a role might require a performer to eagerly enact the values idealized by observers (i.e., that interns deserve a lower status than employees), even if those values "accord to the performer a lower position than he [*sic*] covertly accepts for himself." In this case, interns must appear to accept, if not also accentuate, their position as "just the intern"; they must remain unbothered by employees' characterization of interns as scavengers who shamelessly gobble up free food whenever they can (in part because they are working for free), and refrain from pointing out that some employees do the same, while also receiving a salary.[2] Thus, although they are currently stuck at the bottom of the occupational ladder, possibly bored, and occasionally humiliated, interns must maintain a positive demeanor and exude enthusiasm, not to mention work hard and assume almost total responsibility for their own training.

Elise, a citizen of France, paid about a thousand dollars out of pocket for a J-1 visa to come to New York City as a full-time unpaid intern at Major Records USA, working for free in an expensive city for most of an academic year. After only a month at the company, she had forged a close relationship with her supervisor, and by December, halfway through her internship, she seemed to know nearly everyone in the building. Whenever I see Elise walking down the hallway, she is bantering with employees and fellow interns; I later discover that when her workload allows, she volunteers to help other departments with mailings, errands, or anything else they need. Over the course of the year, her workload becomes more and more challenging, and she eventually takes on projects that involve interacting directly with high-profile artists, such as facilitating artist interviews with the international press.

One of the only times I see Elise overtly break from her enthusiastic demeanor is shortly after the company sends an internal email with pictures from the holiday party—a party that, for cost-saving reasons, we were told, interns could not attend. She marches angrily down the hall and shows me a picture of a young woman at the party. Aware that others are within earshot, she switches to French and asks, "Do you know who this is?" Because the person looks so young, it seems she is likely an intern who had somehow gotten to attend the party (later that day, however, we learn that she is a newly hired assistant to an executive). Knowing she must keep up her performance as a happy intern, Elise seeks to hide her frustration by speaking in French (a language in which, in that part of the office, only she and I are fluent).

Building on chapters 2 and 3, which established that employees generally presume interns are incompetent and uncommitted and employees expect interns to respect the mailroom model of training—work hard, be humble, and create their own opportunities—this chapter delves into the strategies interns use, sometimes successfully, in hopes of landing a job. Knowing, or at least sensing, the obstacles to gaining employment, how do job-seeking interns attempt to overcome the ambiguity of the breaking in process?[3]

The data from my interviews and participant observation, including statements from three groups—job-seeking interns in the process of becoming employees, interns who tried but ultimately never got hired in the music industry (Elise is in this category), and employees who had witnessed interns making this transition (many of them former interns themselves)—show that aspirants seek to build employees' trust in their commitment and competence by aligning themselves with what I call the "ideal intern norm." Adopting the ideal intern norm, however, only makes it likely someone will be deemed a "good intern," and does not necessarily lead to a job offer. Thus, in addition to fulfilling these ideal expectations, interns pursue three key strategies—tactful proactiveness, relationship building, and extended investment—as they try to transition from intern to employee, with varying degrees of success.[4]

Each of the three strategies involves navigating through ambiguity. Interns who engage in tactful proactiveness seek to exhibit just the right level of initiative. They strive to balance working independently and soliciting training from employees; they must also determine when and how to enthusiastically seek more work responsibilities without coming off as annoying, entitled, or overly eager. In relationship building, interns focus on finding the right level of affinity and self-assurance. They must come off as "natural" and interested rather than overtly strategic or instrumental. Additionally, they need to interact with employees confidently while embodying the requisite humility of the intern role (i.e., they cannot be perceived as thinking they are "too good" to be an intern). In the third strategy, extended investment, interns must strike the right balance in allocating their time and energy to their internship and their other responsibilities (e.g., school or work). These decisions offer an opportunity to show commitment but also entail other costs (e.g., debt or lower grades) that serve as significant obstacles for less privileged aspirants.

In short, interns who can signal commitment and competence and can enact these strategies will ostensibly be able to make the most of their internship; importantly, however, a detailed examination of these three strategies reveals how this breaking-in system reproduces inequalities. These three strategies broadly map onto cultural capital (tactful proactiveness), social capital (relationship building), and economic capital (extended investment), key resources that better equip some aspirants to break in. These three types of capital overlap in that they are found most prominently among aspirants with class privilege. Therefore, while some critics of the intern economy suggest that only the most economically advantaged aspirants can afford to do an unpaid internship, this chapter shows how navigating the path to gaining employment more pervasively advantages newcomers from class-privileged backgrounds.

The Ideal Intern: Signaling Commitment and Competence

Sociologists of work and organizations have found that employers base their perceptions of an aspiring employee's potential performance, in part, on signals about the aspirant's competence and commitment.[5] Experiments in which employers evaluate potential job candidates show that gatekeepers rely on these signals, such as work histories, to assess workers' competence while also making judgments based on personal attributes such as age, race, gender, and education.[6] These judgments are also shaped by the "ideal worker norm" in that employers prefer workers who appear fully committed to working long hours at the expense of nonwork concerns (such as family).[7] Sociologists have shown that these employer assessments, while seemingly resting on neutral organizational policies and practices, are rife with bias, leading to systemic labor market inequities that notably harm racial/ethnic minority, working-class, and women workers.[8]

Once hired, biases about which workers are committed and competent, at times euphemistically described as having the "right stuff" or fitting in, persist and function as cultural barriers.[9] Whether fellow employees and supervisors see a worker as a "natural fit" for a role depends not only on the signals that the worker sends intentionally—the educational credentials they amass, the long hours of work they put in, and so forth—but also on (at times) less purposefully curated signals such as their interactional skills, their appearance and personal style, and shared affinities.[10]

While these theories apply to job-seeking interns, their situation differs somewhat from that of more experienced job seekers. Especially for college student interns in their late teens or early twenties who have less extensive work histories, the challenge of breaking in is far from limited to the problem of access (getting the internship). While previous experience (e.g., involvement at a college radio station) and referrals from trusted sources can help open the door for aspirants—since, respectively, these signal some level of competence and commitment—once inside the organization, interns must continue to demonstrate competence and commitment by acting like an ideal intern.

Much like how the ideal worker norm seems neutral and therefore without bias against any group, the ideal intern norm (for the aspiring employee) also obscures built-in biases and disadvantages.[11] Grace, a twenty-two-year-old employee who selects and supervises interns at a prestigious indie record company, summarizes the seemingly neutral, meritocratic nature of internships:

> [Employees] are really responsive to the kind of person you are. If you seem like a creative, intelligent, ambitious person then people are going to want to gravitate toward you to give you a bigger responsibility. If you're more inward and, you know, a little awkward or you don't seem that into doing the work there then no one's going to ask you for a lot of stuff.

However, the process of evaluation—when selecting interns and, later, when assessing whether interns are creative, intelligent, and ambitious—is rife with biases, in this case notably by social class (as discussed in the forthcoming sections), but also by age, gender, and race.[12]

In a youth-oriented industry like music, being young is a salient element of looking and sounding right for the part.[13] While some people do internships later in life to facilitate a career change, these cases are still relatively unusual.[14] The comedic film *The Internship*, starring Owen Wilson and Vince Vaughn, starts with the incongruity of forty-somethings doing internships as its premise (predictably, a flurry of age-related jokes ensues). Therefore, while possible, getting a music industry internship in one's late twenties or older is difficult. As an employee who selects interns at a major record company told me: "I get emails from people who are out of grad school being like, 'Can I come intern for you?' It's like wow . . . you're *way* too far ahead for this! Like, what are you doing?" For slightly older aspirants who secure an internship, some report difficulties in enacting the ideal intern norm. Mark was pursuing a master's degree in music business and was able to intern (for credit) at a prominent independent label at the age of twenty-six. As his recollections illustrate, to be an older intern adds another layer of humility to the experience.

> I was there with nineteen-year-old kids. I just felt like an asshole the whole time because a lot of times they don't have anything for you to do so you're just kind of waiting around for someone to—maybe someone who's younger than you—to give you some *task*. It's kind of humiliating in a way.

Humbly yet enthusiastically seeking additional tasks challenges one's ego to an extent, but to do so surrounded by younger people potentially of higher status creates another level of difficulty.

As I further discuss later, relatively rapid assessments on the part of employees regarding which interns are worth their investment, or some incremental promotions in status, lend themselves to preferring aspirants based on "gut assessments." These types of rapid assessments regarding who fits in or not, studies show, often rely on similarities between the chooser and the chosen in terms of characteristics such as class, gender, and race.[15] Aspiring workers in the music industry are channeled into "race appropriate" departments through the suggestion of fit;[16] sometimes this occurs subtly, like to Danielle, a Black intern who claims she has not noticed any racial prejudice in the music business yet later also tells me employees incorrectly "assume I'm more into hip-hop than other genres." Several employees also described a gendered division of labor where men tend to dominate A&R and women work in publicity and administrative positions.

Beyond the division of labor, though, at times women face other challenges in adopting the ideal intern norm, such as how to act in an appropriately assertive way while building informal work relationships and promoting one's accomplishments (particularly in fields dominated by men).[17] As I mentioned in chapter 1, due to the ambiguous legal standing of unpaid interns, they generally do not have the same legal protections from sexual harassment and discrimination as employees. This legal void creates additional challenges for women; as one former intern told me, she was often unsure how to react to comments either directed at her or interactions among men she could overhear about women's physical appearance and concluded: "I was uncomfortable at least once a day."

Biases in the process of evaluation can interact by race, gender, class, and so on. For example, during a follow-up interview with Greg, when he had been working in the sales department of a major record company for nine months, he complained about his interns' performance. Although music industry personnel put down the importance of "book learning," they tend to link the prestige of a school with an intern's preparation for basic tasks. In this case, Greg links interns' education, class, and race:

GREG: I had a couple interns over my time, ranging from some awful, awful, awful interns to some *decent* ones. I don't think I ever had one that I was like, "He's great!" I had one that I liked the most . . . the other ones I wasn't as invested in them, but I could tell right away that they weren't going to work there so it wasn't worth my time to invest in them at all.

AF: How could you tell or sense that people were not interested in working there?

GREG: We weren't interested in having *them*. You could just tell right away. Even just not being good with the computer, not being able to write and speak well. It's like really basic stuff. . . . A lot of interns that would come in from more of those inner-city schools and they basically didn't jive with us that well. . . . I don't think [HR] did a good enough job getting interns from some of the better business schools around. That place should have been fully staffed with NYU kids from the Tisch program and from Stern School of Business every semester. And they always got kids from Brooklyn College.

I ask Greg what he means by "inner city schools" and he corrects himself, saying he means community colleges (though Brooklyn College is not a community college, it is a public university serving a highly racially diverse, often first-generation student population). He then provides an example of an intern who "didn't have a great educational background" but was graduating in six months and conveyed a strong interest in getting a job in the music industry:

> I said—"Get out there and *meet* people and make connections." And he just didn't really. He would [walk away, come back] and say, "I just talked to the head of promotions!" And I'd be, "Alright tell me what he does" . . . I'm a big believer, I usually know within a minute if I want to hire somebody or not. I know that's really crass to say, but it's just, not based at all on any racial or . . . but just talking to them about their experiences and what they understand about the job and if I can tell that they don't understand the job, that they're capable of explaining the job and see if they can do it, but it's just, whether or not their personality will click with what they want to do, I can usually tell pretty quickly.

The intern was unable to rapidly convey a sense of competence to Greg, who attended one of the country's more prestigious colleges. As with other research on cultural similarities in the hiring process, Greg's evaluation of "jive" and "click" or lack thereof suggests potential limitations in the intern's soft skills which may belie differences in background.[18]

Below I highlight how interns and employees describe what it means to enact commitment and competence as an intern. However, although the data below suggest that interns attempt to be "ideal interns" and use these individual strategies to at least lessen the ambiguity of the breaking in process, there are often unspoken barriers these aspirants cannot control or address. While "trying out" aspirants could offer a way for minority or minoritized job seekers to "overcome" employer biases and break in, there is reason for doubt.[19]

Enacting Commitment

To some interns, the work arrangement they step into seems designed to ensure a lack of commitment—they receive limited training, encounter challenging relationships with supervisors, and complete unsatisfying tasks; any of these conditions might prompt them to quit. According to the mailroom model of training, however, even in extreme circumstances, a job-seeking intern must signal their commitment by expressing enthusiasm about being there, and showing they are intent on staying there. Interns who seem displeased with mundane tasks annoy employees, who interpret insufficient enthusiasm as a lack of commitment to meeting organizational goals.

In the previous chapters, I provided many examples of interns who enacted commitment. With enthusiasm, Paula used FedEx boxes to create poster mailing tubes. Ryan described being happy to sort demo CDs (a tedious task) for the good of his department and to increase his chances of getting a job. Early on in his internship, Nate embraced the repetitive duty of stuffing envelopes for promotional mailings, even while wearing a cast, adding: "I just wouldn't stop, I'd just go everywhere. If they needed something done, I'd just get it done." Nate recounts how, after a few months of interning, he was instrumental in helping the small record company move to another building: "I really came down as a superstar because I packed up damn near the entire office and unpacked damn near the entire office." To enact commitment partly means accepting the notion that no task is too small.

Importantly, performing enthusiasm goes beyond a willingness to execute menial tasks. The ideal job-seeking intern signals their commitment more broadly by going the extra mile at the office to the detriment of their schoolwork, paid job, or personal life. Danielle, a recent graduate with a bachelor's degree in music business, recalls a recent internship where she tried to become part of the team. Rather than limiting her time in the office to the scheduled hours (10 a.m. to 6 p.m. with a lunch break) she regularly extended her hours: "I can't even tell you when I left at six. I left closer to seven. And I ate [lunch] at my desk." She recounts that employees eventually began to include her as a member of the team by inviting her to their happy hour gatherings, which she happily joined. She also jumped at every opportunity to attend other company events and complete additional assignments. To embody the ideal intern norm can lessen the barrier between an intern and employees, though this happens incrementally over a prolonged period of time.

Enacting Competence

In addition to communicating their commitment, interns must embody competence. After three internships, Danielle is aware of employees' stereotypical notions about an intern as someone who is "kind of clueless." Her goal as an intern, she notes, is to surpass this presumption by demonstrating her ability to do good work, often independently—in effect, she aims to comport herself like an employee.

Unfortunately, this is not always easy. At one internship, Danielle did not receive training on how to navigate the FedEx website, and as a result, made many embarrassing mistakes when shipping packages. Eventually, however, Danielle had more successful attempts. For example, she shares that when a highly respected marketing employee asked her to write a press release, the employee was so pleased with the final product that she did not change a single word. Danielle triumphantly concludes, "In all of my experiences I got to a place where I was trusted to do things."

A key way interns can display competence and gain employees' trust is by intuiting when to work independently and when to ask questions. Oliver, one of the employees I spoke with, recalls an intern filing documents and realizing there are two differently placed files for a company: "Just going, 'Hey wait a second, this is marked *Company X* but there's another file that exists in another folder with this name . . . what should I do?' It's like, awesome that you ask. Fantastic!" He continues, "If [the intern] had just decided to [file] it in one, it could have been the wrong spot. If [the intern] weren't here on the day I needed to find it, I'd be in a world of trouble." Nancy, another employee, offers a similar perspective, portraying a good intern as someone who "will take the hint to just figure out, solve a problem themselves rather than ask a million questions, but also has the insight to know once in a while you do need to stop and ask." Taking a hint requires soft skills like tact, awareness, and intuitiveness.

Another way interns can demonstrate competence is to save employees time by anticipating tasks. Emily explains that at her last internship, she worked on a spreadsheet with two other interns; they would work on three versions of the document, each charged with different rows. She says, "I let my boss know we're all done with it. [He said:] 'Hey can you combine it?' I say, 'It's already done, I combined it, I put them all on there, we have one spreadsheet that's accurate.'" She adds, "Knowing what's supposed to be done, doing it, not having [a supervisor] be like, 'Can you do this, can you do this, can you do this' [matters]. You have to be somewhat intuitive." Ideal interns are productive while limiting how often they ask for guidance.[20]

Danielle also points to the value of understanding when to speak up and when to remain quiet, describing her experience sitting near two vice presidents (separated by dividers, not walls): "Part of your job is knowing when you overhear something and you can . . . acknowledge it, or knowing when you're supposed to pretend you're not there because they're pretending you're not there." She describes the employees expecting her to promptly jump in when needed:

> I could just tell—if it's something where we need to gather research, a phone call needs to be made. . . . They're kind of casually talking about how they have to travel. I'm supposed to know whether I'm doing something or not, that that means start looking on American Airlines because he's going to need to blah blah blah. You know, and they get impatient if you're not on top of that.

As osmosis pedagogy dictates, interns must learn without explicit instruction, acting like a fly on the wall, waiting for appropriate moments to tactfully interject. Learning to successfully navigate these interactions can signal competence.

To build and prove competence and commitment in the process of breaking in, interns use three strategies: tactful proactiveness, relationship building, and extended investment. These strategies allow some interns to not only be seen as good interns, but also to potentially navigate the ambiguities inherent in this breaking-in system. Critically, some interns, particularly from privileged socioeconomic backgrounds, come equipped with dispositions that enable them to improve their odds in the transition to breaking in. For example, more privileged college students feel more comfortable proactively interacting with authority figures and building relationships.[21] Therefore, through these three strategies interns *might* overcome the ambiguities of this breaking-in system, but to do so advantages those with resources, including (but far from limited to) having family support to secure an internship and live in an expensive city.

Strategy One: Tactful Proactiveness

As discussed in chapter 3, the mailroom model of training dictates that an intern who sits and waits for more work to be assigned or for employees to initiate conversation will probably not last long in the industry. In this context, an intern must be at least a bit of a "pushy punk" to make the most of their experience. The comments of two interns, Monique and Shane, offer a helpful overview of the need to be proactive.

Monique, who is pursuing a bachelor's degree in music business in hopes of building a career in music, recalls feeling underutilized and unengaged as she struggled to make something of her two A&R internships at a major record company. She recounts, "It's easy to just do an internship sometimes and really not [learn] . . . oh, I learned how to make thirty copies." She laughs, and goes on, "Or I learned how to make coffee. I don't know, so sometimes you really need to be proactive and make the best out of the situation; get the most that you can out of it." Monique observes that while some of her classmates said they had internships where they did and learned a great deal, at her current position, "you need to push to have something to do instead of just busy work. And you always have to ask questions and be proactive." In hindsight, she calls internships a "weird position," describing the social chasm between employees—a group of people who have been together for some time—and an influx of interns who come in and out of the office every few months. At first, she felt intimidated about approaching employees for more work, but eventually she asked if she could contribute more. Her efforts were not completely successful—her assigned tasks did not change much—but her outreach signaled her interest to employees, who rewarded her by speaking with her more and (at her request) sharing stories and life lessons from their music careers.

Shane similarly illustrates the challenge of proactively making more of an internship, stating, "I think you have to be . . . persistent. You have to really try to really get a lot out of the internship." He describes his two years as an intern at a small indie record company positively, but, at least at first, he was only assigned mundane tasks. After a few weeks, he realized the employees had neither the time nor the inclination to update the company website; he told them he had experience updating websites and suggested he could take this work off their hands. From that point on, Shane recounts, "they started to really see what kind of value I could add." He began updating the website, which the employees appreciated, and he incrementally started to demonstrate his competence and gain more responsibilities. He is now an employee at that same record company and continues to stress the importance of interns being proactive.

> You can't do it passively. You really can't. I've seen a lot of passive interns that I've worked with at [this company]. You really can't because if you're passive you're just going to sit there. I'm going to forget about you.

Shane also mentions the dangers of being too persistent: "I think there's a balance that an intern will strike between being persistent, showing that you're there to help, and trying to do as much as you can to help, but also not being in the face *too much*." As Monique's and Shane's descriptions illustrate, a key challenge of breaking in is enacting the tactful proactiveness necessary to respect the humility of the intern role while entrepreneurially seeking new responsibilities and opportunities to build trust with employees.

Finding More Work or Seeking Training, in Just the Right Way

As described in earlier parts of this chapter, interns often make efforts to take on additional tasks, even anticipating the needs of employees. Emily consolidated spreadsheets to ease her supervisor's workload while Shane identified and filled a need to update the company's website. Other interns recall doing things such as tidying up the storage room and nearby areas or looking for and reporting any incorrect content on their record company's website. Finding small tasks like these to do, and executing them independently, is an important way of being proactive.

When interns volunteer for more work or ask for more training, however, they must time and articulate their efforts thoughtfully. Someone who can read the room and understand when their enthusiasm is welcome and when it is an annoyance is in a better position to break in. Understanding the appropriate frequency, timing, and phrasing of offers to help can lead to significant benefits. One intern, evidently aware of the hidden curriculum, recalls asking an employee if she needed help with an industry showcase that evening; the intern ended up helping with on-site logistics and built rapport with the employee.

The intuitive, albeit minor, contributions of the tactfully proactive intern are what Nate refers to as "efficient drive" or "smart motivation" rather than the "dumb blind" motivation of an intern who, for example, incessantly asks for more to do. Employees report appreciating an eager intern more than an unengaged one who simply accepts downtime, but, as Nate suggests, the way an intern asks for more to do can signal their potential.

> You need to do that intelligently somewhat and that shows a lot about you, too. If you can figure out like—"It seems like you're on the spreadsheet a lot, is there any way I can learn this and I can take this over for you?" Rather than [speaking in a deeper, dumber-sounding voice], "I don't have anything to do! Do you

> have anything? I don't have anything to do. Do you have anything?" That can get annoying.

Greg, a former intern who was eventually hired by Major Records USA, offers a similar assessment. We met as fellow interns at the company; by then, he was completing his fourth internship. He explains that over time, especially at his first two internships, he developed a sense of what was expected of interns. He figured out that he needed to do small tasks to show his competent enthusiasm, and he needed to approach it in just the right way.

> You get in there the first day and at first you want to be like, "I want to help with this, help with that." But it's . . . about *realizing* what they want you to do. . . . It's not always good to [suggest], "Hey can I do this?" because you might just be getting into somebody's way. But then you have to realize like, "Hey, every time my boss orders lunch, he asks me to get him a plate, so maybe I'm just going to bring him a plate with lunch." Stupid things like that go a long way.

The Necessity of "Optional" Activities

A key aspect of the tactful proactiveness strategy is understanding that what seems optional is often a prerequisite for the job-seeking intern aiming to break in. Shane recalls agreeing to do any work assignment as an intern, even optional ones that extended beyond his normally scheduled hours: "Just anything extra, [I'd] just jump at it. I would always offer to do more and stay as late as they needed me. If they asked me to come in specially to do a mailing, I'd always do it." Some interns describe helping employees in other departments, for example, a marketing intern helped the Major Records USA sales department mail T-shirts to stores.

Interns who exhibit a willingness to do anything and widen their responsibilities tend to stick out. Shane mentions a recent example of interns who came to a show featuring one of the company's artists even though attendance was optional, and even handed out promotional postcards to people in the audience: "That means a lot. I think it shows a commitment, so we all hung out and it was fun." Similarly, Isabel praises a group of interns who agreed to distribute promotional items at 6:30 a.m.

> I had *Artist X* on the *Today Show* and we had a handful of interns come at 6:30 in the morning and hand T-shirts and posters out to the crowd. . . . At the end of the day, I'll remember those handful of interns that pony it up, got up at five in the morning to come and do that.

Although it is not necessarily explicitly stated to interns, those who respond to invitations to do more, even if this work goes beyond their regularly scheduled hours, earn a reputation among employees as more committed.

Taking It Too Far: The Risk of Seeming Entitled

While interns must be proactive, an intern who is too insistent runs the risk of seeming overbearing and coming off as annoying to employees. When unsatisfied with their responsibilities, an intern's first impulse could be to volunteer to do higher-level tasks. However, interns must be careful not to come off as too pushy—or, worse yet, entitled. Nate describes how he has supervised (or dealt with) "entitled" interns at his previous job:

> It used to annoy the hell out of me when these kids would come in and think they were all entitled. They'd come in with a sense of entitlement that I used to like to beat out of them. . . . Mostly I would just give them hard labor. If they came in with *that* attitude, coming in already entitled, I'd give them hard labor. "Really? You want to do a marketing plan? Go clean up the storage room, I'll see you in a few hours." That would be it.

As Nate illustrates, if interns are too pushy about doing "more important" work or give off the impression that they are not willing to pay their dues by doing mundane tasks, employees can ignore or discipline them.

Interns who push too hard run the risk of violating the sense of an intern's "place." Both employees and fellow interns recognize and reinforce the idea of an intern's "place." For example, at Major Records USA I overheard two interns and two employees complaining about a problematic intern in their department; this intern, absent at that moment, had considerable music industry experience and seemingly expected to do higher-level work rather than the simple tasks he and fellow interns were routinely assigned. Not only can it be difficult for employees to manage such an intern, but such behavior potentially offends fellow interns. When I later pull aside one of the interns, Elise, she calls the problematic intern "full of himself" for complaining about doing low-level tasks as if they were below him, while she completes them daily. Annoyed and somewhat amused, she rhetorically adds that this pompous intern somehow does not understand why people in the department do not like him.

Even interns who have more seniority than others and have ascended to higher-level duties at a company must be sure not to come off as overly confident and condescending—in one case, at another company, a full-time intern seemed uninterested in helping newer, part-time interns complete a mailing, and employees took notice; two employees told me the intern did not understand his place (and he was never hired). An employee at a major record company described a similar case and compared his department to a basketball team, saying, "You've got to play your position." For interns, playing their position means fulfilling their workplace responsibilities but also acting according to the formal and informal expectations of colleagues who believe aspirants must "pay their dues," even if they already have considerable experience.

Even if interns avoid being labeled as entitled, their proactiveness might go too far. Greg (during his first year as an employee) tells me about a Major Records USA intern who showed considerable enthusiasm but did not act according to the intern role: "He didn't really know his place. He was eager, but sometimes in the *wrong* way." Interns are expected to complete their basic tasks and then they might be assigned further work. In the A&R department, interns might suggest artists to their supervisors, who research and develop relationships with potential new additions to the company's roster; however, employees view this intern task as somewhat of a perk. Discussing an intern who failed to grasp the intricacies of his role, Greg says, "He would be like, 'Hey check out this band that I brought in,' and not do stuff that [the boss] had asked him to do." The intern Greg describes showed enthusiasm, but the inattention to other duties made the proactive efforts come off as the "wrong" type of enthusiasm.

Brian, while working in A&R at a prestigious indie record company, similarly oversaw an intern who he describes as taking things too far. The intern printed his own business cards, which could be seen as a sign of commitment, but Brian portrays the effort as "a little bold." The intern put the company's logo on the card, personal cell phone number and email address, and "indicated that he did A&R." Brian calls this behavior "presumptive," suggesting that "that's someone who's putting the cart way ahead of the horse." Instead of slowly learning the trade and working his way up, Brian suggests, the intern is "probably spending too much time doing things like that and not enough time just doing the work."

The aspects of tactful proactiveness highlighted above suggest that this approach requires, or at least is much easier with, class privilege. Being aware of the hidden curriculum, and having a flexible schedule unhindered by a paid job or other responsibilities, is consistent with class advantage. For aspirants with the appropriate cultural capital, the breaking-in system appears less ambiguous—they are aware of how to act, how and when to approach authority figures, and seem comfortable in the process.[22]

Strategy Two: Relationship Building

Being tactfully proactive potentially fosters employees' trust and their perception of an intern as competent and committed. An overlapping and, according to some, even more crucial individual strategy for breaking in rests on the intern's ability to network and develop relationships with employees. While connections are generally important in finding work, social networks are especially salient in the cultural industries where there is a low educational barrier for entry and hiring decisions are strongly tied to trust.[23] Some job-seeking aspirants try to connect with record industry employees on social media, attend workshops where they can meet industry professionals, or secure brief informational interviews through family contacts or by cold calling, but these opportunities pale in comparison to the chance to build trust with employees as an intern.

Becoming an intern offers a literal foot in the door and a pathway to building relationships with members of an occupational community, or so interns are told. There is a large social gap between interns and employees—as I describe below, this is a key challenge for job seekers to overcome when networking—but being an intern ideally offers a form of access (e.g., some built-in proximity to employees) and legitimacy (from an official affiliation with a company) that are difficult for non-intern aspirants to attain.[24] Even beyond the confines of the office, an intern can claim, "I work at *Company X*" when interacting with an industry professional at a show or elsewhere, thereby leveraging the affiliation to signal status, especially if interning at a highly respected firm. In this section I show how interns and employees make sense of the role relationships play in breaking in, and highlight some of the ways interns forge these relationships, as well as the challenges they face while doing so.

The accounts I heard of gaining paid employment in the music industry had a common focus on aspirants' aptitude—often quite explicit and strategic[25]—for networking. The people I met describe three sequential phases to relationship building: the beginning, when the intern must ensure that proximal employees know who they are; during the internship, when interns must deepen and broaden these relationships; and after the internship, when interns must work to maintain relationships. The aptitude for networking, at all stages but particularly during the internship, involves being subtly strategic and possessing a well-timed ability to show some personality (temporarily suspending the hierarchical relationship through informality and/or familiarity). As I discuss below, while relationship building aligns with what sociologists describe as social capital, one's cultural capital (and, relatedly, economic capital) overlaps with the ease with which one navigates the internship—relationship building involves a mixture of comfort with authority and the ability to skillfully appeal to preexisting shared interests.

Early Impressions

When I started my internship at Major Records USA, working under the assistant to a senior executive, I assumed that senior personnel would not learn my name. Several interns I interviewed reported feeling ignored, especially at major record companies, and suspected that no one except their direct supervisor had bothered to learn their names. Nonetheless, on my second day at the company, as I was shuffling papers on my desk in the hallway, the senior executive in the department put his hand on my shoulder and said, "Excuse me, Alex" as he walked by. I had been introduced to him briefly earlier that week and he had addressed me by name continuously since then. Of course, my case is not representative—an intern pursuing a PhD is rare. While a few interns report having experiences similar to mine, others, such as Monique, report needing to train employees to learn her name: "At the beginning of the [Major Records USA] internship I kind of had to [say], 'I'm Monique! I'm Monique!'" Then, pretending to be an employee, she adds, "'*Monique*, sorry I forgot your name.'" In this way, interns must ensure that people know who they are, since such recognition is not a given.

Making an early, strong impression can shape the internship experience. Employees report quickly identifying those interns who seem to "get it" and offering them better assignments and closer mentoring. As an extreme example, the A&R department of the major record company where Ben works as an entry-level employee hosts an unusually large number of interns (ten to fifteen at once) and all of them report to him. Because the interns are seated apart from employees, they have limited opportunities to interact with him, let alone more senior employees. To ease communication with the interns and the burden of managing them, Ben (who was also a recent intern in that department), in consultation with the employees above him, chooses a "head intern" within a week or two of the semester's start. He siphons work for the group through the head intern—when a new assignment comes in, he contacts the head intern who then shares the assignment, oversees the work of fellow interns, and reports back to him directly. Ben describes the process as "almost like a reality show," adding, "It's about rising to the top. . . . There's always going to be one in a group of interns who really stands out."[26] Early impressions are not set in stone, Ben adds, but these are confirmed in most cases, and the head intern remains in this role throughout the semester.

Employees underscore the usefulness of self-promotion from the very beginning of the internship to get face time with employees and build relationships. Putting the impetus on interns to come off as competent immediately, and employees' stated emphasis on gut assessments when making rapid judgments of interns, further highlights how a highly informal breaking-in system reproduces inequities. Choosing a head intern or deciding that someone is especially worthy of training based on a rapid gut assessment lends itself to preferring people who seem to "fit in" and therefore who resemble employees in terms of characteristics such as class, gender, and race.[27]

During the Internship

Moving beyond the initial stage of achieving name recognition and quickly gaining some status with employees, interns report that as their internships continue, they make efforts to deepen relationships with supervising employees and broaden their networks within the company and industry. Ben emphatically stresses the importance of mentors for finding the next internship or getting hired: "When it comes time for [finding] another internship or to graduate it's those people who'll vouch for you and say, 'Hey, let me help you.'" He adds that the rewards from simply meeting people are limited—interns must also develop trust: "There's a lot of people who go out and give out their [business] cards . . . and there's no point in that. You know? Sure, they'll know your name—awesome. And then what?" There were two main ways interns described approaching this phase of relationship building: being subtly strategic and showing some personality.

Subtly strategic. Notably, both employees and interns believe it is best if these efforts to forge deeper relationships are not overtly instrumental and do not take up too much of an intern's time or energy. Companies also explicitly warn interns about the limitations of networking. The one-page intern guide I received from Major Records USA, for example, notes that interning represents an opportunity to network, but specifies, "Don't make this your main priority"—in other words, make sure to get your work done and do not bother the employees. Given that employees tend to frown upon an impersonal, overtly instrumental approach to developing relationships, and yet interns must bridge the symbolic—and at times physical—distance from employees, interns must be subtly strategic.

As Ben and I continue our conversation, I ask if he is saying he "networked" with employees. In response, he grimaces and says, "I think networking is kind of a horrible word. Networking, I think, at the base of it, is using people. I think there's a difference between networking and really just making friends." Rather than instrumentally seeking out contacts in the industry who could help him, or appearing to do so, Ben describes a process in which bonds develop more organically. He says that as an intern, he quickly connected with people who had musical passions just like his, especially a junior employee in his department. He would often "nerd out" about music with the employee, frequently staying late and attending shows with him, and in the process also became friends with fellow interns and other employees. He credits these friendships with his later success.

> What I think attributes to a lot of where I am now is the fact that I was friends with everyone I worked with and worked for. . . . Those people then all liked me and then we were friends and, you know, you help your friends.

Ben's depiction of relationship building is consistent with an occupational identity driven by shared passion and camaraderie.[28] Over time, he became a trusted, competent, and amiable fixture in the office. Employees even invited him to tag along in meetings with colleagues, without asking his supervisors first, and Ben quickly began to contribute by offering his thoughts on artists. Another A&R employee who took part in some of these meetings describes Ben (as an intern) to me as someone who always has something smart to say.

The need to be subtly strategic becomes clear to me at Major Records USA when I want to get to know the head of the department, Bill, a senior executive whose desk is only a short walk away but with whom I have limited built-in contact. My supervisor, Hank, is often a relatively generous mentor, but as Bill's assistant he wants to maximize his face time with Bill to ask occasional questions and, I suspect, to maintain their strong bond. On my second week in the office, when I sign for a package for Bill, Hank jumps out of his seat and, even though he is on the phone, says, "I'll take that," as he rescues the package from my hands and immediately brings it to Bill's office. When he returns, Hank informs me that he always brings packages to Bill.

Eventually, I come up with a way to interact with Bill; in addition to replenishing drinks in the department employees' personal fridges in the mornings before they arrive in the office, I take it upon myself to also do so around lunchtime. This is greeted as a thoughtful initiative but functions as a subtly strategic way to build rapport with employees and strike up conversation. Before I step into Bill's office, I listen to make sure he is not speaking on the phone. If he is working quietly, I come in with a few extra bottles of water and his preferred sodas and if Bill looks at me with an expression remotely approaching a smile, I occasionally start a brief conversation (e.g., "How are you today?") as I open the fridge near his desk.

Isabel describes a comparable series of subtly strategic interactions from her point of view as a senior employee. She tells me about a current intern who walked into her office on multiple occasions to allegedly ask a question, "forgot" the question, and nonetheless sparked a conversation. When Isabel's assistant learned about these incidents, she offered to discipline the intern, but Isabel claimed she did not mind the interruptions and was impressed by the intern's boldness. Because interns often[29] report to an assistant, and their contact with more senior employees—often better positioned to hire them or offer powerful recommendations—is relatively limited, Isabel empathizes with interns' plight. To some employees, if an intern makes the effort to reach out to them, this is a sign of their interest and commitment.

At times, interns' intentional efforts to build relationships went beyond the people in their department. Nate recalls being an intern in the "wrong" department at a record company but approaching employees in the [hip hop-related] department that interested him. The desirable department was next to the supplies closet. Every time he walked by to get envelopes, he commented on the hip-hop record that was playing: "I'd be like, 'I love that record. I hate that record.' Then we'd start talking . . . that's how I got my in." Eventually, Nate started doing work for employees in the other department when he was not too busy.[30] As Ben, Isabel, and Nate show, interns can develop relationships with employees outside their immediate surroundings—from senior employees in their department to people in other departments—however, doing so requires some courage and will yield uneven results.

Particularly at larger companies, interns are informally encouraged to be more explicit about relationship building by walking around, within reason, and occasionally introducing themselves to employees. However, what is within reason, in terms of breaching the boundary between intern and employee, is up for debate. At times, interns stumble over this boundary. One intern, for example, recalls approaching an employee at an indie record company's kitchen area during lunch. The two had what she (the intern) thought was a pleasant conversation. Later that day, she was horrified when she received an email from her supervisor informing her not to bother employees during their lunch breaks. Greg also describes the challenges of such interactions, commenting, "You have to have a lot of balls to do that kind of stuff. I actually did [introduce myself] a couple times as an intern, to varying results." It takes guts and some tact to network as an intern because it is uncertain how employees will respond; some will be receptive to these efforts, while others will not.

Thus, although strolling around the office in search of new mentors might sound promising, it is quite challenging because aspirants must contend with the stigma of the intern role and therefore navigate the difference in status between themselves and employees. Breaching the symbolic order can be intimidating and even counterproductive. Some interns address this problem by asking their supervisors to facilitate introductions and others recount asking fellow interns to introduce them to employees in their respective department.

The quiet and the loud. Engaging in consistent day-to-day interactions with employees offers interns the chance to show who they are, for example, by demonstrating a good sense of humor, in-depth knowledge of music, and infectious enthusiasm. Interns with enough tact and charisma to draw employees into conversation or to extend an interaction when an employee briefly speaks with them, may earn more face time with employees and signal their competence no matter what tasks they are assigned. Nate describes using this approach, specifically by engaging employees in conversation and joining them at shows:

> Your best chance of proving your intelligence is in regular conversation. It's just by creating a relationship with these people where they actually get to know you. Going out with them after work and all that and they get to know you and they realize, "He's a smart kid and he can do things."[31]

Beyond displaying some level of competence, as Nate notes, the job-seeking intern must express their personality while remaining tactful. However, many interns feel anxious about trying to balance humility with confidence and thus go too far in the former direction, embracing the "just the intern" label too tightly. These "nervous" or "scared" interns who stay quiet, as Isabel describes them, are less likely to be hired as employees because "personality's a lot of it. . . . We've had really kind of faceless, quiet interns who do a good job, but I might not remember who they are the next semester."

Employees sometimes try to help interns break out of their shell. A few weeks into my internship at Major Records USA, for example, Hank notes that I tend to stay quiet, telling me, "You remind me of other interns I've had who did a really good job at everything, but they were too quiet. At the end of the internship, no one really knows them." He continues, as if to warn me, "Now, there are some interns, like Carlos, maybe sometimes they're a little *too* loud—you can hear them all the way down the hall—you have to watch out about that, too." While some interns take up too much room, charging into the office like a bull in a china shop, according to employees, most interns fall at the other extreme, remaining overly quiet or shy. Interns who are overwhelmed, humbled, or scared may attempt to play it safe, keep their heads down, and quietly excel. This approach may work for a student in the classroom, but it yields few dividends if maintained for the duration of an internship.

Finding the balance between humbly accepting an intern's low status and proactively developing rapport with employees can be challenging, however. As Amanda expresses, performing the intern role therefore requires an elusive mix of humility and coolness (or industry cool): "You're supposed to be, at the same time, very humble and very quiet and very put in your place, but then also very cool and interesting, and endlessly fascinating . . . I don't know how you mix those two together." As Amanda, who is now twenty-two years old and employed (with pay) outside the music industry, looks back at her two recent music industry internships, she recalls experiencing them as stressful auditions: "You're just uncomfortable being there because you're always performing in some way. Like, performing being a lot more cool and relaxed than you really are or just pretending to be much more . . . I don't know, something else." Only now that she is employed, she adds, can she articulate the challenges of performing as an intern: "At my job now, people think I'm so interesting and funny and I felt the opposite [as an intern]. You know, you're always the least interesting person and you *always* had to be proving something."[32] Interns may attempt to build relationships by balancing being just the intern while also moving beyond the limits of the role, though the safest option is to stay quiet.

After the Internship

Even if an intern develops strong bonds with employees, these relationships weaken quickly due to the temporariness of the position.[33] Karl, an employee at an indie record company who works in a small office and meets every intern, describes the habitual churn of interns as a "constant revolving door." Consequently, as he puts it, "it's a fleeting relationship." Every few months, interns leave and, as time goes by, although the intern's experience may feel vividly recent, employees like Karl struggle to remember much about these transitory colleagues.

> There are some interns that I had that, say [four years ago], that if they wrote me and said, "Hey I need a recommendation for this job" or whatever, while I would still probably do it, I may not even remember anything about what it was like working with them. You know, you're talking, six, seven, eight interns a year over the last four years, naturally there are some of them that I don't really remember.

Karl reports keeping in touch with a few interns, connecting with some on social media while others reach out to him occasionally by email, but they are a minority: "For every one intern that I still keep in touch with a little bit there's five interns I can't even remember their names." He laughs slightly as he recalls a colleague calling him to ask about one of his former interns, but after being told the name, he could not remember this person.

Some job-seeking interns, however, are aware of this challenge. Like other interns I met, Monique praises the merits of having a network to rely on when she graduates.[34] Although, for her, the ideal outcome to an internship is to receive a job offer, she acknowledges that even if the company does not hire her, "You meet people and when you graduate at least you have something to fall [back] on. You know, send out an email to everyone you've interned for asking if they know anybody or if they need anybody, if they're hiring." She also describes the benefit of keeping in touch with industry contacts. Like those interns who sometimes email Karl, Monique occasionally emails her former intern hosts: "Like, 'Hey I saw Artist Y's album. Blah blah blah.' So, they remember who you are." Other former interns tell me they do the same, as well as sending cards for holidays, birthdays, and whatever else might be well received.

Maintaining relationships can lead to employment, as confirmed by Isabel. Isabel's assistant was an intern for approximately a year but eventually needed to find paid work; he found a job outside the music industry but kept in touch with Isabel and was eventually hired at the record company. From a job-seeking standpoint, however, leaving an internship also entails some risk. Much as "who you know" is a familiar dictum describing music industry hiring, stories of breaking in almost invariably contain a version of the expression, "right place, right time." An aspirant who leaves a company before being hired runs the risk of being replaced in the metaphorical queue by a similarly competent and seemingly more committed intern—a solution to this predicament, as the next section discusses, is to extend the internship indefinitely.

Strategy Three: Extended Investment

Employees and ex-interns overwhelmingly claim that a key strategy for interns to move up the hierarchy within their office, gain visibility, and do more meaningful work is to extend their internship (or "stick around"). Interns who come in more hours or days than others, and especially those who stay for numerous semesters, typically gain in status and seniority compared to fellow interns. As I briefly described in the previous section, at many companies there is a clear hierarchy of interns where one or two become head interns (or "super interns"). Interns in this special class may not only be assigned preferred tasks, in many instances they train new interns, serve as a representative for other interns, and act as the intermediary through which employees delegate work. In some cases, the more senior intern is first in line for perks such as concert tickets or even job recommendations. Although in some instances interns ascend to this status after a brief period (by showing what employees describe as "early promise"), more often, they rise to this status through seniority. In this case, interns must assume and grow into this iteration of the intern role—a welcome challenge for the job-seeking intern. Interns who extended their investment by sticking around describe reaping benefits in terms of eventually passing as an employee, thereby building trust and relationships.[35]

After completing two internships at small indie record companies, and with graduation from college just a year away, Bela decided to invest all the time and energy she could into her third internship at a larger, especially prestigious indie record company. She registered for as many evening courses as possible, leaving her four full days each week to intern. By her second semester at the company, she recalls, "I was like the internship coordinator . . . I was just managing the interns, telling them what to do." She credits her achievement of this special status to her ability to show up more than other interns: "I did create strong relationships with the other people in the company . . . I was there pretty often. I was practically a part-time employee." By the time she left, Bela was even interviewing potential summer interns. Now that she has a paid position, when Bela interviews interns, she stresses the importance of extending their hours as much as possible.

> I tell them, "Look, we can't pay, but it behooves you to be there. The more that you're there, the more that you're going to get out of it. And the more you're going to feel like an employee. The more people trust that you're going to be there, the more that they're going to give you to do."

Her experience is consistent with Greg's time as an intern at Major Records USA. By sticking around, he also developed stronger relationships with employees and earned better work assignments. He recalls, "It just takes some time for people to warm up to you more because right off the bat no one's going to give you the benefit of the doubt." As an intern for over seven months, he reports attending shows several times each week and says, "When I was there for a little longer people would realize, 'This intern, he's here all the time, he talks to people, he goes out of his way to meet people and go to shows.'" Greg concludes that "people start to trust you" during your second semester at the company.

Some interns extend their investment only slightly, and unofficially, but this practice still helps them distinguish themselves. After her two-semester internship officially ended, for example, Agatha continued to show up at Major Records USA for half a day every week as a "guest"—she did not gain additional responsibilities or become a head intern, but she maintained face time with employees and eventually returned as an intern in her preferred department. For Shane, coming into the office after he left his internship at an indie record company was impossible because his university was thousands of miles away. However, he volunteered to continue managing the label's website over several months. This work allowed him to signal his continued commitment and stay in touch with employees. Upon graduating, he landed a paid position at the company.[36]

Further extending their investment allows interns to gain competence. Monique describes a fellow intern she encountered who had been with a company for one year and, by then, he "could pass for an employee, almost." The company uses special software to track sales, she recounts, and this intern "knows it like the back of his hand." Employees let this intern oversee these critical data, while other interns do not receive this level of trust. Therefore, interns who stick around can overcome the challenge of being delegated only "easy" or low-risk work.

Similarly, by spending more time at an internship and especially extending it across several semesters, interns are sending a signal that they are committed to becoming employees. Several interns noted that their commitment to interning limited their ability to concentrate on school and maintain a part-time job. Some interns who did not break into the music industry told me they asked their internship hosts for days off to help prepare for exams, or said they could only intern one or two days per week because of their classes and part-time jobs. A frequent trend among interns who did break in was a willingness to invest almost fully in the internship and deprioritize other pursuits, such as letting their grades drop to B's or C's or sacrificing sources of income. Rita, a former intern who was eventually hired, brings up this juggling act between school, job, and internship, and concludes:

> I think it's possible [to juggle]. I just think that if you're doing an internship while you're in college, something's going to suffer. Something's going to suffer, whether it's the internship, which I would hope is the last thing to suffer. Whether it's your school, or whether it's that other job that's actually paying the bills, something's going to suffer, because you can't divide yourself that much.

While an extended investment can pay off, former interns describe how this strategy can cause frustration and reproduce inequality, namely: aspirants are unable to fully escape the stigma of being an intern; many aspirants experience harsh disappointment when they fail to break in; and a higher status for one intern often blocks opportunities for other interns.

While extended investment might offer significant rewards, it has its symbolic limits. As Bela recounts her days as head intern at an indie record company, she describes her inability to completely overcome the intern/employee boundary. By the end of that internship, she came to the office every weekday, managed the department's interns, and took on higher-level tasks. She considered herself an employee in every sense but the official job title (and the commensurate pay). She says she often stayed late to finish work, but on one occasion when almost everyone had left the office, an employee walked by and seemed surprised to see her: "[He said] 'Intern, go home! We don't pay you, go! Leave! Get out of here!' And I was like, 'Um, I'm just finishing something.' And he's like, 'Everyone has gone home. And we pay them.'" The employee's statement disappointed Bela because he referred to her as "intern" despite her status as head intern and her efforts to move beyond the intern role (and her hope of being thought of as "Bela" rather than "intern"). In this way, the more committed interns or head interns can feel like they are hitting their heads against their position's symbolic ceiling.[37]

Another challenge of extended investment is that pursuing this strategy will likely lead to deeper disappointment if a job-seeking intern is not hired. The intern economy in the music industry is equipped with a built-in cooling out mechanism—people generally know that success is at best uncertain; yet extra commitment can sharpen this disappointment and make cooling out less effective. Although she interned at a company for an entire school year before graduating, Danielle was unable to transition into a paid position at the company. She laments, "I worked so hard and when I should have been writing my [term] papers I was working on your campaign, and I gave you as much effort as if I was an employee. And then, they're not really bound by anything." Unemployed when I first interviewed her shortly after graduation, Danielle expresses bitterness about the intern economy as a whole:

> It's just hard. Every place just wants to suck you dry, take your skill and your experience and your knowledge and not give you anything and you're supposed to feel so lucky just to have the name on the résumé, but it's not that great because it still says "intern."

Extended investment, when it does not lead to getting a job, can breed bitterness and a sense of being exploited—such interns transition from breaking in to feeling broken.

Finally, being chosen as head intern, or a more subtle variation thereof, marks a preferred status and elevates an intern's position within the office, but also has consequences for inequality. Appointing a head intern is organizationally efficient in that paid employees save time and energy they would otherwise have to exert to train and interact with newer interns. Perhaps inadvertently, this hierarchy makes it more difficult for newer interns to prove themselves because head interns consolidate the power of delegating tasks and monopolize the interactional space between interns and employees. Not every aspirant I spoke with was aware of the advantages gained by those who extend their investment as an intern, and conversely, the disadvantages experienced by those who do not.

It is especially difficult for interns who must work part-time, in addition to attending classes, to extend their investment in an internship. Nate tells me about two interns who worked as a bartender and waiter, respectively, before being hired at a record company, though these were exceptions in that, on average, having less availability to intern makes it more difficult to get hired: "I look at a lot of these kids and it's a shame. It's a disadvantage because they *have* to go do this part-time work." While he acknowledges his fellow interns were at a disadvantage because he could afford to work for free almost full-time for several semesters and thus became a trusted figure in the office, he would not necessarily do things differently.

> Am I ashamed to exploit that disadvantage? No. I'm going to use it every way I can get. That's why I say it's a shame. I've seen a lot of people who could have done better who just didn't have the time or the money to be able to do it.

As discussed in chapter 3, the internship as an ennobling rite of passage and the mailroom model of training obscure the "shame" or waste Nate describes. Instead, in this context, some employees construe those who cannot afford to intern for free as insufficiently committed.

Conclusion

This chapter considered how job-seeking interns attempt to navigate their way to a paid job. To overcome the characteristic limits of their role, aspirants must act according to the ideal intern norm and utilize three strategies to enact commitment and competence. These strategies involve finding a sort of balance and navigating through ambiguity, a process that illuminates the importance of personal resources including cultural, social, and economic capital. Specifically, these strategies require interns to be attuned to the typically unspoken expectations of employees. Such awareness probably comes more effortlessly to interns with more cultural capital, that is, who come from social backgrounds similar to those of employees and "fit in" immediately. A close examination of how interns attempt to build and deepen relationships, and an assessment of the costs involved in extending one's investment and moving up the intern hierarchy, reveal how this breaking-in system reproduces inequities. In chapter 5, I further unpack how the characteristics of this breaking-in system impact aspirants unequally, and highlight how interns, higher education personnel, and some employers are attempting to address these inequities by trying to minimize the ambiguity at the core of this breaking-in system.

5

Breaking-In Systems in Transition

IN THIS BOOK I have analyzed internships in the music industry as a case study of what I call breaking-in systems. In the process, the book updates symbolic interactionist accounts of breaking in to better reflect the more precarious new economy. Rather than a straightforward process in which established employees train and socialize aspirants, breaking in occurs as an ongoing yet uncertain process, especially in "open" fields such as the record industry that lack agreed upon educational shortcuts and that are characterized by an oversupply of applicants willing to work for little to no pay. Although this is an extreme case, which differs markedly from other breaking-in systems with high educational barriers to entry (e.g., medicine), the expectation that workers are relatively on their own to build their employability and must navigate ambiguity is far from limited to the cultural industries.

Broad structural shifts in employment conditions and higher education over recent decades have given rise to internships as a widespread way for aspiring workers to build their employability. Over just a few decades, internships went from something a few especially ambitious college students did (except for students in majors that required them) to what feels to many like a requirement to enter or remain in the middle class. The recent pervasiveness of internships is supported by the widespread narrative that they lead to a job. For example, the title of a 2024 article in *Forbes* proclaims, “New LinkedIn Data: Internships Are Really, Really Worth It.”[1] However, while some employers closely vet aspirants, pay interns well, train them rigorously, give them substantive work, or at least some combination of the above, recent decades have also seen the rise of highly exploitative unpaid internships.

As a form of provisional labor, unpaid interns assume the burden of learning an organization’s culture, building skills, and cultivating professional relationships for an indefinite period. This seemingly meritocratic system also means that if an aspirant fails at breaking in, they can be fully assigned the blame. However, fully framing success and failure as in the hands of aspirants ignores that an internship is inherently an ambiguous role; it is a liminal period that involves merging the role of “student” with “worker,” as the aspirant, eventually, aims to transition from the former to the latter.

By studying interns but also looking at how participants within key institutions of this breaking-in system—schools and employers—define and navigate this ambiguity in ways that align with their own interests, I have argued that this ambiguity has been exacerbated by the disparate yet overlapping aims of employers and educational institutions. The education-industrial complex I outlined is notably driven by higher education institutions operating in a highly competitive marketplace (e.g., with schools lobbying for reputation and economic resources) and employers looking out for their own cheap labor supply needs and, occasionally, a pipeline of qualified (or overqualified) aspirants. Employees overall do not describe it as their job to train students; rather, they uphold elements of a mailroom model of training that normalizes the suffering of aspirants while also tasking them with their own training.

Taken together, these findings have important implications regarding social inequality. This breaking-in system compels interns to grapple with ambiguity, whether they realize it or not. To varying extents, interns must figure out what is expected of them, iteratively test out the limits of their role in this setting, and possibly gain experience and develop professional relationships. Not every intern is equally equipped to understand the hidden curriculum within these roles, such as how to be tactfully proactive. Nor does every aspirant have the social capital needed to secure an internship at all. Although some of the higher education personnel in this study sometimes expressed cynicism about this breaking-in system, they also came off as deeply passionate about helping students (e.g., multiple interviewees cried near the end of their interview as they discussed the psychic rewards of their job). But internships-for-all policies, even if they are well-meaning and carried out with empathy, further a breaking-in system that advantages privileged students.

While internships-for-all policies may attempt to address inequities in the breaking-in system, they simultaneously reproduce these inequities by negatively impacting minority and minoritized students.[2] Due to the emphasis on high internship participation rates (partly in the interest of institutional reputation), and a general orientation toward career development, the intern economy is flooded with opportunities of widely ranging quality. Students are guided into doing internships but given only broad (and, at times, insufficient) resources to find strong opportunities. By vaguely and inconsistently vetting and assessing internship hosts, higher education institutions further perpetuate an informal breaking-in system that benefits the most well-connected students.

However, a key question remains, particularly as it concerns addressing inequities among aspirants: Can breaking-in systems change? In the preceding chapters, while I noted that breaking-in systems are constantly in flux, I focused especially on their relatively constant features within my case (the music industry's intern economy). Still, my account of this breaking-in system identified several examples of changes over time. For example, I noted how aspirants, over recent decades, have increasingly been seeking internship experience to build their employability. College students are even becoming serial interns—doing multiple internships to compete with aspirants with similar credentials and sometimes to work their way up to their preferred internship experience.[3]

Higher education institutions and their workers' behavior are also in flux—at their school's behest, career services personnel and colleagues work to boost internship participation rates and hopefully help students build their employability. These practices fit with a long-standing though intensifying pattern of schools aiming to build ties with employers and further their competitive standing within the marketplace of higher education institutions. I also noted that individual employees reproduce the mailroom model of training under the guise of an educational experience but at times try to lessen the dehumanization of aspirants—paving the way for a slightly more educational, and humane, rite of passage. Breaking-in systems shift over time, but they sometimes change more sharply and profoundly than I have fully illustrated thus far.

The Audacity of Hopeful Interns

The possibility of change hit me after a few years of research. Until 2011, only a few newspaper articles (notably op-eds in *The New York Times*) occasionally questioned the fairness of the intern economy.[4] Over the previous decades, the only consistent source of critical analysis of the intern economy in the United States could be found in legal reviews pondering whether unpaid interns should be considered employees.[5] In the spring of 2011, however, Ross Perlin (2011b) published *Intern Nation*, an exposé of the intern economy, decrying the craven attempts of employers to abuse the unpaid or low-paid labor of aspirants and the complicit boosting of questionable educational experiences by colleges and universities. Giving voice to, and helping to explain, the unease of young workers—whose standing was especially precarious in the wake of the Great Recession—the book gained immediate attention from mainstream press outlets and therefore brought more visibility to the exploitation of intern labor as a social issue.

As the book was released, Perlin agreed to meet with me to discuss our respective research. A few weeks later, Perlin suggested that I meet Eric Glatt because he was involved in an emerging group of intern rights activists. The three of us planned to meet at a bar in Brooklyn. I biked to our rendezvous and nabbed an outdoor picnic table for the group. When I met Eric Glatt, the third to arrive at the bar, he was wearing a worn-out white T-shirt featuring an image of Mickey Mouse. Upon noticing the shirt, I smiled to myself and wondered whether his choice of shirt was meant as an homage to Perlin's book, which begins with a critical account of Disney's internship program.

As Perlin (2011b) described in his book, each year the company hosts thousands of college students or recent graduates to intern full-time at Disney World as part of the Disney College Program.[6] The internship program is "touted as a massive and wondrous experiment in experiential education" (Perlin 2011b:22) and yet he depicted it as an exemplary misuse of the ambiguously broad meaning of "intern." The interns do menial tasks for a salary close to minimum wage, sometimes working twelve-hour shifts in roles such as greeters, bellhops, or fast-food operators.[7] The internship program, which was launched in the early 1980s, grew from two hundred to approximately eight thousand interns per year within hardly two decades; during this time, to accommodate Disney's flexible labor needs, the program dropped the requirement that student interns major in a related subject (e.g., hospitality). Thousands of college interns pay their schools for academic credit for the experience, which Perlin portrayed as having highly dubious educational value; for students whose schools refuse to offer credit, Disney helps them find colleges and universities willing to accommodate them in exchange for the interns' tuition dollars. Although Perlin found some critics of the internship program, he depicted a well-oiled, large-scale program that is legal and widely endorsed by higher education institutions—therefore, a deeply entrenched type of pseudo-educational practice that seemed unlikely to change, let alone get transformed.

While Glatt, Perlin, and I discussed the characteristics of the intern economy and questioned the legality of unpaid internships, I did not fully realize that we were approaching a turning point. Glatt had been an unpaid intern, working hundreds of hours on the film *Black Swan* as he attempted to break into the film industry. The movie earned over $300 million worldwide and received five Academy Award nominations, but to Glatt this experience felt disappointing because it offered little in the way of training or future job opportunities. Tasked with the same sort of low-level duties interns routinely assume in the music industry—filing, ordering food, running errands, etc.—Glatt, who was forty-one years old at the time and had two master's degrees, reached out to Perlin to ask if he knew a lawyer who might take on his case.[8] Neither of them shared this background with me, but I found out soon enough. In late September of that year, Glatt and a fellow intern (Alexander Footman) filed a lawsuit against Fox Searchlight Pictures for violating federal and state labor laws.

The lawsuit added to the public scrutiny regarding the questionable fairness of the intern economy, not least in the cultural industries, but it also drew detractors. The ease with which some people disparage interns, and in effect blame them for their challenges in navigating an ambiguous breaking-in system, was perhaps best illustrated by Anderson Cooper, a CNN host who commented about the lawsuit on the air: "Would it be great if all unpaid internships paid really well? Sure. It would also be great if my dog made breakfast for me every morning, but I'm not going to file a lawsuit over it." Quoting Cooper in an article on unpaid internships, legal scholar David Yamada diagnosed, "His dismissive tone reflected a common criticism that lowly interns seeking the minimum wage for their work are acting in an entitled manner."[9] Interns I met often seemed to have internalized Cooper's criticism (consistent with the mailroom model of paying your dues) and were more likely to blame themselves for their bad experiences than question the breaking-in system, though some also noted they feared that speaking up (let alone filing a lawsuit) would blackball them from the industry.

Despite public criticism leveraged toward complainants, a growing number of former unpaid interns began suing companies for back pay (and damages). Two such lawsuits were filed in 2011, seven in 2012, and at least twenty-three in 2013.[10] The cases were mostly filed against the largest companies within the most glamorous parts of the cultural industries—film, television, music, publishing, and fashion companies. The growing public scrutiny of internships escalated in June 2013 when federal judge William Pauley handed the plaintiffs (Glatt and Footman) a summary judgment win against Fox Searchlight Pictures Inc. The judge not only agreed the plaintiffs should be considered employees but also certified a class action suit on behalf of an entire class of employees (i.e., unpaid interns) at the parent company, Fox Entertainment Group.[11]

The possibility of landing large, seven-figure class action victories against media corporations drew interest from members of the legal profession. If someone were to enter "unpaid internships" on a search engine in December 2013 (as I did), they may well have found the Unpaid Interns Lawsuit website (www.unpaidinternslawsuit.com) among the top results. The website was hosted by the law firm representing the *Black Swan* interns. The website's heading read "Should you have been paid for your unpaid internship?" and included information on interns' labor rights and ongoing litigation, encouraging former unpaid interns to reach out to them. Illustrating law firms' pursuit of these class action lawsuits but also the potential backlash complainants might have experienced, a former intern filed a class action suit (working with a different law firm) against CBS and Worldwide Pants. Within a week, the former intern dropped the suit, stating she had been coerced into suing by the lawyers representing her: "While I am ultimately responsible for my actions as an adult, I was caught in a weak, vulnerable time, facing student debt."[12]

The floodgate of litigation abruptly closed in 2015 when the US Second Circuit Court of Appeals in New York vacated Judge

Pauley's decision, privileging a different test for determining an employment relationship (and leading to the *Black Swan* case settling out of court). According to the new standard, an unpaid internship can be legal even if it does not meet the six-part test within the Department of Labor's "Fact Sheet #71" if the intern is deemed the "primary beneficiary" of the relationship (as opposed to the company hosting them). Crucially, the three-judge panel cast the determination of an intern's employment status as highly individualized—therefore, the primary beneficiary test could lead to different results for two interns at the same company. In effect, because of the ambiguity of internships—which can look very different across and within companies and be approached differently by interns (as a Student, Job Seeker, or Enthusiast)—interns are likely too dissimilar to form a "class" in a class action lawsuit to address this very ambiguity. In 2018, the primary beneficiary test was incorporated into a revised "Fact Sheet #71" to become a seven-part test, effectively making unpaid internships legal, especially for interns pursuing academic credit.[13]

Beyond lawsuits, efforts to transform the intern economy were further propelled by a wave of intern rights activism. Students attempted to influence how higher education institutions manage internships—for example, an NYU student circulated a petition to end unpaid internship listings on campus.[14] The Intern Labor Rights group, an outgrowth of the Occupy Wall Street movement, handed out intern swag bags ("Pay Your Interns" tote bags) during winter 2013 Fashion Week. Protesters dressed like Santa and held banners that read "All we want for Xmas is pay" in front of an art gallery hosting unpaid interns. These and several other efforts helped strengthen a sense of public outrage about unpaid internships. When fashion company Alexander McQueen posted an ad for an eleven-month unpaid internship, social media, and eventually the popular media, were alive with outrage. Similarly, Sheryl Sandberg (then COO at Facebook and author of a bestselling book on women in the workplace) was shamed on social media because her foundation posted an ad seeking an unpaid intern—critics pointed out that she made over $90 million by selling Facebook stocks that same week.[15]

Though ambiguity and concerns about exploitation in breaking-in systems are concentrated in certain industries and geographical locations, they are far from solely the domain of cultural industries in New York City.[16] Similar activism emerged among unpaid interns from the United Nations in New York, Geneva, and Vienna, with interns in Vienna wearing white masks at a silent protest to bring attention to their "unseen" labor.[17] Many other groups emerged, such as Génération Précaire (France) and Intern Aware (United Kingdom), as well as efforts to unite globally, such as the International Coalition for Fair Internships and global intern strikes in cities such as Montréal (Canada) and Phnom Penh (Cambodia).[18] After about a decade of intern rights activism, in 2014 new legislation in France detailed further regulation of unpaid internships, notably by limiting their duration; and about a decade later, the European Union is considering how to ban unpaid internships altogether.[19]

Advocacy for a fairer, mostly paid intern economy in the United States has continued in fits and starts over the years. More recently, the nonprofit organization Pay Our Interns successfully lobbied for better intern conditions in the US government, leading to White House interns receiving $18.75 per hour starting in fall 2022.[20] In the next sections, I conclude by further considering efforts to manage ambiguity and bring more fairness to the intern economy.

Inequality and Managing Ambiguity

Since the peak of lawsuits by former interns (2013–15), higher education institutions and employers have made visible changes to how they manage the intern economy. Many of the larger media companies began paying their interns at least a small stipend, whereas other companies suspended or cut their internship programs altogether. For example, five months after two former interns filed a class action suit against Condé Nast Publications, the company chose to eliminate its internship program altogether. The company's decision further propelled debates about unpaid internships, with some labor activists claiming victory while other parties bemoaned the "loss of opportunity" for a generation of future interns.[21] The three major record companies, which were all subject to lawsuits from former interns seeking back pay, now pay their interns.

More broadly, following the increase in fears of litigation, companies are increasingly protecting themselves by making internships at least appear more educational and regimented: at the biggest companies, interns must also be enrolled as college students. Employers I encountered (especially major record companies) are instating stricter guidelines for their internship programs, including measures such as strict employee-to-intern ratios by department, limits on internship duration (one to two semesters), mandatory intern supervising seminars, and ensuring that interns each have access to a company computer. Some companies are increasingly making sure their interns carry out assignments that at least resemble a classroom curriculum, such as a semester-long project (in addition to day-to-day duties) that may culminate with a presentation to members of a department or leadership.

However, I heard multiple employees complain about efforts to formalize internships, especially those involving additional paperwork and the inconvenience of losing trained interns (head interns) due to new duration limits. Worse yet, they complain about the lack of drive of paid interns—for example, in 2019 a major record label employee depicts the unpaid interns he used to work with as "more hungry" (figuratively, though possibly literally) than his recent paid interns: "They were more desperate to work hard and prove themselves compared to now, when they're paid." And yet, a college student who interned before and after some larger media companies started paying interns told me things have gotten "much worse" because now employees treat her even more like a temporary worker and make less of an effort to "pretend this is educational." Unpaid internships are still common in the music industry and in other cultural fields, but the slow transition from unpaid to paid internships at some arts and media employers must also include a cultural shift about how people view and treat interns.

Starting to offer pay to interns sounds like a promising development for lessening social inequality, though this has its risks. Before the rise of lawsuits, Mark (a former intern and junior music industry employee) suggests that due to the high cost of entry, music industry employees are disproportionately "from very affluent backgrounds" and frequently receive parental support, at least as they start their careers.[22] He adds: "How can you do an internship in New York if you're not subsidized? I mean, seriously, there's no logical way to answer that question." The need to work for free in a very expensive city to break into a field is a blatant mechanism for reproducing inequality—though some interviewees highlighted heroic exceptions of upward mobility—but concerns about inequality should go further.

As some internship programs transition from unpaid to paid, they are also cutting the number of internships. This can be a positive development for equity, not least since interns are more likely to receive direct mentorship from employees rather than from senior interns. But such a development shifts the challenge of breaking in from one of sticking out during the internship to one of access. While visiting Hank shortly before the COVID-19 pandemic, he laments that many of the (fewer) internship slots are taken up by "must place" candidates—no matter how their interviews go, employees are told they must place these candidates as interns somewhere at the major record company. Describing "must place" candidates as the children and friends' children of senior employees, Hank also tells me, "So, now you don't have as many interns and the ones we have . . . you have to pay [executives'] rich friends' privileged kids." Therefore, whereas the breaking-in system I described in this book mostly entails aspirants navigating an ambiguous role where they can ideally learn and prove themselves on-site in a slow process of vetting aspirants, the increased competition to land the top (paid) internships further reproduces inequalities.

In the last decade, higher education institutions have also attempted to address the increasingly evident inequalities reproduced by the intern economy. Some interviewees discussed initiatives aimed at helping first-generation students, such as workshops and mentorship programs. Higher education personnel expressed some empathy for international students and dedicate a lot of time to help those who face difficulties in terms of securing and doing internships.[23] Other interviewees described "diversity programming" such as community-building activities among students of color and partnerships with employers to establish internship programs aimed at recruiting more diverse workers. A growing number of higher education institutions draw on alumni and philanthropic support to establish fellowships (usually $2,000 to $3,000) to offer financial support for student interns, especially underrepresented students, though many interviewees readily added that these are "Band-Aid solutions" since only a small percentage of students can access these funds.[24] Moreover, if an internship involves moving to another city for the summer, such a sum is insufficient.

Despite the frequent legality of unpaid internships, some higher education personnel described attempting to offer preferential treatment to paid opportunities—for example, they share paid internship listings with students but relegate unpaid ones to a cluttered collection of online listings. These efforts are important since my research using survey data shows that the type of internship (paid vs. unpaid) significantly influences career outcomes. Paid arts-related internships during college are associated with a closer match between one's college training and first job, as well as shorter postgraduation job searches. In contrast, on average, unpaid internships are not linked with improved career outcomes (compared to not interning at all). Such disparities likely reflect significant variation in the quality and characteristics of paid and unpaid experiences. Paid internships are more likely to provide a satisfying experience, closer mentorship, opportunities for creative input, and substantive work assignments. This suggests that paid internships offer more valuable learning and skill-building opportunities compared to unpaid internships.[25]

As mentioned earlier, the term "intern economy" obscures a key type of variation between *paid* and *unpaid* internships. While prior research suggests that the intern economy looks drastically different by field—with STEM and business majors, for example, benefiting from more orderly and institutionalized (and often paid) pathways to breaking in than arts and humanities majors—there is variation *within* fields as well, with paid and unpaid internships representing two extremes that coexist and reproduce inequalities. Respective breaking-in systems incorporate both extremes; for example, while architecture students likely do paid internships, some undertake unpaid internships in their field. This variation has implications for inequality. As I discussed in chapter 4, research on inequality suggests that minority and minoritized candidates receive uneven rewards for their educational and portfolio-building efforts.[26] Marginalized aspirants are therefore at a disadvantage in terms of getting the most valuable internships and, if they do break into the field, gaining opportunities for higher status work and rewards. Consequently, using SNAAP data, I found that gender and social class play significant roles in shaping internship participation rates and subsequent career outcomes. Continuing-generation women are most likely to report unpaid internship experiences, and first-generation men are least likely to participate in internships of any type.[27] Breaking-in systems reflect the inequities found within the broader society.

Rip It Up and Start Again?

Attempting to transform an ambiguous breaking-in system can be a vexing proposition. As cultural theorist Mary Douglas argued long ago, culture is powerful in mediating people's experience of the world—we collectively create and hold up classifications.

Individually, we can question our assumptions, "but changing categories are public matters. They cannot so easily be subject to revision" (Douglas [1966] 2002:48).[28] These shared cultural categories, Douglas argued, must address anomalies. Beyond the categories of student and worker (or youth and adult), cultural classification systems have long made room for those ambiguously in the middle, though not necessarily treated them kindly. As other scholars of invisible work have argued, the mystification of ambiguous roles and their classification as something other than labor is far from limited to interns—it includes some graduate student workers, college athletes, workfare participants, and prison workers.[29]

The apprenticeship has been around for millennia, and along these lines the internship emerged in the nineteenth century as part of medical education. In the early twentieth century, as bureaucratic capitalism grew, related forms emerged such as cooperative education to further incorporate the transition from classroom learning to work. As I argued in the introduction, the ascent of the internship is consistent with the changing nature of work and careers in the new economy. In this context, internships developed as a more purely market-based regime, as opposed to apprenticeships, which have often been guided or guarded by governments (from local to national), guilds, and unions.[30] More precarious employment arrangements and hypercompetitive education systems (and the education-industrial complex that links them) breed ambiguity.

Therefore, while breaking-in systems transition, partly because individual workers, educators, and employees continuously reinterpret and may attempt to change them, it is important to also note ambiguity's staying power. In conversation with interviewees and friends over the years, people have asked me what the breaking-in system I analyzed in this book would look like if one could somehow rip it up and start again. Along these lines, Nora, who owns a small music PR firm and studied music business in college, suggested that her alma mater—a music business program at a private R1 university—should rename their internship program altogether, calling these arrangements "traineeships" or "mentorships." Nora's suggestion came from the hope that employers would settle on one interpretation of what it means to intern to possibly get "trainees" and host employers to focus solely on "training" or "mentorship." She may have also meant that a new name could allow these aspirants to shed some of the stigma associated with being "just the intern." Since ambiguity refers to the coexistence of multiple interpretations, Nora is advocating for siding with one interpretation (e.g., focus on one-on-one individual training) to reduce the ambiguity inherent in music industry internships.[31] To do so, however, would require going beyond renaming the role. A major record company renamed its internship program, consistent with Nora's suggestion, but, according to interviewees, employees still saw and referred to these aspirants as "interns."

While higher education personnel must manage conflicting pressures, notably in balancing institutional priorities with student needs, I mentioned earlier how one way to further reduce the ambiguity of internships in cultural industries would be for schools and employers to partner more closely in designing educational experiences (though these initiatives are time-intensive and challenging to scale). However, it is difficult to imagine eliminating all tension and ambiguity from experiential learning arrangements. Even traditional apprenticeships, celebrated as exemplars of how to break in aspirants, at times featured considerable periods of mundane work and questionable practices, such as masters taking on too many apprentices as cheap laborers.[32] Research on another relatively well-established, seemingly less ambiguous experience, the teaching practicum, suggests that mentors and student teachers may not share the same perception of "good mentoring," and some call for better coordination between universities and host schools.[33] Study abroad, another form of experiential learning that has grown in popularity in recent decades, also poses challenges for oversight on the part of higher education institutions.[34] Higher education study abroad programs usually rely on a small, relatively consistent set of partners (e.g., a faculty member or firm), whereas there are far more potential internship hosts, which can lead to more heterogeneous student intern experiences. Still, there remain concerns about the misalignment between the educational goals of study abroad programs for schools versus their partners, but these seem easier to manage than ensuring rich, consistent educational experiences for interns.[35]

Despite its challenges, and the inevitability of some lingering ambiguity in liminal roles, there is room and some promise to transforming breaking-in systems. By bringing more visibility to breaking-in systems, perhaps we can point to societal solutions to the seemingly individual problem of establishing a career. Or, at the very least, hopefully this will prompt us to not fully blame the intern.

Methodological Appendix

Before Breaking In

Three experiences inform this study as they allowed me to recognize the importance and challenges of unpaid internships early on during my research. In the first instance, as a teenager, I founded and eventually co-ran a small independent record company from the basement of my parents' home in Québec City. In the subsequent years, the label consumed most of my free time during my undergraduate education, an investment offset by garnering considerable satisfaction, some success, and developing several memorable friendships. Three years into the endeavor, the small record company hosted its first and only intern. By then, the company had moved up in many ways: a handful of releases were college radio hits, our roster of bands was obscure but well respected in the Canadian indie rock industry, and the HQ had moved from the house's basement to the top (i.e., second) floor. The intern, Zvonimir, was a very good, albeit somewhat recent friend. He had expressed interest in helping my twin brother (one of my record label partners) and me with the record company out of passion and interest.

Early on, one of us (perhaps Zvonimir) joked that he was our intern. Somehow, the title stuck. By then I had never been an intern or consciously thought about the intern economy, and yet we joked about Zvonimir running our errands and doing other menial tasks. The work we assigned was not much better. Although

Zvonimir is fluent in three languages, good with people, passionate and knowledgeable, we nonetheless had him primarily cut out articles from magazines to create press releases, count inventory, stuff envelopes for orders, and enter figures in a database we never used. He was also charged with listening to some of the least promising demo recordings we received. On one occasion, my brother and I failed to inform him we would be absent for part of his intern shift, so he worked alone and drank tea with our mother. After a few months, Zvonimir applied for a job at the largest record store in the city and listed me as a reference. When I received a call from a store employee, I praised him vehemently and admitted that his loss would be significant. He landed the job and continued to offer invaluable help, though less frequently and unambiguously as a friend, not an intern. The intern jokes ended, though I reflected many times since about this sensitizing episode and the significance of the intern role.

The second experience occurred when I moved to New York City after graduating from college. Looking for work, I considered getting a job in the music industry. After all, I founded and had been co-running an independent record company in Canada for a few years and thought myself amply willing and capable of performing low-level tasks at a US record company. The week of my arrival I discussed this idea with one of my music industry contacts at an online music retailer. As I stood in the company's office, a huge loft space in the heart of SoHo, the young man, perhaps five years my senior, described the structure of the music labor market, saying that if I wanted to get a job I would have to intern first. He informed me that, despite my experience, to the people in the New York music industry I was basically—professionally speaking—a stranger. A lot of people who intern do not go very far, he added, though the interns who are smart and motivated tend to get noticed and hired. He expressed confidence that I would get hired as an employee after establishing myself as an unpaid intern. Financially, I quickly needed a paid job and therefore could not afford to take an unpaid internship. I applied for the few music industry jobs I saw listed online that summer and never heard back from anyone, eventually working in another industry before attending graduate school.

My earlier experiences within the intern economy made me aware of the challenges of interning. "Intern" became a loaded term, a sensitizing concept, and therefore provided me with "a general sense of reference and guidance in approaching empirical instances" (Blumer 1969:148). Relatedly, the third experience—a pilot study—reinforced my sociological interest in internships. Due to my music industry contacts and credentials I was able to gain access to a research site to complete the requirements of a graduate ethnography class; for one semester, I spent at least two hours per week, usually a whole afternoon, at College Promotions. The firm promotes records on behalf of bands and mainly independent record labels of the indie rock style. I gained access to this site by offering my services as an unpaid intern, stating that I wanted to study how the firm functions as part of a class project. I had known the boss (Kevin) of the four-employee company for many years because I had worked with College Promotions to promote my independent record label's last eight releases. After warning me that my intern tasks would be tedious, I assured him of my serious interest, and he granted me access.

When I started studying this firm, it was not my original intention to focus on the role and experiences of interns; instead, I was interested in the way promotion and PR firms help shape popular tastes in music. However, I was quickly struck by the abundance of interns. The company was hosting five part-time interns who spent the bulk of their time tediously preparing mailings to college and community radio stations. Interns also helped with doing inventory, photocopying, running errands, and—seemingly the highlight of the week—writing short album reviews to be posted on the company's website. In addition, the company hosted an unpaid full-time intern who essentially did the same work as employees, though he kept in touch with personnel at the least important radio stations. I realized there was a hierarchy of interns, with super interns (or "head interns") at the top and next in line for a promotion. After completing my coursework, and much trial and error, I began looking for research sites to analyze the role of internships in the process of breaking into a cultural industry.

Participant Observation: Being an Intern

"Here I go," I think to myself, as I enter the vacant lobby of a nondescript building in Manhattan. As I walk in, I show Tito, the security guard, my ID, and he hands me a sticker with today's date scribbled on it, which grants me access to the building for the rest of the day. I head to the elevators and make my way to the offices of Major Records USA. It is October 2008, and I am in the process of conducting participant observation at two music companies in New York City: two days per week for four months at the sales and marketing department of a major record label I call Major Records USA and at least one day per week for six months at the digital sales department of Indie Distribution, a distribution company specializing in "indie" (or independent) music.

As a PhD student, I gained entry to both research sites as an unpaid intern and was an overt participant observer. However, like the interns I met through this study, I had to "work my way up" to gain access to these preferred sites. After I completed my first music industry internship at College Promotions, I conducted a handful of interviews with interns and employees. Paradoxically, the interns told me they were bored and wanted to do more while the employees complained that they could not find committed, competent interns. Based on these conflicting accounts, I decided to spend more time inside the walls of music companies to investigate how individuals attempt to break into this labor market, while also analyzing how other actors (employers and higher education personnel) shape and interpret those efforts.

Although I was older and more professionally experienced than typical interns, my responsibilities were similar to those of other interns I met over the years. At Indie Distribution, I interned in the digital sales department, interacting primarily with Abby (a twenty-six-year-old white woman), Nate (a twenty-six-year-old Asian American man), and Dana (a thirty-year-old white woman). My responsibilities included tracking the online visibility of new releases; compiling content from a handful of digital sales employees to build and format marketing plans; and various small administrative tasks, which included helping Dana assemble her expense reports, but never fetching anyone coffee or a meal. At Major Records USA, I interned in the sales and marketing department for Hank (a thirty-seven-year-old Black man) and spent most of my working hours stocking refrigerators, running errands in the office, printing reports, checking emails, and occasionally picking up food or coffee orders. My assignments at both sites were intermittent and therefore allowed me to closely observe my surroundings and develop rapport with workers who varied greatly in both seniority (ranging from intern to senior executive) and area of expertise (including A&R, publicity, and sales).

Assuming the position of intern provided a fruitful point of entry to situate internships and careers within the music industry. Ethnographers who assume a highly participatory role in the field, and thus carry out real responsibilities, have been likened to interns in that both roles provide "special opportunities to get close to, participate in, and experience life in previously unknown settings" (Emerson, Fretz, and Shaw 1995:4). Like other sociologists in recent years, I decided to do fieldwork *as* an intern (Childress 2017; Jones 2024; Ocejo 2017; Rivera 2015b; Sallaz 2009; Siciliano 2021). Being an intern enabled me to become socialized to the norms of the sites, to observe and participate in everyday activities, focusing particularly on the visible workplace interactions between (and among) interns and employees. At both companies my tasks as an intern were primarily administrative or research-oriented, though typically not time-sensitive, which made extended observation (and note-taking) from my desk or during occasional walks throughout the office possible. I had built-in reasons for walking around both offices: at Major Records USA I frequently needed to interact with employees or interns down the hall or on another floor; at Indie Distribution I sat down the hall and around the corner from my assigned department, which made movement necessary.

In addition, since employees expect interns to attempt to speak with various employees, they encouraged or seemingly tolerated my additional walks and detours. Grindstaff (2002) and Zafirau (2008) also studied cultural industries by gaining entry as interns; similar to their respective experiences, my low status as "just an intern" (Grindstaff 2002:283) limited my access to certain meetings and people yet also facilitated entry and mitigated some of the typical trust issues between ethnographer and participants. As Zafirau (2008) found during his fieldwork at Limelight, a talent agency in Hollywood, one's status as an intern can overshadow (though not completely) one's status as a researcher. I wrote daily field notes and frequently reread these notes to locate potential themes and gaps in need of further development. The participant observation occasionally brought me beyond the context of the office, extending to music venues, bars, coffee shops, and birthday parties. Participant observation helped build on early interview data to capture contextualized work practices (Barley and Kunda 2001) as well as generate and clarify the themes of inquiry regarding people's attempts to start and sustain careers in the music industry.

Interview Data

While I originally thought the participant observation would be the bulk, and nearly the final stage, of my data collection, the data (and changes to the breaking-in system) steered me in new directions. Between 2008 and 2013, I interacted with hundreds of music industry workers, college personnel, and key informants (e.g., writers, attorneys) and conducted semi-structured interviews with sixty of them. However, several subsequent developments—major lawsuits filed by former interns, intern labor rights activism, and attempts on the part of companies and higher education to further formalize internships (in both cases to improve student outcomes and to protect themselves legally)—prompted me to expand the project considerably. Thus, this book also draws on an additional sixty-two interviews from the "post-lawsuits" period, mostly conducted between 2016 and 2021, including thirty-three interviews with higher education personnel (mostly internship coordinators and career services personnel), to further situate the role of higher education institutions as intermediaries between interns and employers in the intern economy. The interviews with interns and employees were conducted somewhat differently than those with higher education personnel, so I discuss these separately.

I recruited intern and employee participants through messages sent via two local university music-oriented student email lists, through contacts at fieldwork sites, and via snowball sampling. While the sample was not randomly selected and thus is not representative of the music industry, it is arguably illustrative of practices in the commercial New York City rock/pop record industry, focusing especially on "major" record companies and smaller independent ("indie") companies. Participants mostly worked or interned in the following departments at major or indie record companies: A&R (artists and repertoire, who scout talent and act as a liaison between the artists and record company), publicity (cultivates publicity for artists/releases), and sales/marketing (these duties overlap and are not completely separated at most record companies encountered in this study).

Music industry interviewees ranged from eighteen to fifty-four years old and skewed young (average age = twenty-nine years old) per industry trends. I formally interviewed twenty of the workers more than once as they transitioned in and out of music industry employment; all but three of these interviews were digitally recorded and transcribed. Interviews mostly lasted ninety minutes or more, though they ranged from thirty-eight minutes to over three hours in duration. Interview questions uncovered participants' demographic characteristics, career challenges, perceptions about the music industry, the role of education, and workplace culture.

This book also draws on forty-four in-depth interviews conducted with higher education personnel. Half of these interviews (twenty-two) were conducted by a postdoctoral scholar, Dr. Gillian Gualtieri, with whom I worked closely during the COVID-19 pandemic (2020–22). We deliberately sampled higher education personnel who work as internship coordinators, in career services offices, leadership positions (e.g., deans), and faculty at research universities, liberal arts colleges, and specialized arts schools. We sampled first on institution type, identifying individuals who work at schools in "cultural capitals" (Oakley et al. 2017) in the United States, especially Los Angeles and New York City, and schools that participated in the SNAAP survey since I also collected survey data on internships in creative majors. We also used snowball sampling to identify respondents whom existing participants thought we should interview. The higher education interview sample contains diversity in terms of institution type (seventeen from R1 institutions and twenty-seven interviewees from a variety of R2, special focus arts and design schools, etc.), geographic area (twenty-three in New York City/Los Angeles and twenty-one spread across the United States), and job title (director of career services, internship coordinator, career advisor, etc.).

Higher education interviews were also open-ended, but due to geographical distance and the pandemic, these were mostly conducted via Zoom (seven were conducted in person) and recorded. Interviews typically lasted approximately one hour, though ranged between 52–111 minutes. Guided by respondents' answers and expertise, we asked questions about the organization of internship programs, advising for students throughout the internship process, the role and meaning of internships, the role and responsibility of schools regarding students' careers, constraints experienced by interns and the professionals we interviewed, and metrics of success. This open-ended approach allowed us to tailor our line of questioning to capture respondents' varied experiences and respond to participants as they represented themselves.

Audio recordings of the higher education interviews were all transcribed and coded using inductive methods with qualitative data analysis software program Atlas.ti. I inductively developed a coding scheme for analyzing the interviews—though this was done collaboratively with Dr. Gualtieri for the higher education interviews—through analytic memos (Saldaña 2016). First cycle coding was inductive and thematic. An inductive approach to coding allowed me to let the data "speak for itself" without imposing theoretical assumptions, providing ample opportunity for unanticipated themes and findings to "emerge," especially underlying tensions, constraints, and attitudes. In the second cycle of coding, I reviewed the coding instrument and the results from the coding and refined the scheme, collapsing some primary codes into broader "theoretical" codes (Corbin and Strauss 2015).

For all interviews, while social desirability bias is often a concern with interview research, I addressed these concerns by ensuring that interviews were confidential and by using pseudonyms for participants and their employers. In the book, mostly I use "Artist X" or an equivalent pseudonym when the name of a musical artist comes up during an interview, though at times I use real artist names to retain some of the power of the data. When doing so, I either omit the name of the interviewee, use the name knowing that interviewees often mention artists that are not associated with their label, and in one instance I switch the name of the well-known artist with a similarly positioned artist (e.g., two top rappers or pop stars).

NOTES

Introduction

1. See Bailey, Hughes, and Moore (2004); National Association of Colleges and Employers (NACE) (2022); Perlin (2011b).

2. As further illustration of how internships blur the line between "work" and "education," neither the US Department of Labor nor the Department of Education keep track of official internship statistics. While there is no authoritative source of data on US internship participation, let alone data on how rates have changed over time, the best estimates consistently suggest a dramatic increase in the frequency of internships. See Greenhouse (2010); Hora (2022); NACE (2022); Shandra (2022). Moreover, internships have also become more common among high school students and community college students, but this book focuses on students pursuing bachelor's degrees since this is the most common educational credential among record company interns and employees.

3. Some students even pay for-profit companies to be placed in key unpaid internships, see Perlin (2011b) and Shellenbarger (2009). For more on internship auctions, see Gani (2016) and Olen (2013).

4. Rita became a full-time employee at the magazine almost one year prior to college graduation. It is unusual but not uncommon for aspiring workers in the cultural industries to prioritize "getting in" over finishing their degree since they are unsure when or whether the next opportunity will arise. In this case, Rita (who was already used to managing multiple roles) continued to balance school and work until graduation. Timing is part of the challenge for interns trying to break into fields with less formalized intern-to-employee programs. Whereas in some fields (e.g., consulting) large employers hire graduating workers months in advance, in most cultural industries this is very rare.

5. Catching up with Rita in late 2023, now working at a major record company, she tells me she still calls her interns "intern," though sometimes they seem to be in on the joke—she recently received a holiday card from an intern who signed the card "Intern."

6. Anthropologist A. R. Radcliffe-Brown (1940) referred to such relations as an asymmetrical "joking relationship." Such humor entails a mix of friendliness and antagonism, which sociologists later identified as a potential source of harmony or a form of resistance to current power relations (Goffman 1961b:58; Willis 1977). Also see Collinson (1992).

7. This figure is higher in the arts, culture, and media fields, ostensibly because firms cannot afford to pay interns or do not see the need to do so because there is such strong demand from aspirants. See Ables (2023) and Hora (2022).

8. Apprenticeships extend at least as far back as the Code of Hammurabi (Perlin 2011b). For more on the history of apprenticeships and the growth of work-based learning (leading to the current intern economy), see Frenette (2015).

9. Jacobson and Shade (2018) suggested a typology of internships based on five factors that shape the experience: (1) pay (paid/unpaid), (2) academic credit, (3) for-profit/nonprofit, (4) full-time/part-time, and (5) on-site/off-site. Internships that take place offsite have become far more common since the start of the COVID-19 pandemic in 2020. Also see Vasel (2020).

10. STEM refers to students in science, technology, engineering, and mathematics. See Moss-Pech (2021); Okay-Somerville and Scholarios (2022). I am not claiming that all internships in these fields lead to positive educational and career outcomes; there remains heterogeneity in the quality of internships in all fields, though some college-to-career pipelines are more streamlined than others.

11. See Cachero (2022); Cerullo (2021); Lufkin (2022).

12. I have previously argued (Frenette 2013), building on Perlin (2011b), that the ambiguity of internships—that the experience means many different things across and within fields—is part of what enables the exploitation of interns.

13. See Rao (2023). Although the work can be humbling and at times even degrading, internships at high-end restaurants offer prestige and career advancement to culinary students. See Leschziner (2015).

14. See Farnham (2013).

15. See Chan, Selden, and Pun (2020); Day and Wu (2019).

16. See The Chronicle of Higher Education/Marketplace (2012). Also see Fischer (2013), which further expands on this finding.

17. See CBC News (2013); Hoffman (2013).

18. See Frenette et al. (2015) for more on the growth of unpaid and paid internships in creative fields. Regarding the economic conditions for young workers in the wake of the Great Recession, at this time a greater share of America's youth was enrolled in high school or college than at any period in history (Taylor et al. 2012), yet one in seven of the nation's 16–24-year-olds were neither at school nor working (Edwards 2013). Those who did attend college mostly took out student loans, which exacerbated fears of a "college debt crisis" (Cohn 2010) and growing interest in how the nation's record-setting \$1.2 trillion in college debt affected young workers, families, and the economy as a whole (Denhart 2013). During the Great Recession, the employment rate fell for students as well as nonenrolled young people; between 2007 and 2011, the employment rate went from 47.6 percent to 40.7 percent for youth enrolled in school and 73.2 percent to 65 percent for the nonenrolled (Taylor et al. 2012). As of the September 2013 jobs report, the country's unemployment rate "only" fell to a disappointing 7.2 percent, but the rate for 20–24-year-olds remained in the double digits at 12.9 percent (Kasperkevic 2013). Also in this post–Great Recession period, according to a Pew Research Center survey, only 30 percent of young workers (between 18–30 years old) consider their current job a "career"; the figure drops to 11 percent for workers aged 18–24 years old (Taylor et al. 2012).

19. For other academic accounts of the rise of ambiguous, often unpaid internships as a challenge to transitions from higher education to work, see Grant-Smith and McDonald (2018); Jacobson and Shade (2018); Tomlinson (2024).

20. See Oakley and O'Brien (2016); Perlin (2011b); de Peuter, Cohen, and Brophy (2012).

21. See Taketa (2014).

22. See Walker (2016).

23. See Glaeser (2013). This uncritical embrace of unpaid internships as a solution to the plight of youth unemployment went beyond US borders. For example, during a news conference around the same period, Stephen Poloz, Bank of Canada governor, similarly stated that unemployed young people (including college graduates) should pursue some "real-life experience," adding: "If your parents are letting you live in the basement, you might as well go out and do something for free to put the experience on your CV" (Medeiros 2014).

24. See NACE (2022).

25. See Frenette et al. (2015).

26. For a summary of the rise of lawsuits filed by unpaid interns, see Frenette (2015).

27. See Raymond (2015). These lawsuits were clustered in the cultural industries, especially at large media companies in music, television, film, publishing, and fashion.

28. For a discussion of "do what you love" as a career ideal, especially in creative fields, see Duffy (2017) and Tokumitsu (2015). For a broader analysis of passion in relation to occupational identities and career choices, see Cech (2021); DePalma (2021); Wilson (2022).

29. See Frederick (1997); Klein (2000); Perlin (2011b). Cultural industries are involved in the creation and dissemination of symbolic goods such as film, television, music, publishing, and fashion. Some cultural industries, such as architecture and parts of the design field, are more likely to pay interns. But overall cultural industries historically feature the predominance of unpaid intern labor, particularly in recent decades (see Frenette et al. 2015).

30. See Messitte (2015); Raymond (2015); Siegemund-Broka (2013).

31. For more on the limited career payoffs of unpaid internships, see Frenette et al. (2015) and Hunt and Scott (2023). *The New York Times* profiled a handful of college alumni in their twenties who had completed internships in music, television, fashion, film, or publishing; several years after graduation most were still working at internships instead of paid positions. So common is this predicament—the inability of recent college graduates, across various sectors, to achieve career footholds—that the article dubs educated millennials the "permanent intern underclass" (Williams 2014).

32. See Jones (2024) for more on the experiences of interns in US Congress. Jones finds that Black and Latino people, as well as aspirants from less economically privileged backgrounds, are underrepresented as interns in Congress and face additional barriers to entry (e.g., in the process of building social networks).

33. See Frenette, Gualtieri, and Robinson (2021); NACE (2022); Shandra (2022).

34. For a review of studies primarily portraying an individualist view of job searching as an autonomous, self-regulated process, see Wanberg, Ali, and Csillag (2020). This individualist view is consistent with long-standing, dominant cultural understandings of the American Dream (see Chinoy 1955).

35. See Lave (1996); Lave and Wenger (1991); Van Maanen (1976); Van Maanen and Schein (1979).

36. Such models stand in contrast, especially, to functionalist views of socialization whereby newcomers are "empty vessels" uniformly filled up by socialization (Merton, Reader, and Kendall 1957). Along these lines, Pugh (2014:81) argued that an "undercurrent of implied determinism" in the term socialization can obscure conflicts and heterogeneity in this process. Guhin, Calarco, and Miller-Idriss (2021) then suggested that this critique partly explains why the concept has received little sociological attention in recent decades. See Colomy and Brown (1995).

37. While I argue in this book that the classic studies of "breaking in" need to be updated to account for the socially induced ambiguity encountered by interns navigating through the education-industrial complex, the rich sociological tradition of studying how newcomers learn or "become" nonetheless remains contemporary. For example, such studies from recent decades capture how one becomes a tour guide (Wynn 2011b), an opera fanatic (Benzecry 2011), a Hollywood agent (Roussel 2017), a blues musician (Grazian 2003), a master of craft (Ocejo 2017), and a police officer (Simon 2024).

38. See Colomy and Brown (1995); McCall and Simmons ([1966] 1978).

39. See Frenette et al. (2021).

40. It is not uncommon—and certainly not new—for a workplace role to be highly flexible and ambiguous. Over sixty years ago, Dalton (1959:27,68) described the "Assistant-to" position as an "elastic role" that officially "serves to relieve the executive of routine work" yet also fulfills numerous other purposes:

> It serves as a reward, as an unofficial channel of information, as an informal arm of authority, as a safety valve for the pressures generated by a necessary surplus of able and ambitious developing executives, as a protective office for loyal but aging members rendered unfit by changes they cannot meet or from other failures, as a training post, etc.

41. See Meyer and Rowan (1977). Also, see Hallett and Ventresca (2006) for a discussion of the lineage of this skeptical approach, from symbolic interactionism to inhabited institutionalism.

42. See Moore (2013).

43. As organizational scholars would frame this paradox, higher education is a hub that connects and must appeal to many different publics (e.g., students, their parents, employers, the state) and maintain multiple identities (e.g., offering liberal arts education to engaged citizens and training people for careers—two distinct though overlapping identities). Higher education institutions are compelled to simultaneously symbolize their commitment to being places of learning and to being springboards to good jobs. For more on higher education as a "hub," see Stevens, Armstrong, and Arum (2008). For more on institutional pluralism and efforts within higher education institutions to manage multiple identities, see Besharov and Smith (2014); Eaton and Stevens (2020); Kraatz and Block (2008).

44. For a review of the hidden curriculum and its application to first-generation college students, see Gable (2021).

45. At some companies the curriculum of interns is more thorough and organized. An A&R department at one company, for example, organizes a weekly meeting

where interns learn to "pitch" unsigned artists they researched that week. Some companies organize regular speaker series for their interns or ensure short one-on-one interviews with staff members.

46. The mailroom framework is an instantiation of the way interns are evaluated as winners or losers, an example of what Lamont, Beljean, and Clair (2014) described as how organizations deploy routine practices to assign value to individuals.

47. See Armstrong and Hamilton (2013); Jack (2019); Stuber (2011).

48. See Lucas (2001); also see Hamilton, Roksa, and Nielsen (2018).

49. See Hamilton et al. (2018).

50. See Armstrong and Hamilton (2013); Hamilton et al. (2018); Jack (2019).

51. See Duffy (2017); Kuehn and Corrigan (2013).

52. Leschziner (2015) described how the aspirational status of interns buffers the low status of their tasks. Also see Baker and Faulkner (1991) on how a role can serve as a resource.

53. See Cappelli (1999).

54. See Jacoby (1985); Kalleberg (2009).

55. See Mills (1951); Whyte Jr. (1956).

56. See Chinoy (1955).

57. Although the period following World War II generally offered more stability for white- and blue-collar workers, not everyone had access to these jobs. Women and members of racial minority groups were notably excluded from such "good" jobs. Also, academic and popular accounts of post-WWII jobs arguably overlook some of their negative features (job security and a living wage were often paired with feeling stuck and doing repetitive tasks). See Aronowitz (1992); Chinoy (1955); Hollister (2011); Milkman (1997); Smith (1997).

58. See Kalleberg (2009, 2011).

59. See Beck (2000); Boltanski and Chiapello (2006); Ross (2003); Sennett (1998); Smith (2001).

60. For more on the factors leading to the transformation of work and careers since the 1970s, see Cappelli (1999); Kalleberg (2009, 2011).

61. See Hatton (2011); Hipple (2001); Kalleberg (2011); Matusik and Hill (1998); Smith (2001).

62. See Cottom (2017); Kalleberg (2011); Smith (2001).

63. See Liu (2019); US Bureau of Labor Statistics (2023). Also see Arthur and Rousseau (1996).

64. See Harris (1993).

65. See Halpin and Smith (2017).

66. See Cappelli (2015); Cottom (2017); Waddoups (2016).

67. See Gershon (2017); Kalleberg (2011); Neely (2020); Skaggs (2019b); Smith (2010).

68. See Schaeffer (2022); Taylor, Fry, and Oates (2014).

69. See Collins (2002); Horowitz (2018); Kalleberg (2011). On the claim that employers increasingly expect job-ready workers for entry-level jobs, see Titus (2021) and Weber and Korn (2014).

70. See Arum and Roksa (2014); Ayala-Hurtado (2025); Binder, Davis, and Bloom (2016); Cottom (2017); Rivera (2015b); Roksa and Silver (2019); Streib (2023).

71. See Brown (2018). On the increases in the costs of attending college, also see National Center for Education Statistics (2021a).

72. See Espeland and Sauder (2007) and Sauder and Espeland (2006, 2009) for more on reactivity as an organizational response to being evaluated.

73. See Rosenbaum (2001).

74. See Arum and Roksa (2014); Berman and Paradeise (2016).

75. See Berman and Paradeise (2016); Besbris and Petre (2020); Brint et al. (2005); Geiger (2019).

76. See Moss-Pech (2021); Shandra (2022).

77. See O'Mahony and Bechky (2006) for more on how workers overcome the career progression paradox.

78. See Rivera (2015b).

79. See Vallas and Christin (2018).

80. See Gershon (2017).

81. See Gershon (2017); Sharone (2013); Smith (2001).

82. While the exact payoffs of social capital in the job market are contested—for example, see Lin (1999) and Mouw (2003)—an array of studies has identified a significant association between social capital and finding a job. See Dowd and Pinheiro (2013); Granovetter ([1974] 1995); Lin (1999); Marsden and Campbell (1990); Martin, Frenette, and Gualtieri (2023); Mouw (2003).

83. See Gershon (2017); Sharone (2017).

84. See Chen (2015); Halpin and Smith (2017); Sharone (2013).

85. See Gershon (2017).

86. See Altomonte (2020); Deener (2017); Levine (1985); Weick (1995).

87. The line between "student" and "employee" is blurry, even when an intern is paid. In *Mayo Foundation for Medical Education and Research et al. v United States*, the Supreme Court ruled (#09–837, decided January 11, 2011) that medical residents do not fall into a special (tax-exempt) "student" category in the Treasury Department's tax regulation since their standing resembles employment more so than an educational activity. Moreover, the legality of internships has even been contested in fields with long traditions of work-based training that resemble apprenticeships, such as cosmetology and the equestrian industry (see Morris 2023).

88. See Weick (1995). For additional nuance regarding the relationship between information (or lack thereof) and ambiguity, see Martin (1992). For more on how social actors attempt to agentically navigate ambiguous situations, see Emirbayer and Mische (1998).

89. See Jones (1996); Menger (1999).

90. J. Lee (2016) described aspiring rappers' brief brushes with famous people as "momentous interactions" that reenergize and supply hopes of "blowin' up." Faulkner (1983) referred to the odd combination of nearness and remoteness as characteristic of film composers working on the periphery.

91. See Banks (2017).

92. See Frenette and Dowd (2020); Menger (1999). Though, this does not mean that education credentials are without merit. As sociologists Childress and Gerber (2015) found regarding the MFA for creative writers, a "useless" credential still signals a professional identity to themselves and the world, showing they are more than simply a hobbyist.

93. See Dowd (2006); Hracs (2012); Scott (1999).

94. See Anonymous (1959, March 16).

95. See Peterson (1990).

96. See Bielby and Bielby (1994); Caves (2000).

97. See Hirsch (1972); Lingo and O'Mahony (2010); Wohl (2021).

98. See Childress (2017); Gerber (2017); Mears (2011); Lingo and Tepper (2013); Skaggs (2022).

99. See Banks (2007); Cornfield (2015); Hesmondhalgh and Baker (2011); Jones (1996); Peterson and Anand (2002).

100. See Peterson and Anand (2002); Pham (2011).

101. See Hesmondhalgh and Baker (2011); Neff, Wissinger, and Zukin (2005); Stahl (2012).

102. See Becker (1982); Bourdieu (1993); Frenette (2019).

1. The Education-Industrial Complex

1. See Lipka (2010).

2. The Department of Labor's Wage and Hour Division, which was born from the Fair Labor Standards Act (FLSA) of 1938, is responsible for promoting and enforcing labor standards, including the federal minimum wage. "Fact Sheet #71" relates only to interns at for-profit organizations; the statement retains the general exception for unpaid interns working without expectation of compensation in the public sector and for nonprofit charitable organizations.

3. According to the Fair Labor Standards Act (FLSA; the 1938 federal legislation regulating employment), interns should be paid. However, this point seems to be a matter of interpretation. An employee is defined in a spectacularly broad way; as Senator Hugo Black noted shortly before the FLSA became law, the definition of an employee is "the broadest definition that has ever been included in any one act" (Curiale 2010:1539, quoting 81 Congressional Record 7657, 1937). An "employee" is defined as "any individual employed by an employer," and "employ" means "to suffer or permit to work" (29 USC section 203). The term "employee" was further clarified in 1947 when the Supreme Court ruled on *Walling v. Portland Terminal Co.* (330 US 148), a case opposing railway trainees and a railway company. To become eligible for employment as railway brakemen, trainees first took part in a program that lasted seven to eight days. Applicants chosen by the company to take part in this program worked with railway yard employees over this period, progressing from generally observing activities to doing some work under close supervision (Yamada 2002). Trainees claimed they should be paid minimum wage during their training, but the Supreme Court ultimately disagreed, finding:

> The definition "suffer or permit to work" was obviously not intended to stamp all persons as employees who, without any express or implied compensation agreement, might work for their own advantage on the premises of another. Otherwise, all students would be employees of the school or college they attended, and as such entitled to receive minimum wages. So also, such a construction would sweep under the Act each person who, without promise or expectation of compensation, but solely for his personal purpose or pleasure, worked in activities carried on by other persons either

> for their pleasure or profit. (*Walling v. Portland Terminal Co.*, 330 US 148, 152, 1947)

For more on the history of internships, the six-factor test derived from the 1947 *Walling v. Portland Terminal Co.* decision, and more recent court decisions from circuit courts in the United States, see Curiale (2010); Ford (2021); Frenette (2015); Yamada (2002).

4. See US Department of Labor, Wage and Hour Division (2010).

5. One of the letter's authors, Joseph E. Aoun, the president of Northeastern University, expanded on the national importance of internships in a follow-up opinion piece. See Aoun (2010).

6. Without employment status, unpaid interns are not entitled to the same legal protections from sexual harassment and discrimination as employees. Title VII of the Civil Rights Act of 1964 protects "employees" from workplace harassment or discrimination, but courts have not found that the act covers unpaid interns (Fox 2014; LaRocca 2006; Ortner 1998; Yamada 2002). Further, the courts are unlikely to find internship sponsors, such as colleges and universities, liable in such harassment and discrimination cases (Edwards and Hertel-Fernandez 2010). This standing leaves student interns "in a legal void, falling between the cracks of legal protections for workers and legal protections for students" (Yamada 2002:2).

7. See Lieber (2022); Perlin (2011a). Beyond charging tuition dollars and fees without necessarily offering regular class meetings with permanent faculty, schools also generate revenue by renting out summer housing to interns.

8. Yet, as I note later and expand upon elsewhere (Frenette 2019), some paid employees state that they draw on the cutting-edge consumptive knowledge and experiences of passionate young interns. Some companies, especially A&R departments at major record companies, aim to host the most knowledgeable music fans possible to serve as a source of knowledge and enthusiasm, though experienced employees may not readily admit this point.

9. The rise of music business programs aligns with the resurgence of what Steven Brint called "practical arts" majors, which are oriented explicitly toward training college students for occupations as opposed to the "learning for learning's sake" emphasis of liberal arts education. Specifically, Brint (2002:232) defined liberal arts as "the basic fields of science and scholarship housed in colleges of arts and sciences—physics, chemistry, history, English, political science, and others" whereas the "practical arts" refer to "occupational and professional programs often housed in their own schools and colleges—business, engineering, computer science, nursing, education, and other fields oriented to preparing students for careers." In 1970, the practical arts represented less than half of four-year bachelor's degrees, but by 2000 that figure had grown to approximately 60 percent.

Also, see Brint et al. (2005) for more on the long-standing coexistence of "market-based utilitarianism" and "liberal arts" traditions within higher education.

10. Brian's comments on the rise of music business programs are consistent with the mailroom model of training I discuss in chapter 3. He observed, "It's interesting because a lot of universities across the country have set up music business programs, which means they are trying to provide a practical, clear path for students to get to a certain position in music, but I'm not sure what the success rate of that is because

I still find that the formal education aspect of it might be helpful but it doesn't really replace actually just getting in there and doing it."

11. These shifts are part of the well-documented "marketization" of higher education in which higher education institutions have been forced to contend with market pressures, much like any other type of business. Broader economic, social, and political neoliberal forces in the latter half of the twentieth century prompted a decline in public funding of US higher education institutions, with the federal government shifting from funding schools to funding individual students, and student aid transitioning from grants to loans. Thus, as the price of higher education has risen considerably, the cost has increasingly become the responsibility of students and their families. See Berman and Paradeise (2016); Bok (2003); Geiger (2019); Roksa and Silver (2019).

12. For more on "high-impact practices" in higher education, see Kuh et al. (2010); Pascarella and Terenzini (2005).

13. For more on the educational benefits of internships, see Binder et al. (2015) and Parker et al. (2016) on improved academic performance; Barr and McNeilly (2002) on leadership abilities; and Divine, Miller, and Wilson (2006) on soft skills.

14. See Guarise and Kostenblatt (2018); Luecking and Fabian (2000).

15. Since there is some variation in how higher education institutions market themselves, describe their goals, and justify their legitimacy, in this chapter—and in the methodological appendix—I identify interviewees based on whether the school is public or private, and their Carnegie classification. Regarding the latter, "R1: Doctoral Universities" are the most "research active" and typically the most prestigious schools; it is therefore unsurprising that interviewees from the R2 public universities and Special Focus (arts and design schools) private institutions are slightly more explicitly vocational in their approach.

16. Some of the programs in Sebastian's department have more of a liberal arts orientation whereas others are more vocational (i.e., teach technical skills that seemingly align directly with industry). Still, Sebastian describes the more career-oriented view of college as widely shared across all of these majors.

17. Sebastian is one of the more educationally rigorous respondents I interviewed. While it is not uncommon for students who take internships for college credit to write reflection papers based on their experiences, most interns write these without receiving in-depth feedback from an educator to better understand what they observed. To paraphrase another faculty member I interviewed, by sending students into a workplace and simply tasking them with observing the complexities around them, it is as though students are asked to read works by Shakespeare on their own without the benefit of working through these texts in a class.

18. There are many exceptions to this claim. For example, college programs that are more vocational in orientation offer students a more straightforward preparation for technical jobs in music and film. Nevertheless, the oversupply of aspirants in these fields still makes breaking in challenging.

19. See Berman and Paradeise (2016); Einstein (2015); Harrison et al. (2022); Roksa and Robinson (2022).

20. See Askin and Bothner (2016); Brankovic, Hamann, and Ringel (2023); Chu (2021).

21. Other studies also illuminate how higher education personnel, including career services employees, must balance institutional pressures with student needs; see Damaske (2009); Davis and Binder (2016).

22. The ROI ranking the article reported on compares the cost (tuition and fees) for attending a variety of higher education institutions (broken down by major) in relation to the average incomes in the twenty years after graduation; Maureen's school's creative majors ranked as among the worst for "return on investment."

23. At the extreme, the US government has been cracking down on exploitative for-profit higher education institutions that cravenly mislead prospective students, selling them expensive degrees and portraying inflated career outcomes. See Cottom (2017).

24. Similarly, a body of empirical research shows that higher education institutions increasingly market themselves by emphasizing the individual career advancement of their graduates, rather than learning and democratic equality. See Hartley and Morphew (2008); Saichaie and Morphew (2014).

25. The marketing benefits of demonstrating a history of strong internship placements overlap with schools' place-specific value proposition. Music-related programs at schools in cultural centers, such as New York, Los Angeles, and Nashville for the record industry, specifically market their proximity to industry players. As one interviewee in a cultural center explains, "Universities have figured out we can give our student an advantage . . . and so, for a university in [CITY] with a [music business] program like we have, we would be remiss to not take advantage of the industry that we are literally in the middle of."

26. See Frenette et al. (2021).

27. See Frenette et al. (2021); Hora et al. (2021). For more on the relationship between social class and participation in campus and social activities (notably for less privileged students whose schedules are constrained due to paid jobs), see Martin (2012).

28. While I present evidence in this chapter about how higher education institutions promote interning, students' interest in internships can also come from observing peers; data from Binder et al. (2016) suggest that these two forms of influence are intertwined. The authors found that higher education institutions help students learn status distinctions between occupational fields and, in so doing, their findings suggest that schools and peers socialize these aspirants to the expectation that they must intern to get a job (e.g., students watch most of their peers apply for internships, facilitated by on-campus recruitment events, and in turn begin to do the same).

29. In a SNAAP survey of arts alumni that was fielded in 2015–17, respondents were asked how they found their most significant arts-related internship (they could choose between two personal and three school-related options). Overall, a slight majority (54 percent) of graduates selected a school-related option (faculty connection, career development office, or alumni network) rather than a personal option (personal research or through friends/family). However, historical patterns highlight the growing importance of personal resources in finding an internship. For more, see Frenette et al. (2021).

30. Searching for an internship usually means looking for listings on websites and through word of mouth, though in a minority of instances this means convincing an

entity to start hosting interns (i.e., creating an internship program). Urging companies to start hosting interns was more common among people who interned in the 1990s or early 2000s than it was for more recent interns.

31. See Hamilton et al. (2018). For more context on parental investment in children from early childhood through college, see Bandelj (2023); Hamilton (2016).

32. See Frenette et al. (2021).

33. See Calarco (2014); Jack (2016, 2019); E. Lee (2016); Stuber (2011).

34. See Moss-Pech (2021).

35. For a more detailed discussion of these three reasons for hosting interns, see Frenette (2013). Further, when analyzing the interview data, I realized that employees downplay the creative contributions of interns. For an examination of how companies broadly utilize a variety of formal and informal practices to learn from interns, a process I call leveraging youth, see Frenette (2019).

36. See Gray (2021); Pianko (1996); Sterling and Merluzzi (2019).

37. Research and popular writings from recent decades widely portray internship programs as a cost-efficient way to screen, mold, and recruit new talent across a variety of industries. See Divine et al. (2008); Gerken et al. (2012); Muhamad et al. (2009); Rothman and Lampe (2010).

38. First, availability is not the only qualification that matters for landing an internship, but employees often noted it as an important prerequisite. Second, this finding further supports the claim from critics that unpaid internships reproduce class inequality because only those with sufficient economic resources can afford to work for free. See Frederick (1997); Klein (2000); Perlin (2011b). Doing provisional labor, including building a portfolio of experience and gaining connections over an extended period, requires resources beyond those needed to finance a brief unpaid or low-paid internship, and thus has broader class-based effects. Significantly, being available also implies being able to afford to be flexible.

39. Through ensuring that unpaid interns are receiving school credit, for-profit employers are reducing the risk of getting sued for back pay. I further discuss the emerging legal standing of unpaid interns in chapter 5; also see Frenette (2015).

40. A few interviewees specifically referred to the eight core competencies that the National Association of Colleges and Employers concluded are crucial to a career-ready workforce. See NACE (n.d.), "What Is Career Readiness?," https://www.naceweb.org/career-readiness/competencies/career-readiness-defined/.

41. In the face of vague legal standards for an unpaid internship, higher education institutions enact policies and practices in a variety of ways (i.e., actors can inhabit institutions differently). Much like Gualtieri (2020) found in the enactment of Title IX policies, here I suggest that higher education employees with more visibility, perhaps because they are at smaller schools or programs—and therefore, with more accountability from students—are more likely to do oversight (if they have the resources) rather than symbolically attend to student needs.

42. McGoey (2012) suggests that ignorance functions as an organizational resource—in this case, by lacking knowledge about internship experiences, schools can plausibly deny any lack of oversight.

43. In contrast, other higher education interviewees describe being sticklers about credit hours—with some explicitly stating that a student would be in trouble for working so many extra hours—but unless the intern or employer report these extra hours, no penalty can be enforced.

44. See Sweet (2019); Williams (2021).

2. Dealing with an Ambiguous Role

1. Although Faulkner's (1974) research focused on professional hockey players and symphony orchestra musicians, the concept is similar to the "fog of youth" described in Joseph Hermanowicz's (1998) study of scientists. All these workers must contend with the disconnect between their aspirations, their abilities, and the opportunity structure they encounter. As an "internal career" evolves, workers adjust their subjective self-conceptions (Schein and Van Maanen 2016).

2. See Becker et al. (1961); Hughes (1956); Van Maanen (1976).

3. Although this is the typical profile of a record industry intern, there are occasionally younger interns, and more frequently "older" interns (in their mid- to late twenties). This variation is due to several factors: (1) as companies begin to pay interns at least minimum wage, some have waived the college enrollment requirement; (2) to help ensure tidy college-to-career transitions, some postsecondary institutions allow graduates to sign up for "no credit" enrollment to complete internships well after graduation; (3) some interns are enrolled in graduate school (e.g., in the field of music business); and (4) many undergraduate students are not 18–21 years old; see National Center for Education Statistics (2021b).

4. I borrow the phrase "motley assemblage" from Paul Cressey, who used it in his classic ethnography *The Taxi-Dance Hall* (1932) to describe the diverse group of men who patronized these urban nightlife establishments.

5. I developed these ideal types (Weber [1968] 1978) based on the defining qualities that emerged from participants' descriptions of their experiences. The people I encountered in the study, for example, did not necessarily refer to the "student type" of intern, but frequently mentioned educational motivations for internships. A typology can illuminate how differently positioned interns make a claim to different motivations. For a detailed discussion of the development and use of typologies in qualitative research, see Wynn (2011a).

6. Similarly, the roles of "runner" and "gofer," particularly in Hollywood, have allowed newcomers to get a sense of what they do and do not want to pursue in the film and television industry. When interviewed about his early career, television writer and producer Mitchell Hurwitz (Pretentious Film Majors 2014) recounted starting as a runner on the show *The Golden Girls*, describing the position as "trying to find out what you don't want to do for a living . . . really seeing what people are like that do those jobs." However, unlike many cultural industry internships, runner and gofer positions are typically paid.

7. Amanda reported feeling embarrassed when she made a mistake or was uncertain about how to act, but otherwise she could not identify any negative consequences, including in terms of academic outcomes. With some exceptions, a bad internship experience is unlikely to earn a student a poor grade because academic

assessment is usually the responsibility of the school rather than the employer. Also, Amanda interned for six semesters (including two summers) but only paid for school credits one-third of this time, which means most of her time was "off the books" and therefore even if things had gone poorly, the experience would not have impacted her academic standing.

8. College student interns are in the process of transitioning into adulthood, and since they are typically the youngest people in the office they often feel (or are made to feel) like "kids." About a dozen times in this book, I quote employees referring to interns as "kids"—I take their use of this term as a reference to interns' relative youth (even if interns and employees are sometimes only a few years apart), but the term also has negative and somewhat positive connotations. Sometimes employees (and higher education personnel) infantilize interns by referring to them as kids and thus emphasize their relative inexperience and cluelessness, though sometimes "kid" comes off as a term of endearment.

9. Perks are an important form of compensation in professional and other social contexts (McClain and Mears 2012; Mears 2015). In the cultural industries, perks such as physical objects and the meaning gained from involvement in an artistic field are conceptualized as "psychic rewards" (Frenette 2016; Menger 1999) that help sustain an individual's participation despite the lack of meaningful monetary payment. Similarly, Lloyd (2006:132) found that service sector workers in a culturally desirable haunt describe working for the "community" more than the pay. More broadly, the "intangible benefits" described by Paula are consistent with the pull of passion that draws newcomers to fields where they can "do what they love" (Cech 2021; DePalma 2021; Wilson 2022).

10. The division between the Student and the Job Seeker in terms of their desire for career clarification is notably blurry. Students are primarily interested in learning whether they want to work in a specific field, whereas Job Seekers focus on learning which type of company or department in the music industry best fits their abilities and interests.

11. This is, by definition, what I call provisional labor. As I note later, what further muddies the waters (or exacerbates ambiguity) for Job Seeker interns is the fact that not every intern sees what they are doing as provisional labor—this ambiguity makes Job Seeker interns' signal to potential employers less clear (consistent with Mai [2021] on unclear signals in the labor market).

12. "Employment management work" entails the full process of deciding which labor market to enter, seeking relevant education and experience, decoding hiring and recruitment procedures, assessing one's fit for potential jobs, withstanding periods of unemployment, and (re)drawing plans (Halpin and Smith 2017). Job Seeker interns have already decided which labor market they wish to enter and, depending on their situation, they alternate between other aspects of employment management work (e.g., assessing their potential fit).

13. Student interns also take on risk, in the sense that they assume some of the burden for their own training and longer-term career (Neff 2012). However, interns who aimed to secure employment in the record industry described this risk more keenly because the potential return on their investment in a music career was uncertain, yet their timeline until graduation proceeded unabated.

14. See Goffman (1959). Also, the typology emphasizes the justifications people offer for doing internships, functioning as a kind of "motive talk" that puts prior actions in alignment with what people think is normal or expected for the situation. However, such motives overlap with, and at times are, "motivations" (inner drivers toward certain lines of action). See Winchester and Green (2019) for more on the distinction between motives and motivations.

15. Data from the Strategic National Arts Alumni Project (SNAAP) suggest that the Job Seeker motivation has gained prominence over the last two decades, overcoming the Student motivation as the most frequently emphasized reason for pursuing an internship. I designed a module of the SNAAP survey, which received responses from over ten thousand arts alumni who graduated between 1980 and 2017. Reflecting on their internship experiences, recent graduates (from 2008–17) were significantly more likely to select career-oriented reasons for interning ("build up my résumé" and "develop a professional network") than earlier graduates, who were more likely to indicate they had interned for educational reasons ("fulfill a graduation requirement" and "expand on what I learned in the classroom"). This pattern does not reflect a trend of arts programs eliminating internship requirements for graduation—indeed, the evidence suggests a rise in arts internships—but rather that arts graduates are increasingly likely to intern even if it is not required by their program and are more likely to emphasize the career-oriented reasons for pursuing such experiences. For more, see Frenette et al. (2021).

16. When working with interns they perceive as strongly committed, employees may share insights from their own career paths, provide in-depth histories and descriptions of the industry's landscape, introduce them to colleagues at the company as well as at other firms or institutions, and possibly offer them more free stuff (e.g., concert tickets).

17. There is variation in terms of employees treating less committed interns more harshly. Some interns that employees deem uncommitted will be simply ignored (which is its own form of harshness) whereas, at times, some committed interns deemed as promising potential employees will be held to a higher standard, which might include more "tough love" such as sternly correcting missteps (as opposed to ignoring the uncommitted intern's errors).

18. To build on the selection of interns based on availability, which I discussed in the previous chapter, employees also describe partly selecting interns based on their display of passion for music, ideally specifically for the genre or artists linked to their company. This rationale is consistent with employers hosting interns for their cheap labor since, according to employees, interns who are passionate about music are more likely to enthusiastically take on any task thrown at them. According to employees, selecting interns who seem passionate about music may limit the presence of completely uncommitted interns.

19. Interns seek a position at the record company, in part, to get closer to the magic or coolness of the backstage. Per Walter Benjamin's ([1936] 1969) concept of aura, the journey that interns and employees take to the workplace is akin to a pilgrimage to the source, an effort to seek closeness with the original. Their achieved proximity to this source of coolness offers them what sociologist Violaine Roussel

(2017:59) calls "vocation by proxy," the accomplishment of uniqueness and social status through association with artistic talent.

20. I use "organizational goals" broadly to include the goals of either the larger organization or the "relevant group," a distinction noted by John Van Maanen (1976). The goals of the former might include being productive in the interest of the company's profits, while the goals of the latter might include working in a way that aligns with the culture of the department or work unit, at times to the detriment of the employer's goals—for example, an intern who shows up to the office an hour before their departmental colleagues and works later than them might well meet the company's goal in the interest of profitability, but such behavior would possibly draw the ire of colleagues who feel the intern's hard work makes them look lazy.

21. The accusation of being a "groupie" is gendered; any time an employee described interns motivated by wanting a closer affiliation with artists, they mentioned women. In contrast, they portrayed men who showed excitement for music as passionate music nerds.

22. For example, in an opinion piece titled "The Six Principles of Stupidity," *New York Times* columnist David Brooks (2025) decried the stupidity of a "memo that reads like it was written by an intern."

23. According to a social media post in 2021 by HBO Max, an intern accidentally sent a test email to a portion of the company's mailing list. The post then specified, "We apologize for the inconvenience, and as the jokes pile in, yes, it was the intern. No, really. And we're helping them through it." This post, acknowledging the recognizable "blame the intern" joke, albeit relatively kindly phrased in this case, was met with an outpouring of support for the unnamed intern on social media, including from Monica Lewinsky, whose relationship with President Bill Clinton in the mid-1990s while an intern led to arguably the most memorable intern-related scandal. See Spangler (2021).

24. Additionally, part-time status signals an intern's potential lack of commitment, warranted or not, just as it does for part-time employees (Epstein et al. 1999). Moreover, the presumed incompetence (or mild competence) of interns overlaps with similarly negative perceptions of workers with nonstandard employment (e.g., part-time or temporary workers) more broadly (Boyce et al. 2007; Brooks 2011; Pedulla 2016). For more on employer concerns about the commitment and competence of these nonstandard workers, see Pedulla (2020:51–55).

25. See Becker (1972); Van Maanen (1978).

26. Multiple studies point to discrepancies between interns' expectations and experiences. See Muhamad et al. (2009); Narayanan, Olk, and Fukami (2010); Taylor and de Laat (2013). Giomboni (2024) further illustrates the importance and potential payoffs of interns making sense of their role's implicit and explicit expectations.

27. See Ho (2009); Kunda (1992); Neely (2022).

28. Taylor and de Laat (2013) report a similar "sink or swim" onboarding approach in their study of interns at feminist organizations.

29. The precise expectations of industry cool vary by company and even by department, with some settings embracing stricter guidelines and others offering more latitude. Nevertheless, the presence of newcomers such as interns makes visible the

expectations of "demeanor," which Goffman (1956:489) referred to as "that element of the individual's ceremonial behavior typically conveyed through deportment, dress, and bearing, which serves to express to those in his immediate presence that he is a person of certain desirable or undesirable qualities." Regarding clothing in the music industry, the rules of demeanor are asymmetrical, allowing more freedom for established employees than entry-level workers.

30. This process of mostly unspoken socialization and ensuing ambiguity is similarly captured in Michel Anteby's (2013) study of Harvard Business School, although in this case the aims of socialization go beyond the surface-level. Anteby refers to socialization via mostly implicit instructions ("vocal silence"), albeit rigorously enforced through nudges, winks, and a preponderance of other cues, leading to a "productive ambiguity."

31. The interns and former interns in this study generally referred to interning as "work," even if it was an unpaid internship.

32. There are two caveats to the acceptance of formal but stylish clothing for senior employees. First, there is a strong class-based component to Hank wearing expensive suits that fit him impeccably, like the clothes worn by some of the star acts signed to the record company, which embodies an elite aesthetic. Nevertheless, an experienced employee who dresses up in less aesthetically "accomplished" attire is not deemed clueless, though they do not necessarily receive such compliments. Second, the dress code varies across the industry; for example, at a small indie record label even Hank's calculated and expressive form of overdressing would likely be seen as inappropriate, particularly given the strong DIY ethic in these environments. Friedman and Laurison (2019:139) similarly found that the fit, or lack thereof, between an individual's style and what they call an organization's "studied informality" shapes whether someone becomes an integrated member of the organization.

33. As I noted previously, assessments of musical enthusiasm are prone to gender bias—Brandon's description of screaming "girls" reflects a tendency to devaluate the passion of young women (at times calling them "groupies") compared to more positive descriptions of musically inclined young men.

3. The New Mailroom

1. Being "betwixt and between" is a key characteristic of liminality as outlined by anthropologist Victor Turner (1967). As the typology of intern motivations presented in chapter 2 illustrates, interns are viewed and view themselves as students, fans, workers, or, most commonly, a combination of the above.

2. Internships differ markedly from the status transitions typically examined in classic anthropological studies. Whereas in earlier eras most rites of passage concerned transitions that were universal within a community (e.g., movement from adolescent to adult), today young adults often opt into under-institutionalized liminal roles such as internships, which entail less robust and therefore less immediately legitimate narratives. As organizational scholars Herminia Ibarra and Otilia Obodaru (2016) argued, to varying extents, contemporary "liminars" must either draw on and adapt the narrative of an organization or a culture or construct their own cultural script.

3. In her study of hospitals' surgeon-training programs, Katherine Kellogg (2011) detailed an "old-school" system in which "Iron Men" embody a macho, almost superhuman persona; these workers hold a set of beliefs that include the idea that interns must suffer to learn.

4. See Rensin (2004:xvii).

5. "Copy boy" in journalism and "runner" in film and television are also romanticized positions that traditionally involve low-level work but can serve as a launching pad; see Ashton (2015); Tuchman (1973). No matter the role, the claim that one will work their way up from the bottom and tolerate anything has been a prominent narrative among aspirants in the cultural industries for decades. For example, before working as a film director in the early 1930s, Jean Vigo wrote to "everybody" in film for a job as an assistant, pronouncing: "I'm willing to sweep up the stars' crap" (Truffaut [1978] 1994:26).

6. A few of the more experienced record industry employees I encountered worked their way up from mailroom jobs (although not formal mailroom training programs, which, to my knowledge, never existed at record companies), but with the outsourcing of mail distribution and other clerical and support work to independent firms, these rare stories have become almost unfathomable. At one major record company I encountered in my fieldwork, although mailroom employees are physically close to music employees, they are distanced in status because the former wear uniforms and work for another firm. When I asked if mailroom employees could ever hope to get a job at the record company, a middle-management employee thought I was joking and laughed, exclaiming, "Could you even imagine?" See Drucker ([1989] 2005).

7. Mailroom trainee programs are viewed as the primary pathway to becoming an agent (see Roussel 2017). However, in recent years the pay-your-dues approach has grown increasingly incompatible with many companies' goals of equity and inclusion. Consequently, in 2021, CAA, a talent agency founded by Michael Ovitz, transformed their venerable mailroom program to provide more field-relevant business training. See Sun (2021).

8. For example, in 1933, NBC introduced the Page Program, which continues to this day. Pages receive a one-year paid fellowship position and rotate across assignments at NBCUniversal. The program is described as a pathway to an entry-level job and is credited for launching the careers of Regis Philbin, Michael Eisner, and (more recently) Aubrey Plaza, but with an acceptance rate as low as 1.5 percent it is a remarkably competitive program. For more, see Johnson (2011).

9. See Kamenetz (2006).

10. See Frederick (1997:302).

11. As scholars of meritocratic discourse have previously noted (e.g., Banks 2017; Mijs 2016) and consistent with what I show later in the chapter, such discourse often legitimates (and reproduces) forms of social inequality.

12. The people who walked to Brooklyn to fetch cheesecake were not interns but rather members of Da Band, a musical group on season two of the reality television show *Making the Band* (Pearlman et al. 2002) who were hoping to land a record contract. See Donnelly (2019).

13. O'Mahony and Bechky (2006) quoted a film crew intern who complained about doing nothing but assembling fruit baskets but eventually began receiving better assignments.

14. The intern was twenty-three years old and considered this mistreatment part of a larger pattern in which several employees asked her to do inappropriate tasks. Because she had prior interning experience, she understood she needed to start at the bottom. However, she also believed this employee was going too far. She worried that other, less experienced interns would not know this was abnormal treatment, explaining, "It hurts me to know that someone else is going to come here and think it's normal that you treat them this way. So, it's good that I've never been treated this way before, because I know that it's not right. But imagine if it's someone's first [position], like 'Oh, it's normal maybe to treat me like that.'"

15. See Rolston and Herrera (2000).

16. While her analogy may highlight a real problem, it overlooks how schools adjust their curricula as industries transform. Library schools now teach digital archiving, and music business programs try to prepare students for the digital music landscape. Journalism schools face similar problems in trying to prepare students for a mostly digital industry in which print media is rapidly declining and employment is uncertain (see Besbris and Petre 2020). Thus, the rise of music business programs arguably represents an attempt by higher education to prepare students for precarious lives in the music industry.

17. Abby's description of music business curricula is inaccurate and, some would argue, unfair—my interviews with higher education personnel indicate that such programs are constantly shifting and trying to incorporate new and imminent trends—but my fieldwork indicates that her characterization of curricula as at least a step or two behind trends is pervasive among music industry personnel (at least those without a music business degree).

18. Friedman and Laurison (2019) described a similar bias against TV/film degrees among television industry professionals.

19. As Ryan's comment illustrates, expertise involves more than mastering knowledge. Expertise is relational in that it is done (or performed) rather than held, and one's status as an expert is tied to one's social status in the immediate and broader contexts. See Anteby and Holm (2021); Carr (2010); Occhiuto (forthcoming).

20. Nate expresses the commonly held view, consistent with anthropologist Victor Turner's (1969) work on rites of passage, that to attain the "high" (in this case, the position of music industry employee), a neophyte must experience the "low" (as an intern or perhaps an equivalent position).

21. Music business students at one school, for example, must write a pass/fail paper as part of their internship. Students from other programs describe taking part in a seminar related to their internship. While some scholars believe internships represent a promising pedagogical practice (e.g., Bailey et al. 2004), this section focuses on how music industry personnel conceive of internship training and the consequent experience of interns.

22. The use of the term "osmosis" in this context, in a literal sense, is flawed since osmosis typically results in a kind of equivalence, which is not the case between employees and interns. The employees I met during this study did not all equally embrace the idea of osmosis pedagogy—some put more care in onboarding and continuously training interns than others—but overall, this was a widespread justification that I argue helps obscure the exploitation of interns.

23. To get an "add" refers to a radio promotion employee, at a record company or from an outsourced firm, convincing radio station personnel to play certain songs ("add" them to the rotation of songs at the station).

24. Violaine Roussel's (2017:67) talent agency respondents also described the benefits of socialization via overhearing, citing the example of assistants and mailroom trainees hearing how agents build and sustain relationships over the phone. Overhearing offers the opportunity to learn a wide range of knowledge and skills, including the vocabulary of the industry, negotiation tactics, and the navigation of ethical dilemmas.

25. These documents are called marketing plans or digital plans at Indie Distribution but are actually very short summaries of targets at various vendors. For example, under the name of a digital music store, one bullet point might read: "Pitch release for feature on new releases page." The term "marketing plan" is therefore used loosely at Indie Distribution; in the wider business world, such documents are typically longer, more detailed, and consciously strategic.

26. Much like some employees describe trying to make internships less exploitative than what they experienced, some indicate that they try to occasionally or even systematically share industry insights with interns. Hank, my supervisor at Major Records USA, occasionally makes a point of quizzing interns—for example, he asks them how many Spotify "plays" of a song counts for a track sale. However, the point remains that a belief in learning by being in the room is widespread and taking on the role of "teacher" is limited or brief among employees.

4. Laboring to Earn

1. According to sociologist Everett Hughes, the frequently mundane tasks done by some interns, such as stuffing hundreds of packages for mass mailings, reflects a moral division of labor around "dirty work" in which the workers of higher standing take on the most desirable work and push more degrading tasks to those with lower status. Consequently, those doing dirty work may embrace dignifying rationalizations (e.g., "I am doing this for a larger goal") to convince themselves that they are merely *doing* dirty work and that this does not define *them*. See Ashforth and Kreiner (1999); Emerson and Pollner (1976); Hughes (1962).

2. Goffman (1963:3) defined stigma as an "attribute that is deeply discrediting." As a social process, stigma is malleable—what is stigmatizing in one setting or given period is not necessarily always so (Manago, Davis, and Goar 2022). Therefore, there is room to debate whether an intern is always stigmatized, but in contexts such as where and when Elise interned, the experience meets the sociological criteria of stigma. Interns are labeled as different (and lesser) and these differences are negatively stereotyped (e.g., presumed incompetent). Although interning can be a positive step in the process of breaking in, to become an intern exposes the aspirant to experiencing status loss, at least in the status hierarchy of the workplace, since interns are kept at a symbolic distance from "regular" employees. For more on stigma as a social process, see Clair (2018); Link and Phelan (2001); Manago et al. (2022).

3. I use the term "job-seeking intern" more broadly than Job Seeker intern (from chapter 2)—the former refers to an intern who claims to seek employment in the

industry, whereas the latter refers to a *type* of motivation (i.e., an abstraction of the job-seeking motivation distilled into its purest form).

4. Interns who are not primarily interested in getting hired might also use these three strategies (e.g., to deepen their learning), but in this chapter I focus especially on the process of breaking in for job seekers.

5. See Mai (2021); Spence (1973).

6. See Correll, Benard, and Paik (2007); Pedulla (2016).

7. According to the concept of the ideal worker norm, while judgments about who is deemed worthy of employment and advancement rest on seemingly neutral organizational bases—such as the ability to work long hours, productivity, busyness, and the ability to flexibly respond to the unexpected (Kelly et al. 2010)—these judgments are gendered. The assumption that the worker should never deviate from being fully committed to their work is perceived as being, and frequently is, more attainable for men (Acker 1990; Williams 2000). Research since then has found that not only are employers' evaluations of competence and commitment gendered (Rivera 2017), at times women face additional barriers to entry, such as the need to seem "likeable" (Quadlin 2018). Motherhood also negatively impacts perceptions of competence and commitment (Ridgeway and Correll 2004). Even young women who are not mothers but perceived as *potentially* becoming mothers in the future prompt colleagues to question their commitment and competence (Stokes 2017; Thébaud and Taylor 2021). In some instances, men are perceived as less competent than women for some roles, though this is rarely the case for high-status work; a notable exception is fashion modeling, where bookers from agencies see men as less competent than women (Mears 2011:232).

8. Research along these lines demonstrates broad inequalities in perceptions of competence by race, gender, class, and age (Alegria and Banerjee 2024; Ridgeway and Fisk 2012; Rivera and Tilcsik 2016; Roscigno et al. 2007). For more on how these biases are racialized, see Acker (2006); Maume et al. (2014); Moss and Tilly (2001); Ray (2019).

9. For example, according to Blair-Loy and Cech's (2022) study of STEM professors, cultural schemas about commitment (work devotion schema) and competence (schema of scientific excellence) shape workers' experiences and career outcomes; the former contributes to workers interpreting mothers as less committed to their STEM jobs, while the authors link the latter to the devaluation of scientific contributions by women and faculty of color.

10. See Ashcraft (2013); Friedman and Laurison (2019); Luhr (2024); Nichols, Pedulla, and Sheng (2023); Rivera (2015b); Tilly (1998). Also see Grugulis and Stoyanova (2012) on fitting in and social capital. Finally, in cultural industries there are many aspirants who very purposefully curate their personal style (e.g., Mears 2011), but not all aspirants possess the same cultural capital (e.g., the intern who shows up at a record company wearing a suit and tie, therefore not adhering to the "industry cool" code of conduct I discussed in chapter 2).

11. Rao (2020) also extends the ideal worker norm to the realm of job seekers by proposing the "ideal job-seeker norm" as a concept to explain how neoliberal logics permeate the reality of marriage. In this way, Rao shows how married men benefit from more time and resources to search for work than women do.

12. See Lamont et al. (2014) for more on the process of evaluation. Moreover, see Shade and Jacobson (2015:190) for more on how access to internship placements is "classed, raced, and gendered."

13. See Warhurst and Nickson (2001); Williams and Connell (2010). Moreover, the ideal intern norm varies within and across fields. In other, less youth-oriented fields, and industries requiring a graduate degree, the ideal intern may well be older.

14. While some media articles point to the increasingly prevalent practice of doing internships in middle age or later in life (sometimes called a "returnship" if this is meant to reenter the workforce), such articles still suggest these are unusual and therefore potentially challenging arrangements. See Bird (2025); Farnham (2012); Stanton (2016).

15. See Kanter (1977); Luhr (2024); Nelson and Vallas (2021); Nichols et al. (2023); Rivera (2015b).

16. See Negus (1999); Roy and Dowd (2010).

17. For more on how "social capital operates as a gendered resource" (Martin et al. 2023:2) see Luhr (2024); Mickey (2022); Neely (2020). Moreover, prior research shows that identical behaviors by men and women can be evaluated differently. For example, managers value "taking charge" more highly for men than for women workers (see Correll et al. 2020).

18. See Rivera (2015a, 2015b).

19. Sterling and Fernandez (2018) propose that "tryouts" in the form of internships could decrease the gender wage gap in starting salaries since women could prove themselves during the internship and therefore give employers more information to challenge their preexisting assumptions or biases about candidates. However, Sterling and Merluzzi (2019) also express some doubts about the equalizing potential of tryouts, suggesting that internships could diversify applicant pools while employers may opt not to convert those internships into full-time jobs.

20. An ideal intern is, in this context, similar to how Smith and Neuwirth's (2008) study portrays a "good temp"—both groups are low-level temporary workers with at least a bit of skill and a decent work ethic and who require little supervision. A key difference is that contrary to a good temp, an intern rarely stays indefinitely without aspiring to a permanent job.

21. See Jack (2016, 2019); E. Lee (2016); Stuber (2011).

22. On the often class-based sources of cultural capital, and the resulting comfort in interaction with peers and authority figures, see Jack (2016, 2019); Khan (2011); and E. Lee (2016).

23. See Becker (1982); Blair (2001); Grugulis and Stoyanova (2012); Menger (1999).

24. As noted previously, there are other paths to breaking in that put an aspirant in touch with music industry professionals, for example, assuming an active role at a college radio station. However, employees say that unless someone has close friends or family connections to the industry, it is nearly impossible to secure paid employment without doing some type of provisional labor to accrue experience and build industry relationships.

25. Some interns make a strategic choice not to network. One intern at a music PR firm, for example, thought he would develop bonds with music journalists but quickly decided he was not interested in doing PR and opted not to nurture these relationships.

Interns sometimes retroactively criticize their lack of strategic action; particularly among interns who did not gain employment, there is a tendency to self-blame and note how they should have further taken advantage of opportunities to network, for example, by attending company events and mingling with those in attendance.

26. Head interns are not necessarily on a trajectory to a music industry career. When I first met Ben, the head intern in his department at the time was an undergraduate student from an Ivy League university who hoped to attend law school after graduation (which she did, and she never returned to the music industry). She described interning in music as a fun experience she wanted to have before pursuing a law degree—primarily an Enthusiast type of orientation—yet she was poised and professional, projecting a sense of competence and responsibleness. This head intern struck me as adept at building rapport; she was at ease when interacting with new people and finding musical common ground. Toward the beginning of our interview, she turned the spotlight back onto me and asked what kind of music I had been listening to. I talked a bit about obscure 1980s synthesizer-driven music, and though she appeared to know little about this esoteric genre, she skillfully pivoted to discussing Duran Duran, a pop band from that era that incorporated synthesizers.

27. See Kanter (1977); Luhr (2024); Nelson and Vallas (2021); Nichols et al. (2023); Rivera (2015b).

28. Ben's understanding of building relationships as making friends with professional benefits is consistent with accounts from other creative workers, such as comedians (Jeffries 2017) as well as musicians and songwriters (Coulson 2012; Skaggs 2019a), who acknowledge the economic benefits of networking but stress the cooperative (community building) and pleasurable (fun) elements of sociality (see also Cornfield 2015).

29. Following the rise of lawsuits from former unpaid interns, some companies—including major records companies—have attempted to require manager-level employees and higher to oversee interns, rather than assistants. In practice, this does not always work out because it is easy for employees to sidestep this rule.

30. While a minority of interns take part in such arrangements, some people do become "shared interns" who divide their time between the department where they are officially assigned and another department where they aspire to go next. Especially when the workload in the host department is not too onerous, or if an intern can commit to doing additional hours of work, employees express a willingness to split an intern's time. Some employers, especially after an intern's first semester, are open to sharing an intern with another department or even another company—especially a peer company (e.g., two similarly positioned record companies) or a collaborator (e.g., a record company and a PR firm)—in effect to help the intern's career but also to further solidify bonds between employees of the firms. For example, Kevin, then an employee at a small music marketing firm, proudly helped connect interns with prominent record companies that were also clients, thereby helping his most promising aspiring interns break in while also strengthening his employer's bonds with key clients. By helping interns in this way, the host company also further signals its quality as a place to break in, which helps attract future interns.

31. As I discuss in the concluding chapter, the perspective that Nate describes—going out to shows with supervisors or otherwise trying to socialize with employees

after hours—puts some interns in a difficult situation. Several young women who were recent or current interns noted, usually "off the record," that at times they cut short or avoided such social occasions due to concerns about unwanted advances from employees.

32. Joel Podolny (2005:10) refers to the difficulties of newcomers (in relation to established professionals) as one of deference relations where newcomers must prove themselves before garnering the same social respect. He uses the example of golfer Lee Trevino, who allegedly remarked, "When I was a rookie, I told jokes, and no one laughed. After I began winning tournaments, I told the same jokes, and all of a sudden, people thought they were funny."

33. Similarly, Barley and Kunda (2011) showed that freelancers, even highly credentialed and experienced ones, also need to purposely sustain relationships. Godart and Mears (2024) used the case of fashion modeling to show how the "transitory ties" that emerge from brief yet meaningful professional relationships can yield recurrent professional collaborations over time. Finally, although classic research on social networks indicates that dormant or neglected ties lose their value (Burt 1992; Coleman 1990), recent research conducted by Levin, Walter, and Murnighan (2011) suggests that reconnecting with dormant ties can generate benefits similar to those from current ties.

34. Several interns I met similarly expressed a sense of reassurance at having a web of contacts—each of whom had their own networks—they could potentially call on after graduation. Research from the Strategic National Arts Alumni Project (SNAAP) finds that social capital developed during college is associated with a greater likelihood of both breaking into the arts and remaining in the arts years later (Frenette and Dowd 2020; Martin et al. 2023; also see Fine 2017 on "the first network").

35. Interns and employees report some instances when long-term interns received symbolic promotions along the way. One intern at a small music marketing firm was instructed to say she was an employee—for example, in interactions with clients—with the promise that she would soon transition from "fake hired" to "hired" in a matter of weeks (though this never occurred). One intern at a major record company, after multiple semesters of interning, began receiving a weekly stipend of fifty dollars and was told to call himself a "scout," though scouts usually earn more (and he was not, technically, an employee of the company). About the symbolic benefits of the promotion, the intern noted: "This is a business built on image—if people think you're an employee, you're an employee."

36. In Richard Arum and Josipa Roksa's *Aspiring Adults Adrift* (2014), about one-quarter of the sample of nearly one thousand college graduates claimed to have found postgraduation employment via interning, volunteering, or a previous job by either staying in touch or, like Shane, remaining on part-time.

37. While embodying the ideal intern norm and using strategies such as extended investment allow some hopeful job seekers to pass as employees, Bela's experience also illustrates the enduring quality of stigma.

5. Breaking-In Systems in Transition

1. See Perna (2024).
2. See Jack (2019); Jang-Tucci, Hora, and Zhang (2025); Stuber (2011).

3. For more data on this phenomenon among arts graduates, see Frenette et al. (2021). See Wolfgram and Ahrens (2022) for more on doing multiple internships more broadly.

4. A notable exception emerged briefly in 2010 after the US Department of Labor's Wage and Hour Division published the "Fact Sheet #71" statement, as I discussed previously.

5. For example, see Curiale (2010); Gregory (1998); Ortner (1998); Yamada (2002).

6. As of 2011, Perlin suggests that Disney World hosts seven thousand to eight thousand interns per year. According to some sources, while the Disney College Program was on hiatus during the peak of the COVID-19 pandemic, as of 2024 it accepts twelve thousand paid interns out of fifty thousand applications. The interns typically pay Disney to live on-site in conditions resembling college dorms. See "What Is the Disney College Program?" The Best Schools, October 8, 2024, https://thebestschools.org/magazine/disney-college-program/.

7. Intern salaries are now closer to $16 per hour, which is well above the federal minimum wage but close to the typical salary of food service workers. Beyond pay, Perlin (2011b) notes that interns are subject to draconian management practices and do not know in advance which roles they will have. These conditions are consistent with previous experiences of seasonal workers at Disney, often college students themselves; see Van Maanen (1991).

8. See Perlin (2013) for his description of his initial interaction with Glatt.

9. See Yamada (2016:394).

10. See Frenette (2015).

11. See Greenhouse (2013).

12. See Siegemund-Broka (2014).

13. For more on the 2015 decision and its implications, see Perlin (2015); Yamada (2016). For more on the revised "Fact Sheet #71," see Babendir (2018); Greenfield (2018).

14. See Griffee (2013).

15. See Goff (2013); Page (2013); Sheriff (2013); Yamada (2016).

16. See Frenette et al. (2015) for more on the geographical location of arts-related internships in the United States.

17. See Jordan (2017).

18. For more on such a strike across Québec, see Olson (2019).

19. See Kassam (2024).

20. See Sternlicht (2022).

21. See Gurfein (2013).

22. Such an assertion is not without empirical support. See Brook, O'Brien, and Taylor (2020); O'Brien et al. (2016).

23. Some employers are reluctant to work with international students due to potentially more administrative paperwork, whereas school interviewees noted some complexities in terms of work authorization for off-campus internships, which scare off some employers. Also, international students sometimes face more scrutiny in terms of vetting—their internships must align more closely to their major, and some interns are told they must do the internship for credit (i.e., pay tuition and fees), whereas some report reluctance about whether they are allowed to do paid

internships (in case this could be construed by authorities as paid employment). To the chagrin of higher education personnel, many students (not international) side-step official rules and do internships off the books, which means they do not alert the school, pay tuition and fees, and contribute to strong school statistics on internship participation. But doing off-the-books internships is often not an option (or a riskier one if something goes wrong) for international students.

24. The growth of educational institutions offering financial support to unpaid or low-paid interns also exacerbates inequality in that better endowed schools (which already feature more privileged students) can better support student interns.

25. See Frenette et al. (2021).

26. See Acker (2006); Lindemann, Rush, and Tepper (2016).

27. See Frenette et al. (2015); Frenette et al. (2021).

28. For updated accounts on categorization and its power, see Hannan et al. (2019); Lamont (2012). Also see related work by McDonnell, Stoltz, and Taylor (2021) on (re)classification.

29. See Crain, Poster, and Cherry (2016); Hatton (2020, 2025); Ruppel (2024).

30. For more on the history of apprenticeships, internships, and work-based learning more broadly, see Bailey et al. (2004); Frenette (2015); Perlin (2011b).

31. Similarly, Mary Douglas ([1966] 2002) noted how siding with one interpretation reduces ambiguity.

32. See Frenette (2015).

33. See Lawson et al. (2015); Trent (2010).

34. See Frenette et al. (2021); Redden (2018).

35. See Vande Berg (2007) for more about educational concerns regarding study abroad programs.

REFERENCES

Ables, Kelsey. 2023. "Unpaid Internships Have Been Criticized for Years. Why Are They Still Around?" *Washington Post*, June 22. https://www.washingtonpost.com/business/2023/06/22/unpaid-interns-employment/.

Acker, Joan. 1990. "Hierarchies, Jobs, Bodies: A Theory of Gendered Organizations." *Gender & Society* 4(2):139–58.

———. 2006. "Inequality Regimes: Gender, Class, and Race in Organizations." *Gender & Society* 20(4):441–64.

Alegria, Sharla, and Pallavi Banerjee. 2024. "Time Won't Give Me Time: Intersections of Racialized and Gendered Organization of Work in Tech." *Social Problems*: spae047.

Altomonte, Guillermina. 2020. "Exploiting Ambiguity: A Moral Polysemy Approach to Variation in Economic Practices." *American Sociological Review* 85(1):76–105.

Anon. 1959. "The Musical Businessman: Goddard Lieberson." *Time*, March 16. https://content.time.com/time/subscriber/article/0,33009,937031-2,00.html.

Anteby, Michel. 2013. *Manufacturing Morals: The Values of Silence in Business School Education*. University of Chicago Press.

Anteby, Michel, and Audrey L. Holm. 2021. "Translating Expertise Across Work Contexts: US Puppeteers Move from Stage to Screen." *American Sociological Review* 86(2):310–40.

Aoun, Joseph E. 2010. "Protect Unpaid Internships." *Inside Higher Ed*, July 12. https://www.insidehighered.com/views/2010/07/13/protect-unpaid-internships.

Armstrong, Elizabeth A., and Laura T. Hamilton. 2013. *Paying for the Party: How College Maintains Inequality*. Harvard University Press.

Aronowitz, Stanley. 1973. *False Promises: The Shaping of American Working Class Consciousness*. McGraw-Hill.

Arthur, Michael B., and Denise M. Rousseau, eds. 1996. *The Boundaryless Career: A New Employment Principle for a New Organizational Era*. Oxford University Press.

Arum, Richard, and Josipa Roksa. 2014. *Aspiring Adults Adrift: Tentative Transitions of College Graduates*. University of Chicago Press.

Ashcraft, Karen L. 2013. "The Glass Slipper: 'Incorporating' Occupational Identity in Management Studies." *Academy of Management Review* 38(1):6–31.

Ashforth, Blake E., and Glen E. Kreiner. 1999. "'How Can You Do It?': Dirty Work and the Challenge of Constructing a Positive Identity." *Academy of Management Review* 24(3):413–34.

Ashton, Daniel. 2015. "Making Media Workers: Contesting Film and Television Industry Career Pathways." *Television & New Media* 16(3):275–94.

Askin, Noah, and Matthew S. Bothner. 2016. "Status-Aspirational Pricing: The 'Chivas Regal' Strategy in US Higher Education, 2006–2012." *Administrative Science Quarterly* 61(2):217–53.

Ayala-Hurtado, Elena. 2025. "The Expectational Liminality of Insecure College Graduates." *Sociology of Education* 98(1):27–43.

Babendir, Bradley. 2018. "Let Them Eat Experience." *Jacobin*, February 22. https://jacobin.com/2018/02/trump-unpaid-internships-labor-department.

Bailey, Thomas R., Katherine L. Hughes, and David T. Moore. 2004. *Working Knowledge: Work-Based Learning and Education Reform*. Routledge.

Baker, Wayne E., and Robert R. Faulkner. 1991. "Role as Resource in the Hollywood Film Industry." *American Journal of Sociology* 97(2):279–309.

Bandelj, Nina. 2023. "America's Parenting Economy: How the Ideal of Parental Investment Scaffolds Family-Hostile Policy." *Sociological Forum* 38(4): 1349–60.

Banks, Mark. 2007. *The Politics of Cultural Work*. Palgrave Macmillan.

———. 2017. *Creative Justice: Cultural Industries, Work and Inequality*. Rowman & Littlefield.

Barley, Stephen R., and Gideon Kunda. 2001. "Bringing Work Back In." *Organization Science* 12(1):76–95.

———. 2011. *Gurus, Hired Guns, and Warm Bodies: Itinerant Experts in a Knowledge Economy*. Princeton University Press.

Barr, Terri F., and Kevin M. Mcneilly. 2002. "The Value of Students' Classroom Experiences from the Eyes of the Recruiter: Information, Implications, and Recommendations for Marketing Educators." *Journal of Marketing Education* 24(2):168–73.

Bechky, Beth A. 2021. *Blood, Powder, and Residue: How Crime Labs Translate Evidence into Proof*. Princeton University Press.

Beck, Ulrich. 2000. *The Brave New World of Work*. Polity Press.

Becker, Howard S. 1972. "A School Is a Lousy Place to Learn Anything In." *American Behavioral Scientist* 16(1):85–105.

———. 1982. *Art Worlds*. University of California Press.

Becker, Howard S., Blanche Geer, Everett C. Hughes, and Anselm L. Strauss. 1961. *Boys in White: Student Culture in Medical School*. University of Chicago Press.

Benjamin, Walter. [1936] 1969. "The Work of Art in the Age of Mechanical Reproduction." In *Illuminations*, edited by H. Arendt. Translated by H. Zohn. Schocken Books.

Benzecry, Claudio E. 2011. *The Opera Fanatic: Ethnography of an Obsession*. University of Chicago Press.

Berger, Lauren. 2012. *All Work, No Pay: Finding an Internship, Building Your Resume, Making Connections, and Gaining Job Experience*. Ten Speed Press.

Berman, Elizabeth P., and Catherine Paradeise. 2016. "Introduction: The University Under Pressure." *Research in the Sociology of Organizations* 46: 1–22.

Besbris, Max, and Caitlin Petre. 2020. "Professionalizing Contingency: How Journalism Schools Adapt to Deprofessionalization." *Social Forces* 98(4): 1524–47.

Besharov, Marya L., and Wendy K. Smith. 2014. "Multiple Institutional Logics in Organizations: Explaining Their Varied Nature and Implications." *Academy of Management Review* 39(3):364–81.

Bielby, William T., and Denise D. Bielby. 1994. "'All Hits Are Flukes': Institutionalized Decision Making and the Rhetoric of Network Prime-Time Program Development." *American Journal of Sociology* 99(5):1287–1313.

Binder, Jens F., Thom Baguley, Chris Crook, and Felicity Miller. 2015. "The Academic Value of Internships: Benefits Across Disciplines and Student Backgrounds." *Contemporary Educational Psychology* 41:73–82.

Binder, Amy J., Daniel B. Davis, and Nick Bloom. 2016. "Career Funneling: How Elite Students Learn to Define and Desire 'Prestigious' Jobs." *Sociology of Education* 89(1):20–39.

Bird, Beverly. 2025. "How Old Is Too Old to Be an Intern and Is a Returnship Right For You?" *Investopia,* May 27. https://www.investopedia.com/internships-too-old-11731253#toc-challenges-for-older-interns.

Blair, Helen. 2001. "'You're Only as Good as Your Last Job': The Labour Process and Labour Market in the British Film Industry." *Work, Employment and Society* 15(1):149–69.

Blair-Loy, Mary, and Erin Cech. 2022. *Misconceiving Merit: Paradoxes of Excellence and Devotion in Academic Science and Engineering*. University of Chicago Press.

Blumer, Herbert. 1969. *Symbolic Interactionism: Perspective and Method*. University of California Press.

Bok, Derek. 2003. *Universities in the Marketplace: The Commercialization of Higher Education*. Princeton University Press.

Boltanski, Luc, and Eve Chiapello. 2006. "The New Spirit of Capitalism." *International Journal of Politics, Culture, and Society* 18(3):161–88.

Bourdieu, Pierre. 1993. *The Field of Cultural Production: Essays on Art and Literature*. Columbia University Press.

Boyce, Anthony S., Ann Marie Ryan, Anna L. Imus, and Frederick P. Morgeson. 2007. "'Temporary Worker, Permanent Loser?' A Model of the Stigmatization of Temporary Workers." *Journal of Management* 33(1):5–29.

Brankovic, Jelena, Julian Hamann, and Leopold Ringel. 2023. "The Institutionalization of Rankings in Higher Education: Continuities, Interdependencies, Engagement." *Higher Education* 86(4):719–31.

Brint, Steven. 2002. "The Rise of the 'Practical Arts.'" In *The Future of the City of Intellect: The Changing American University*, edited by S. Brint. Stanford University Press.

Brint, Steven, Mark Riddle, Lori Turk-Bicakci, and Charles S. Levy. 2005. "From the Liberal to the Practical Arts in American Colleges and Universities: Organizational Analysis and Curricular Change." *Journal of Higher Education* 76(2):151–80.

Brook, Orian, Dave O'Brien, and Mark Taylor. 2020. *Culture Is Bad for You*. Manchester University Press.

Brooks, David. 2025. "The Six Principles of Stupidity." *New York Times,* January 30. https://www.nytimes.com/2025/01/30/opinion/trump-executive-orders.html.

Brooks, Robert A. 2011. *Cheaper by the Hour: Temporary Lawyers and the Deprofessionalization of the Law*. Temple University Press.

Brown, Anna. 2018. "Most Americans Say Higher Ed Is Heading in Wrong Direction, but Partisans Disagree on Why." Pew Research Center, July 26. https://pewrsr.ch/2mHHHS0.

Burt, Ronald S. 1992. *Structural Holes: The Social Structure of Competition*. Harvard University Press.

Cachero, Paulina. 2022. "Interns Are Making Over $16,000 a Month as Wall Street Talent Wars Heat Up." *Bloomberg*, April 14. https://www.bloomberg.com/news/articles/2022-04-14/how-much-are-wall-street-interns-paid-some-make-over-16-000-a-month?embedded-checkout=true.

Calarco, Jessica M. 2014. "Coached for the Classroom: Parents' Cultural Transmission and Children's Reproduction of Educational Inequalities." *American Sociological Review* 79(5):1016–37.

Cappelli, Peter H. 1999. *The New Deal at Work: Managing the Market-Driven Workforce*. Harvard Business School Press.

———. 2015. "Skill Gaps, Skill Shortages, and Skill Mismatches: Evidence and Arguments for the United States." *ILR Review* 68(2):251–90.

Carr, E. Summerson. 2010. "Enactments of Expertise." *Annual Review of Anthropology* 39:17–32.

Caves, Richard E. 2000. *Creative Industries: Contracts Between Art and Commerce*. Harvard University Press.

CBC News. 2013. "Unpaid Bus Person Internship Offered at Vancouver Hotel." *CBC*, September 12. https://www.cbc.ca/news/canada/british-columbia/unpaid-bus-person-internship-offered-at-vancouver-hotel-1.1705150.

Cech, Erin A. 2021. *The Trouble with Passion: How Searching for Fulfillment at Work Fosters Inequality*. University of California Press.

Cerullo, Megan. 2021. "These Companies Pay Interns More than $8,000 a Month." *CBS News*, April 14. https://www.cbsnews.com/news/tech-finance-interns-salary-100000/.

Chan, Jenny, Mark Selden, and Ngai Pun. 2020. *Dying for an iPhone: Apple, Foxconn, and the Lives of China's Workers*. Haymarket Books.

Chen, Victor T. 2015. *Cut Loose: Jobless and Hopeless in an Unfair Economy*. University of California Press.

Childress, Clayton. 2017. *Under the Cover: The Creation, Production, and Reception of a Novel*. Princeton University Press.

Childress, Clayton, and Alison Gerber. 2015. "The MFA in Creative Writing: The Uses of a 'Useless' Credential." *Professions and Professionalism* 5(2):1–16.

Chinoy, Ely. 1955. *Automobile Workers and the American Dream*. Doubleday & Company.

Chu, James. 2021. "Cameras of Merit or Engines of Inequality? College Ranking Systems and the Enrollment of Disadvantaged Students." *American Journal of Sociology* 126(6):1307–46.

Clair, Matthew. 2018. "Stigma." In *Core Concepts in Sociology*, edited by J. M. Ryan. Wiley-Blackwell.

Cohn, Scott. 2010. "The Debt That Won't Go Away." *CNBC*, December 20. http://www.cnbc.com/id/40680905.

Coleman, James S. 1990. *Foundations of Social Theory*. Harvard University Press.

Collins, Randall. 2002. "Credential Inflation and the Future of Universities." In *The Future of the City of Intellect: The Changing American University*, edited by S. Brint. Stanford University Press.

Collinson, David L. 1992. *Managing the Shopfloor: Subjectivity, Masculinity and Workplace Culture*. Walter de Gruyter.

Colomy, Paul, and J. David Brown. 1995. "Elaboration, Revision, Polemic, and Progress in the Second Chicago School." In *A Second Chicago School? The Development of a Postwar Sociology*, edited by G. A. Fine. University of Chicago Press.

Corbin, Juliet, and Anselm Strauss. 2015. *Basics of Qualitative Research: Techniques and Procedures for Developing Grounded Theory*. 4th ed. Sage.

Cornfield, Daniel B. 2015. *Beyond the Beat: Musicians Building Community in Nashville*. Princeton University Press.

Correll, Shelley J., Stephen Benard, and In Paik. 2007. "Getting a Job: Is There a Motherhood Penalty?" *American Journal of Sociology* 112(5):1297–1339.

Correll, Shelley J., Katherine R. Weisshaar, Alison T. Wynn, and JoAnne D. Wehner. 2020. "Inside the Black Box of Organizational Life: The Gendered Language of Performance Assessment." *American Sociological Review* 85(6):1022–50.

Cottom, Tressie McMillan. 2017. *Lower Ed: The Troubling Rise of For-Profit Colleges in the New Economy*. The New Press.

Coulson, Susan. 2012. "Collaborating in a Competitive World: Musicians' Working Lives and Understandings of Entrepreneurship." *Work, Employment and Society* 26(2):246–61.

Crain, Marion G., Winifred R. Poster, and Miriam A. Cherry, eds. 2016. *Invisible Labor: Hidden Work in the Contemporary World*. University of California Press.

Cressey, Paul G. 1932. *The Taxi-Dance Hall: A Sociological Study of Commercialized Recreation and City Life*. University of Chicago Press.

Curiale, Jessica L. 2010. "America's New Glass Ceiling: Unpaid Internships, the Fair Labor Standards Act, and the Urgent Need for Change." *Hastings Law Journal* 61:1531.

Dalton, Melville. 1959. *Men Who Manage: Fusions of Feeling and Theory in Administration*. John Wiley & Sons Inc.

Damaske, Sarah. 2009. "Brown Suits Need Not Apply: The Intersection of Race, Gender, and Class in Institutional Network Building." *Sociological Forum* 24(2):402–24.

Davis, Daniel, and Amy Binder. 2016. "Selling Students: The Rise of Corporate Partnership Programs in University Career Centers." *Research in the Sociology of Organizations* 46:395–422.

Day, Matt, and Debby Wu. 2019. "Chinese Foxconn Factory Making Amazon Gear Misused Teenage Interns." *Los Angeles Times*, August 9. https://www.latimes.com/business/story/2019-08-09/foxconn-factory-china-making-amazon-gear-misused-temp-workers-and-teenage-interns.

Deener, Andrew. 2017. "The Uses of Ambiguity in Sociological Theorizing: Three Ethnographic Approaches." *Sociological Theory* 35(4):359–79.

Denhart, Chris. 2013. "How the $1.2 Trillion College Debt Crisis Is Crippling Students, Parents and the Economy." *Forbes*, August 7. http://www.forbes.com/sites

/specialfeatures/2013/08/07/how-the-college-debt-is-crippling-students-parents-and-the-economy/.

DePalma, Lindsay J. 2021. "The Passion Paradigm: Professional Adherence to and Consequences of the Ideology of 'Do What You Love.'" *Sociological Forum* 36(1):134–58.

de Peuter, Greig, Nicole Cohen, and Enda Brophy. 2012. "Interns Unite! (You Have Nothing to Lose—Literally)." *Briarpatch*, November/December, 8–12.

Divine, Richard, Robert Miller, and J. Holton Wilson. 2006. "Analysis of Student Performance in an Internship Program in a US University." *International Journal of Quality and Productivity Management* 6(1):1–14.

Divine, Richard, Robert Miller, J. Holton Wilson, and JoAnn Linrud. 2008. "Key Philosophical Decisions to Consider When Designing an Internship Program." *Journal of Management and Marketing Research* 2(1):1–8.

Donnelly, Matthew S. 2019. "#TBT: That Time 'Making The Band' Served a Giant Slice of Humble Pie." *MTV*. https://www.mtv.com/news/b470x3/making-the-band-juniors-cheesecake-tbt.

Douglas, Mary. [1966] 2002. *Purity and Danger: An Analysis of Concepts of Pollution and Taboo*. Routledge.

Dowd, Timothy J. 2006. "From 78s to MP3s: The Embedded Impact of Technology in the Market for Prerecorded Music." In *The Business of Culture: Strategic Perspectives on Entertainment and Media*, edited by J. Lampel, J. Shamsie, and T. K. Lant. Psychology Press.

Dowd, Timothy J., and Diogo L. Pinheiro. 2013. "The Ties Among the Notes: The Social Capital of Jazz Musicians in Three Metro Areas." *Work and Occupations* 40(4):431–64.

Drucker, Peter F. [1989] 2005. "Sell the Mailroom." *Wall Street Journal*, November 15. https://www.wsj.com/articles/SB113202230063197204.

Duffy, Brooke E. 2017. *(Not) Getting Paid to Do What You Love: Gender, Social Media, and Aspirational Work*. Yale University Press.

Eaton, Charlie, and Mitchell L. Stevens. 2020. "Universities as Peculiar Organizations." *Sociology Compass* 14(3):127–68.

Edwards, Kathryn A., and Alexander Hertel-Fernandez. 2010. "Not-So-Equal Protection—Reforming the Regulation of Student Internships." Economic Policy Institute.

Edwards, Mark. 2013. "Disconnected Youth: A Challenge for Our Country, But One We Can Tackle." *Huffington Post*, November 5. http://www.huffingtonpost.com/mark-edwards/disconnected-youth-a-chal_b_4182794.html.

Einstein, Mara. 2015. "Nothing for Money and Your Work for Free: Internships and the Marketing of Higher Education." *tripleC: Communication, Capitalism & Critique* 13(2):471–85.

Emerson, Robert M., Rachel I. Fretz, and Linda L. Shaw. 1995. *Writing Ethnographic Fieldnotes*. University of Chicago Press.

Emerson, Robert M., and Melvin Pollner. 1976. "Dirty Work Designations: Their Features and Consequences in a Psychiatric Setting." *Social Problems* 23(3):243–54.

Emirbayer, Mustafa, and Ann Mische. 1998. "What Is Agency?" *American Journal of Sociology* 103(4):962–1023.

Epstein, Cynthia F., Carroll Seron, Bonnie Oglensky, and Robert Sauté. 1999. *The Part-Time Paradox: Time Norms, Professional Life, Family and Gender*. Routledge.

Espeland, Wendy N., and Michael Sauder. 2007. "Rankings and Reactivity: How Public Measures Recreate Social Worlds." *American Journal of Sociology* 113(1):1–40.

Fair Labor Standards Act. 29 USC Sec. 203.

Farnham, Alan. 2012. "And Now, the 50-Year-Old Intern." *ABC News*, April 2. https://abcnews.go.com/blogs/business/2012/04/and-now-the-50-year-old-intern/.

———. 2013. "Don't Work So Hard, Employers Tell Interns." *ABC News*, November 3. https://abcnews.go.com/Business/work-hard-employers-interns/story?id=20760559.

Faulkner, Robert R. 1974. "Coming of Age in Organizations: A Comparative Study of Career Contingencies and Adult Socialization." *Sociology of Work and Occupations* 1(2):131–73.

———. 1983. *Music on Demand: Composers and Careers in the Hollywood Film Industry*. Transaction Publishers.

Fine, Gary A. 2017. "A Matter of Degree: Negotiating Art and Commerce in MFA Education." *American Behavioral Scientist* 61(12):1463–86.

Fischer, Karin. 2013. "The Employment Mismatch." *Chronicle of Higher Education*, March 4. https://www.chronicle.com/article/the-employment-mismatch/.

Ford, Rachel. 2021. "No Money, All Problems? A Review of Unpaid Internship Standards in the US." *University of Cincinnati Law Review*, May 10. https://uclawreview.org/2021/05/10/no-money-all-problems-a-review-of-unpaid-internship-standards-in-the-u-s/.

Fox, Emily J. 2014. "Unpaid Interns Not Protected from Sexual Harassment." *CNN Money*, January 25. https://money.cnn.com/2013/10/09/news/economy/unpaid-intern-sexual-harassment/.

Frederick, Jim. 1997. "Internment Camp: The Intern Economy and the Culture Trust." *The Baffler* (9):51–58.

Frenette, Alexandre. 2015. "From Apprenticeship to Internship: The Social and Legal Antecedents of the Intern Economy." *tripleC: Communication, Capitalism & Critique* 13(2):351–60.

———. 2016. "'Working at the Candy Factory': The Limits of Nonmonetary Rewards in Record Industry Careers." In *The Production and Consumption of Music in the Digital Age*, edited by B. J. Hracs, M. Seman, and T. E. Virani. Routledge.

———. 2019. "Leveraging Youth: Overcoming Intergenerational Tensions in Creative Production." *Social Psychology Quarterly* 82(4):386–406.

Frenette, Alexandre, Amber D. Dumford, Angie L. Miller, and Steven J. Tepper. 2015. *The Internship Divide: The Promise and Challenges of Internships in the Arts. SNAAP Special Report*. Indiana University and Arizona State University, Strategic National Arts Alumni Project.

Frenette, Alexandre, and Timothy J. Dowd, with Rachel Skaggs and Trent Ryan. 2020. *Careers in the Arts: Who Stays and Who Leaves? SNAAP Special Report*. Indiana University, Strategic National Arts Alumni Project.

Frenette, Alexandre, Gillian Gualtieri, and Megan Robinson. 2021. *Growing Divides: Historical and Emerging Inequalities in Arts Internships. SNAAP Special Report.* Indiana University, Strategic National Arts Alumni Project.

Friedman, Sam, and Daniel Laurison. 2019. *The Class Ceiling: Why It Pays to Be Privileged.* Policy Press.

Gable, Rachel. 2021. *The Hidden Curriculum: First Generation Students at Legacy Universities.* Princeton University Press.

Gani, Aisha. 2016. "Trump Summer Internship Asks for $100,000 on Charity Auction Website." *The Guardian,* April 22. https://www.theguardian.com/us-news/2016/apr/22/trump-organization-summer-internship-auction-charitybuzz.

Geiger, Roger L. 2019. *American Higher Education Since World War II: A History.* Princeton University Press.

Gerber, Alison. 2017. *The Work of Art: Value in Creative Careers.* Stanford University Press.

Gerken, Maike, Bart Rienties, Bas Giesbers, and Karen D. Könings. 2012. "Enhancing the Academic Internship Learning Experience for Business Education—A Critical Review and Future Directions." In *Learning at the Crossroads of Theory and Practice: Research on Innovative Learning Practices,* edited by P. Van den Bossche, W. H. Gijselaers, and R. G. Milter. Springer Netherlands.

Gershon, Ilana. 2017. *Down and Out in the New Economy: How People Find (or Don't Find) Work Today.* University of Chicago Press.

Giomboni, Joseph R. 2024. "Early Career Workers Granted Creative Autonomy: Agency Shifts Intern Debate Towards Industry Expectations." *Journal of Education and Work* 37(1–4):292–308.

Glaeser, Edward L. 2013. "High Value in Unpaid Internships." *Boston Globe,* October 30. https://www.bostonglobe.com/opinion/2013/10/30/unpaid-internships-unpopular-solution-real-problem/KqHbPLxfgdjuhcVN0xL6XJ/story.html?s_campaign=sm_tw.

Godart, Frédéric, and Ashley Mears. 2024. "Transitory Ties: A Network Ecology Perspective on Job Opportunities in Fashion Modeling." *Social Networks* 77:129–38.

Goff, Keli. 2013. "Sheryl Sandberg 'Leans In' to Another Controversy." *Washington Post,* August 14. http://www.washingtonpost.com/blogs/she-the-people/wp/2013/08/14/sheryl-sandberg-leans-in-to-another-controversy/.

Goffman, Erving. 1956. "The Nature of Deference and Demeanor." *American Anthropologist* 58(3):473–502.

———. 1959. *The Presentation of Self in Everyday Life.* Anchor Books.

———. 1961a. *Asylums.* Anchor Books.

———. 1961b. *Encounters: Two Studies in the Sociology of Interaction.* Bobbs-Merrill.

———. 1963. *Stigma: Notes on the Management of Spoiled Identity.* Simon & Schuster.

Granovetter, Mark. [1974] 1995. *Getting a Job: A Study of Contacts and Careers.* 2nd ed. University of Chicago Press.

Grant-Smith, Deanna, and Paula McDonald. 2018. "Ubiquitous Yet Ambiguous: An Integrative Review of Unpaid Work." *International Journal of Management Reviews* 20(2):559–78.

Gray, Kevin. 2021. "Trends in One-Year, Five-Year Intern Retention Rates." National Association of Colleges and Employers, June 9. https://www.naceweb.org/talent-acquisition/trends-and-predictions/trends-in-one-year-five-year-intern-retention-rates/.

Grazian, David. 2003. *Blue Chicago: The Search for Authenticity in Urban Blues Clubs.* University of Chicago Press.

Greenhouse, Steven. 2010. "The Unpaid Intern, Legal or Not." *New York Times,* April 2. http://www.nytimes.com/2010/04/03/business/03intern.html?ref=stevengreenhouse.

———. 2013. "Judge Rules That Movie Studio Should Have Been Paying Interns." *New York Times,* June 11. http://www.nytimes.com/2013/06/12/business/judge-rules-for-interns-who-sued-fox-searchlight.html?_r=1&.

Greenfield, Rebecca. 2018. "Unpaid Internships Are Back with the Labor Department's Blessing." *Bloomberg,* January 18. https://www.bloomberg.com/news/articles/2018-01-10/unpaid-internships-are-back-with-the-labor-department-s-blessing.

Gregory, David L. 1998. "The Problematic Employment Dynamics of Student Internships." *Notre Dame Journal of Law, Ethics and Public Policy* 12:227–64.

Griffee, Susannah. 2013. "Students Fight Back Against Illegal Unpaid Internships." *USA Today,* May 9. https://www.usatoday.com/story/news/nation/2013/05/09/students-fight-unpaid-internships/2145033/.

Grindstaff, Laura. 2002. *The Money Shot: Trash, Class, and the Making of TV Talk Shows.* University of Chicago Press.

Grugulis, Irena, and Dimitrinka Stoyanova. 2012. "Social Capital and Networks in Film and TV: Jobs for the Boys?" *Organization Studies* 33(10):1311–31.

Gualtieri, Gillian. 2020. "Symbolic Compliance and Student Concerns: Legal Endogeneity and Title IX at American Colleges and Universities." *Sociological Forum* 35(1):207–28.

Guarise, Desalina, and James Kostenblatt. 2018. "Unpaid Internships and the Career Success of Liberal Arts Graduates." National Association of Colleges and Employers. https://www.naceweb.org/jobmarket/internships/unpaid-internships-and-the-career-success-of-liberal-arts-graduates/.

Guhin, Jeffrey, Jessica M. Calarco, and Cynthia Miller-Idriss. 2021. "Whatever Happened to Socialization?" *Annual Review of Sociology* 47:109–29.

Gurfein, Laura. 2013. "How Ending Condé Nast's Internship Program Will Affect Students." *Racked,* November 15. http://ny.racked.com/archives/2013/11/15/how_ending_conde_nasts_internship_program_affects_nyc_students.php.

Hallett, Tim, and Marc J. Ventresca. 2006. "Inhabited Institutions: Social Interactions and Organizational Forms in Gouldner's Patterns of Industrial Bureaucracy." *Theory and Society* 35(2):213–36.

Halpin, Brian W., and Vicki Smith. 2017. "Employment Management Work: A Case Study and Theoretical Framework." *Work and Occupations* 44(4):339–75.

Hamilton, Laura T. 2016. *Parenting to a Degree: How Family Matters for College Women's Success.* University of Chicago Press.

Hamilton, Laura, Josipa Roksa, and Kelly Nielsen. 2018. "Providing a 'Leg Up': Parental Involvement and Opportunity Hoarding in College." *Sociology of Education* 91(2):111–31.

Hannan, Michael T., Gaël Le Mens, Greta Hsu, Balázs Kovács, Giacomo Negro, László Pólos, Elizabeth Pontikes, and Amanda J. Sharkey. 2019. *Concepts and Categories: Foundations for Sociological and Cultural Analysis*. Columbia University Press.

Harris, T. George. 1993. "The Post-Capitalist Executive: An Interview with Peter F. Drucker." *Harvard Business Review* 71(3):114–22.

Harrison, Reema, Lois Meyer, Patrick Rawstorne, Husna Razee, Upma Chitkara, Steven Mears, and Chinthaka Balasooriya. 2022. "Evaluating and Enhancing Quality in Higher Education Teaching Practice: A Meta-Review." *Studies in Higher Education* 47(1):80–96.

Hartley, Matthew, and Christopher C. Morphew. 2008. "What's Being Sold and to What End? A Content Analysis of College Viewbooks." *Journal of Higher Education* 79(6):671–91.

Hatton, Erin. 2011. *The Temp Economy: From Kelly Girls to Permatemps in Postwar America*. Temple University Press.

———. 2020. *Coerced: Work Under Threat of Punishment*. University of California Press.

———. 2025. "Working for Rehab: Labor Expropriation as Treatment for Addiction." *Work and Occupations* 52(3):388–416.

Hermanowicz, Joseph C. 1998. *The Stars Are Not Enough: Scientists—Their Passions and Professions*. University of Chicago Press.

Hesmondhalgh, David, and Sarah Baker. 2011. *Creative Labour: Media Work in Three Cultural Industries*. Routledge.

Hipple, Steven F. 2001. "Contingent Work in the Late-1990s." *Monthly Labor Review* 124:3–27.

Hirsch, Paul M. 1972. "Processing Fads and Fashions: An Organization-Set Analysis of Cultural Industry Systems." *American Journal of Sociology* 77(4):639–59.

Ho, Karen. 2009. *Liquidated: An Ethnography of Wall Street*. Duke University Press.

Hoffman, Meredith. 2013. "Roberta's Pizza Advertises for Unpaid Intern, Upsets Neighborhood." *DNAinfo New York*, April 8. https://www.dnainfo.com/new-york/20130408/bushwick/doh-robertas-pizza-advertises-for-unpaid-intern-upsets-neighborhood/.

Hollister, Matissa. 2011. "Employment Stability in the US Labor Market: Rhetoric Versus Reality." *Annual Review of Sociology* 37:305–24.

Hora, Matthew T. 2022. "Unpaid Internships & Inequality: A Review of the Data and Recommendations for Research, Policy and Practice." Center for Research on College-Workforce Transitions, University of Wisconsin-Madison. https://ccwt.wisc.edu/wpcontent/uploads/2022/04/CCWT _Policy-Brief-2_Unpaid-Internships-and-Inequality-1.pdf.

Hora, Matthew T., Matthew Wolfgram, Zi Chen, and Changhee Lee. 2021. "Closing the Doors of Opportunity: A Field Theoretic Analysis of the Prevalence and Nature of Obstacles to College Internships." *Teachers College Record* 123(12):180–210.

Horowitz, Jonathan. 2018. "Relative Education and the Advantage of a College Degree." *American Sociological Review* 83(4):771–801.

Hout, Michael. 2012. "Social and Economic Returns to College Education in the United States." *Annual Review of Sociology* 38:379–400.

Hracs, Brian J. 2012. "A Creative Industry in Transition: The Rise of Digitally Driven Independent Music Production." *Growth and Change* 43(3):442–61.

Hughes, Everett C. 1956. "Social Role and the Division of Labor." *Midwest Sociologist* 18(2):3–7.

———. 1958. *Men and Their Work*. Free Press.

———. 1962. "Good People and Dirty Work." *Social Problems* 10(1):3–11.

Hunt, Wil, and Peter Scott. 2023. "Stepping Stones or Trapdoors? Paid and Unpaid Graduate Internships in the Creative Sector." *British Journal of Sociology of Education* 44(4):585–605.

Ibarra, Herminia, and Otilia Obodaru. 2016. "Betwixt and Between Identities: Liminal Experience in Contemporary Careers." *Research in Organizational Behavior* 36:47–64.

Jack, Anthony A. 2016. "(No) Harm in Asking: Class, Acquired Cultural Capital, and Academic Engagement at an Elite University." *Sociology of Education* 89(1):1–19.

———. 2019. *The Privileged Poor: How Elite Colleges Are Failing Disadvantaged Students*. Harvard University Press.

Jacobson, Jenna, and Leslie R. Shade. 2018. "Stringtern: Springboarding or Stringing Along Young Interns' Careers?" *Journal of Education and Work* 31(3):320–37.

Jacoby, Sanford M. 1985. *Employing Bureaucracy: Managers, Unions, and the Transformation of Work in the 20th Century*. Columbia University Press.

Jang-Tucci, Kyoungjin, Matthew T. Hora, and Jiahong Zhang. 2025. "Gatekeeping at Work: A Multi-dimensional Analysis of Student, Institutional, and Employer Characteristics Associated with Unpaid Internships." *Higher Education* 89(4):907–36.

Jeffries, Michael P. 2017. *Behind the Laughs: Community and Inequality in Comedy*. Stanford University Press.

Johnson, Jenna. 2011. "Life of an NBC Page Isn't Quite Like '30 Rock.'" *Washington Post*, May 5. https://www.washingtonpost.com/blogs/campus-overload/post/life-of-an-nbc-page-isnt-quite-like-30-rock/2011/05/11/AFiTX00G_blog.html.

Jones, Candace. 1996. "Careers in Project Networks: The Case of the Film Industry." In *The Boundaryless Career: A New Employment Principle for a New Organizational Era*, edited by M. B. Arthur and D. M. Rousseau. Oxford University Press.

Jones, James R. 2024. *The Last Plantation: Racism and Resistance in the Halls of Congress*. Princeton University Press.

Jordan, Brandon. 2017. "Why Doesn't the United Nations Pay Its Interns?" *The Nation*, March 10. https://www.thenation.com/article/archive/why-doesnt-the-united-nations-pay-its-interns/.

Kalleberg, Arne L. 2009. "Precarious Work, Insecure Workers: Employment Relations in Transition." *American Sociological Review* 74(1):1–22.

———. 2011. *Good Jobs, Bad Jobs: The Rise of Polarized and Precarious Employment Systems in the United States, 1970s–2000s*. Russell Sage Foundation.

Kamenetz, Anya. 2006. "Take This Internship and Shove It." *New York Times*, May 30. https://www.nytimes.com/2006/05/30/opinion/30kamenetz.html#:~:text=Instead%20of%20starting%20out%20in,least%20one%20internship%20before%20graduating.

Kanter, Rosabeth M. 1977. *Men and Women of the Corporation*. Basic Books.

Kassam, Ashifa. 2024. "'Ramen Noodles Budget:' EU Moves to End Exploitation of Unpaid Internships." *The Guardian*, January 2. https://www.theguardian.com/world/2024/jan/02/ramen-noodles-budget-eu-moves-to-end-exploitation-of-unpaid-internships.

Kasperkevic, Jana. 2013. "The Millennials' Failure to Launch: Searching the Jobs Report for Answers." *The Guardian*, October 23. http://www.theguardian.com/money/2013/oct/23/young-people-unemployment-jobs-report-answers?INTCMP=ILCNETTXT3487.

Kellogg, Katherine C. 2011. *Challenging Operations: Medical Reform and Resistance in Surgery*. University of Chicago Press.

Kelly, Erin L., Samantha K. Ammons, Kelly Chermack, and Phyllis Moen. 2010. "Gendered Challenge, Gendered Response: Confronting the Ideal Worker Norm in a White-Collar Organization." *Gender & Society* 24(3):281–303.

Khan, Shamus. 2011. *Privilege: The Making of an Adolescent Elite at St. Paul's School*. Princeton University Press.

Klein, Naomi. 2000. *No Logo: Taking Aim at the Brand Bullies*. Taylor & Francis.

Kraatz, Matthew S., and Emily S. Block. 2008. "Organizational Implications of Institutional Pluralism." In *The SAGE Handbook of Organizational Institutionalism*, edited by R. Greenwood, C. Oliver, K. Sahlin, and R. Suddaby. Sage Publications.

Kuehn, Kathleen, and Thomas F. Corrigan. 2013. "Hope Labor: The Role of Employment Prospects in Online Social Production." *Political Economy of Communication* 1(1):9–25.

Kuh, George D., Jillian Kinzie, John H. Schuh, and Elizabeth J. Whitt. 2010. *Student Success in College: Creating Conditions That Matter*. John Wiley & Sons.

Kunda, Gideon. 1992. *Engineering Culture: Control and Commitment in a High-Tech Corporation*. Temple University Press.

Lamont, Michèle. 2012. "Toward a Comparative Sociology of Valuation and Evaluation." *Annual Review of Sociology* 38:201–21.

Lamont, Michèle, Stefan Beljean, and Matthew Clair. 2014. "What Is Missing? Cultural Processes and Causal Pathways to Inequality." *Socio-Economic Review* 12(3):573–608.

LaRocca, James J. 2006. "Lowery v. Klemm: A Failed Attempt at Providing Unpaid Interns and Volunteers with Adequate Employment Protections." *Boston University Public Interest Law Journal* 16:131–44.

Lave, Jean. 1996. "Teaching, as Learning, in Practice." *Mind, Culture, and Activity* 3:149–64.

Lave, Jean, and Etienne Wenger. 1991. *Situated Learning: Legitimate Peripheral Participation*. Cambridge University Press.

Lawrence, T. E. 1955. *The Mint*. Jonathan Cape Ltd.

Lawson, Tony, Melek Çakmak, Müge Gündüz, and Hugh Busher. 2015. "Research on Teaching Practicum—A Systematic Review." *European Journal of Teacher Education* 38(3):392–407.

Lee, Elizabeth M. 2016. *Class and Campus Life: Managing and Experiencing Inequality at an Elite College*. Cornell University Press.

Lee, Jooyoung. 2016. *Blowin' Up: Rap Dreams in South Central*. University of Chicago Press.

Leschziner, Vanina. 2015. *At the Chef's Table: Culinary Creativity in Elite Restaurants*. Stanford University Press.

Levin, Daniel Z., Jorge Walter, and J. Keith Murnighan. 2011. "Dormant Ties: The Value of Reconnecting." *Organization Science* 22(4):923–39.

Levine, Donald N. 1985. *The Flight from Ambiguity: Essays in Social and Cultural Theory*. University of Chicago Press.

Lieber, Ron. 2022. "Why We Still Haven't Solved the Unpaid Internship Problem." *New York Times*, June 11. https://www.nytimes.com/2022/06/11/your-money/unpaid-internships.html.

Liles, Kevin. 2005. *Make It Happen: The Hip-Hop Generation Guide to Success*. Atria Books.

Lin, Nan. 1999. "Social Networks and Status Attainment." *Annual Review of Sociology* 25:467–87.

Lindemann, Danielle J., Carly A. Rush, and Steven J. Tepper. 2016. "An Asymmetrical Portrait: Exploring Gendered Income Inequality in the Arts." *Social Currents* 3(4):332–48.

Lingo, Elizabeth Long, and Siobhán O'Mahony. 2010. "Nexus Work: Brokerage on Creative Projects." *Administrative Science Quarterly* 55(1):47–81.

Lingo, Elizabeth Long, and Steven J. Tepper. 2013. "Looking Back, Looking Forward: Arts-Based Careers and Creative Work." *Work and Occupations* 40(4):337–63.

Link, Bruce G., and Jo C. Phelan. 2001. "Conceptualizing Stigma." *Annual Review of Sociology* 27(1):363–85.

Lipka, Sara. 2010. "Leave Internships to Us, College Leaders Tell Feds." *Chronicle of Higher Education*, April 29. https://www.chronicle.com/article/leave-internships-to-us-college-leaders-tell-feds/.

Liu, Jennifer. 2019. "Nearly Half of Workers Have Made a Dramatic Career Switch, and This Is the Average Age They Do It." *CNBC*, October 31. https://www.cnbc.com/2019/10/31/indeed-nearly-half-of-workers-have-made-a-dramatic-career-switch.html.

Lloyd, Richard. 2006. *Neo-Bohemia: Art and Commerce in the Postindustrial City*. Routledge.

Lucas, Samuel R. 2001. "Effectively Maintained Inequality: Education Transitions, Track Mobility, and Social Background Effects." *American Journal of Sociology* 106(6):1642–90.

Luecking, Richard G., and Ellen S. Fabian. 2000. "Paid Internships and Employment Success for Youth in Transition." *Career Development for Exceptional Individuals* 23(2):205–21.

Lufkin, Bryan. 2022. "The 'Top-Talent' Interns Taking Home Sky-High Wages." *BBC*, May 3. https://www.bbc.com/worklife/article/20220428-the-top-talent-interns-taking-home-sky-high-wages.

Luhr, Sigrid W. 2024. "Engineering Inequality: Informal Coaching, Glass Walls, and Social Closure in Silicon Valley." *American Journal of Sociology* 129(5):1409–46.

Mai, Quan D. 2021. "Unclear Signals, Uncertain Prospects: The Labor Market Consequences of Freelancing in the New Economy." *Social Forces* 99(3):895–920.

Manago, Bianca, Jenny L. Davis, and Carla Goar. 2022. "The Stigma Discourse-Value Framework." *Comparative Sociology* 21(3):275–99.

Marsden, Peter V., and Karen E. Campbell. 1990. "Recruitment and Selection Processes: The Organizational Side of Job Searches." In *Social Mobility and Social Structure*, edited by R. L. Breiger. Cambridge University Press.

Martin, Joanne. 1992. *Cultures in Organizations: Three Perspectives*. Oxford University Press.

Martin, Nathan D. 2012. "The Privilege of Ease: Social Class and Campus Life at Highly Selective, Private Universities." *Research in Higher Education* 53:426–52.

Martin, Nathan D., Alexandre Frenette, and Gillian Gualtieri. 2023. "Campus Connections for Creative Careers: Social Capital, Gender Inequality, and Artistic Work." *Poetics* 96:101763.

Matusik, Sharon F., and Charles W. L. Hill. 1998. "The Utilization of Contingent Work, Knowledge Creation, and Competitive Advantage." *Academy of Management Review* 23(4):680–97.

Maume, David J., Beth A. Rubin, and Charles J. Brody. 2014. "Race, Management Citizenship Behavior, and Employees' Commitment and Well-Being." *American Behavioral Scientist* 58(2):309–30.

McCall, George J., and Jerry L. Simmons. [1966] 1978. *Identities and Interactions: An Examination of Human Associations in Everyday Life*. The Free Press.

McClain, Noah, and Ashley Mears. 2012. "Free to Those Who Can Afford It: The Everyday Affordance of Privilege." *Poetics* 40(2):133–49.

McDonnell, Terence E., Dustin S. Stoltz, and Marshall A. Taylor. 2021. "Revision, Reclassification, and Refrigerators." *Sociological Forum* 36(1):1316–44.

McGoey, Linsey. 2012. "The Logic of Strategic Ignorance." *British Journal of Sociology* 63(3):533–76.

Mears, Ashley. 2011. *Pricing Beauty: The Making of a Fashion Model*. University of California Press.

———. 2015. "Working for Free in the VIP: Relational Work and the Production of Consent." *American Sociological Review* 80(6):1099–1122.

Medeiros, Christian. 2014. "Get Ready to Work for Free." *The Varsity*, November 24. https://thevarsity.ca/2014/11/24/get-ready-to-work-for-free/.

Menger, Pierre-Michel. 1999. "Artistic Labor Markets and Careers." *Annual Review of Sociology* 25:541–74.

Merton, Robert K., George G. Reader, and Patricia Kendall, eds. 1957. *The Student-Physician: Introductory Studies in the Sociology of Medical Education*. Harvard University Press.

Messitte, Nick. 2015. "Universal Music Group Sued By Unpaid Interns." *Forbes*, April 30. https://www.forbes.com/sites/nickmessitte/2015/04/30/universal-music-group-sued-by-unpaid-interns/?sh=36555f3b3a79.

Meyer, John W., and Brian Rowan. 1977. "Institutionalized Organizations: Formal Structure as Myth and Ceremony." *American Journal of Sociology* 83(2):340–63.

Mickey, Ethel L. 2022. "The Organization of Networking and Gender Inequality in the New Economy: Evidence from the Tech Industry." *Work and Occupations* 49(4):383–420.

Mijs, Jonathan J. B. 2016. "The Unfulfillable Promise of Meritocracy: Three Lessons and Their Implications for Justice in Education." *Social Justice Research* 29:14–34.

Milkman, Ruth. 1997. *Farewell to the Factory: Auto Workers in the Late Twentieth Century*. University of California Press.

Mills, C. W. 1951. *White Collar: The American Middle Classes*. Oxford University Press.

Moore, David T. 2013. *Engaged Learning in the Academy: Challenges and Possibilities*. Palgrave Macmillan.

Morris, Lara. 2023. "Looking a Gift Horse in the Mouth: Working Students Under the Fair Labor Standards Act." *Washington and Lee Law Review* 80(1): 445–538.

Moss, Philip, and Chris Tilly. 2001. *Stories Employers Tell: Race, Skill, and Hiring in America*. Russell Sage Foundation.

Moss-Pech, Corey. 2021. "The Career Conveyor Belt: How Internships Lead to Unequal Labor Market Outcomes Among College Graduates." *Qualitative Sociology* 44(1):77–102.

Mouw, Ted. 2003. "Social Capital and Finding a Job: Do Contacts Matter?" *American Sociological Review* 68(6):868–98.

Muhamad, Rusnah, Yazkhiruni Yahya, Suhaily Shahimi, and Nurmazilah Mahzan. 2009. "Undergraduate Internship Attachment in Accounting: The Interns Perspective." *International Education Studies* 2(4):49–55.

Narayanan, V. K., Paul M. Olk, and Cynthia V. Fukami. 2010. "Determinants of Internship Effectiveness: An Exploratory Model." *Academy of Management Learning & Education* 9(1):61–80.

National Association of Colleges and Employers. 2022. "The 2022 Student Survey Report: Attitudes, Preferences, and Outcomes of Bachelor's Degree Students at Four-Year Schools." September. https://www.naceweb.org/store/2022/2022-nace-student-survey-report-and-dashboard-4-year.

———. N.d. "What Is Career Readiness?" https://www.naceweb.org/career-readiness/competencies/career-readiness-defined/.

National Center for Education Statistics. 2021a. "Digest of Education Statistics: 2021." US Department of Education. https://nces.ed.gov/programs/digest/d21/.

———. 2021b. *National Postsecondary Student Aid Study: 2020 Undergraduate Students (NPSAS:UG)*. US Department of Education.

Neely, Megan T. 2020. "The Portfolio Ideal Worker: Insecurity and Inequality in the New Economy." *Qualitative Sociology* 43(2):271–96.

———. 2022. *Hedged Out: Inequality and Insecurity on Wall Street*. University of California Press.

Neff, Gina. 2012. *Venture Labor: Work and the Burden of Risk in Innovative Industries*. MIT Press.

Neff, Gina, Elizabeth Wissinger, and Sharon Zukin. 2005. "Entrepreneurial Labor Among Cultural Producers: 'Cool' Jobs in 'Hot' Industries." *Social Semiotics* 15(3):307–34.

Negus, Keith. 1999. *Music Genres and Corporate Cultures*. Routledge.

Nelson, Jennifer L., and Steven P. Vallas. 2021. "Race and Inequality at Work: An Occupational Perspective." *Sociology Compass* 15(10): e12926.

Nichols, Bethany J., David S. Pedulla, and Jeff T. Sheng. 2023. "More Than a Match: 'Fit' as a Tool in Hiring Decisions." *Work and Occupations* 52(2):175–203.

Oakley, Kate, and Dave O'Brien. 2016. "Learning to Labour Unequally: Understanding the Relationship Between Cultural Production, Cultural Consumption and Inequality." *Social Identities* 22(5):471–86.

Oakley, Kate, Daniel Laurison, Dave O'Brien, and Sam Friedman. 2017. "Cultural Capital: Arts Graduates, Spatial Inequality, and London's Impact on Cultural Labor Markets." *American Behavioral Scientist* 61(12):1510–31.

O'Brien, Dave, Daniel Laurison, Andrew Miles, and Sam Friedman. 2016. "Are the Creative Industries Meritocratic? An Analysis of the 2014 British Labour Force Survey." *Cultural Trends* 25(2):116–31.

Occhiuto, Nicholas. Forthcoming. "Who's an Expert and Why Does It Matter?: How Social and Economic Inequalities Shape the Production and Recognition of Expertise." *Research in the Sociology of Organizations*.

Ocejo, Richard E. 2017. *Masters of Craft: Old Jobs in the New Urban Economy*. Princeton University Press.

Okay-Somerville, Belgin, and Dora Scholarios. 2022. "Focused for Some, Exploratory for Others: Job Search Strategies and Successful University-to-Work Transitions in the Context of Labor Market Ambiguity." *Journal of Career Development* 49(1):126–43.

Olen, Helaine. 2013. "Today's Internship Economy Is Widening the Wealth Gap in America." *The Guardian*, June 4. https://www.theguardian.com/money/us-money-blog/2013/jun/04/unpaid-internship-paying-for-experience-lebron-james.

Olson, Isaac. 2019. "Thousands of Quebec Students Launch Week-long Strike Against Unpaid Internships." *CBC*, March 18. https://www.cbc.ca/news/canada/montreal/unpaid-internship-strike-1.5060666.

O'Mahony, Siobhan, and Beth A. Bechky. 2006. "Stretchwork: Managing the Career Progression Paradox in External Labor Markets." *Academy of Management Journal* 49(5):918–41.

Ortner, Craig J. 1998. "Adapting Title VII to Modern Employment Realities: The Case for the Unpaid Intern." *Fordham Law Review* 66:2613–24.

Page, Libby. 2013. "Intern Protest: 'All I Want for Christmas Is Pay.'" *The Guardian*, December 16. http://www.theguardian.com/education/2013/dec/16/unpaid-internship-christmas-protest-serpentine-gallery.

Parker III, Eugene T., Cindy A. Kilgo, Jessica K. E. Sheets, and Ernest T. Pascarella. 2016. "The Differential Effects of Internship Participation on End-of-Fourth-Year GPA by Demographic and Institutional Characteristics." *Journal of College Student Development* 57(1):104–9.

Pascarella, Ernest T., and Patrick T. Terenzini. 2005. *How College Affects Students: A Third Decade of Research*. Vol. 2. Jossey-Bass.

Pearlman, Lou, Sean Combs, Jonathan Murray, and Mary-Ellis Bunim. 2002. *Making the Band*. ABC/MTV.

Pedulla, David S. 2016. "Penalized or Protected? Gender and the Consequences of Nonstandard and Mismatched Employment Histories." *American Sociological Review* 81(2):262–89.

———. 2020. *Making the Cut: Hiring Decisions, Bias, and the Consequences of Nonstandard, Mismatched, and Precarious Employment.* Princeton University Press.

Perna, Mark C. 2024. "New LinkedIn Data: Internships Are Really, Really Worth It." *Forbes*, June 4. https://www.forbes.com/sites/markcperna/2024/06/04/are-internships-worth-it/.

Peterson, Richard A. 1990. "Why 1955? Explaining the Advent of Rock Music." *Popular Music* 9(1):97–116.

Peterson, Richard A., and Anand, N. 2002. "How Chaotic Careers Create Orderly Fields." In *Career Creativity: Explorations in the Remaking of Work*, edited by M. A. Peiperl, M. B. Arthur, and N. Anand. Oxford University Press.

Perlin, Ross. 2011a. "Unpaid Interns, Complicit Colleges." *New York Times*, April 2. https://www.nytimes.com/2011/04/03/opinion/03perlin.html.

———. 2011b. *Intern Nation: How to Earn Nothing and Learn Little in the Brave New Economy*. Verso.

———. 2013. "*Black Swan* Event: The Beginning of the End of Unpaid Internships." *Time*, June 13. https://business.time.com/2013/06/13/black-swan-event-the-beginning-of-the-end-of-unpaid-internships/.

———. 2015. "Interns, Victimized Yet Again." *New York Times*, July 3. https://www.nytimes.com/2015/07/03/opinion/interns-victimized-yet-again.html.

Pham, Alex. 2011. "EMI Group Sold as Two Separate Pieces to Universal Music and Sony." *Los Angeles Times*, November 12. http://articles.latimes.com/2011/nov/12/business/la-fi-ct-emi-sold-20111112-68.

Pianko, Daniel. 1996. "Power Internships." *Management Review* 85(12):31–33.

Podolny, Joel M. 2005. *Status Signals: A Sociological Study of Market Competition*. Princeton University Press.

Pretentious Film Majors. 2014. "Mitch Hurwitz on Starting Out, Becoming a Writer & Golden Girls (Interview 1/2)." YouTube. Posted by Pretentious Film Majors, October 26. https://www.youtube.com/watch?v=e9AVI2jm5eI.

Pugh, Allison J. 2014. "The Theoretical Costs of Ignoring Childhood: Rethinking Independence, Insecurity, and Inequality." *Theory and Society* 43(1):71–89.

Quadlin, Natasha. 2018. "The Mark of a Woman's Record: Gender and Academic Performance in Hiring." *American Sociological Review* 83(2):331–60.

Radcliffe-Brown, Alfred R. 1940. "On Joking Relationships." *Africa* 13(3):195–210.

Rao, Aliya H. 2020. *Crunch Time: How Married Couples Confront Unemployment*. University of California Press.

Rao, Tejal. 2023. "Fine Dining and the Ethics of Noma's Meticulously Crafted Fruit Beetle." *New York Times*, January 24. https://www.nytimes.com/2023/01/24/dining/noma-fruit-beetle-fine-dining.html.

Ray, Victor. 2019. "A Theory of Racialized Organizations." *American Sociological Review* 84(1):26–53.

Raymond, Nate. 2015. "Warner Music to Pay $4.2 Million to End Intern Wage Lawsuit." *Reuters*, June 10. https://www.reuters.com/article/lifestyle/warner-music-to-pay-42-million-to-end-intern-wage-lawsuit-idUSKBN0OQ2KB/.

Redden, Elizabeth. 2018. "Study Abroad Numbers Grow." *Inside Higher Ed*, November 12. https://www.insidehighered.com/news/2018/11/13/study-abroad-numbers-continue-grow-driven-continued-growth-short-term-programs.

Rensin, David. 2004. *The Mailroom: Hollywood History from the Bottom Up*. Ballantine Books.

Ridgeway, Cecilia L., and Shelley J. Correll. 2004. "Motherhood as a Status Characteristic." *Journal of Social Issues* 60(4):683–700.

Ridgeway, Cecilia L., and Susan Fisk. 2012. "Class Rules, Status Dynamics, and 'Gateway' Interactions." In *Facing Social Class: How Societal Rank Influences Interaction*, edited by S. T. Fiske and H. R. Markus. Russell Sage.

Rivera, Lauren A. 2015a. "Go with Your Gut: Emotion and Evaluation in Job Interviews." *American Journal of Sociology* 120(5):1339–89.

———. 2015b. *Pedigree: How Elite Students Get Elite Jobs*. Princeton University Press.

———. 2017. "When Two Bodies Are (Not) a Problem: Gender and Relationship Status Discrimination in Academic Hiring." *American Sociological Review* 82(6):1111–38.

Rivera, Lauren A., and András Tilcsik. 2016. "Class Advantage, Commitment Penalty: The Gendered Effect of Social Class Signals in an Elite Labor Market." *American Sociological Review* 81(6):1097–1131.

Roksa, Josipa, and Karen J. Robinson. 2022. "From in Loco Parentis to Consumer Choice: Examining the Changing Relationship Between Students and Higher-Education Institutions in the United States." In *Routledge Handbook of the Sociology of Higher Education*, edited by J. E. Côté and S. Pickard. Routledge.

Roksa, Josipa, and Blake R. Silver. 2019. "'Do-It-Yourself' University: Institutional and Family Support in the Transition Out of College." *Review of Higher Education* 42(3):1051–71.

Rolston, Clyde P., and David Herrera. 2000. "The Critical Role of University-Sponsored Internships for Entry into the Professional Music Business: A Report of a National Survey." *Journal of Arts Management, Law, and Society* 30(2):102–12.

Roscigno, Vincent J., Sherry Mong, Reginald Byron, and Griff Tester. 2007. "Age Discrimination, Social Closure and Employment." *Social Forces* 86(1):313–34.

Rosenbaum, James E. 2001. *Beyond College for All: Career Paths for the Forgotten Half*. Russell Sage Foundation.

Ross, Andrew. 2003. *No-Collar: The Humane Workplace and Its Hidden Costs*. Basic Books.

Rothman, Miriam, and Marc Lampe. 2010. "Business School Internships: Sources and Resources." *Psychological Reports* 106(2):548–54.

Roussel, Violaine. 2017. *Representing Talent: Hollywood Agents and the Making of Movies*. University of Chicago Press.

Roy, William G., and Timothy J. Dowd. 2010. "What Is Sociological About Music?" *Annual Review of Sociology* 36:183–203.

Ruppel, Emily H. 2024. "How Work Becomes Invisible: The Erosion of the Wage Floor for Workers with Disabilities." *American Sociological Review* 89(5):907–36.

Saichaie, Kem, and Christopher C. Morphew. 2014. "What College and University Websites Reveal About the Purposes of Higher Education." *Journal of Higher Education* 85(4):499–530.

Saldaña, Johnny. 2016. *The Coding Manual for Qualitative Researchers*. Sage.

Sallaz, Jeffrey J. 2009. *The Labor of Luck: Casino Capitalism in the United States and South Africa*. University of California Press.

Sauder, Michael, and Wendy N. Espeland. 2006. "Strength in Numbers? The Advantages of Multiple Rankings." *Indiana Law Journal* 81(1):205–28.

———. 2009. "The Discipline of Rankings: Tight Coupling and Organizational Change." *American Sociological Review* 74(1):63–82.

Schaeffer, Katherine. 2022. "10 Facts about Today's College Graduates." Pew Research Center, April 12. https://pewrsr.ch/3uATci3.

Schein, Edgar H., and John Van Maanen. 2016. "Career Anchors and Job/Role Planning: Tools for Career and Talent Management." *Organizational Dynamics* 45:165–73.

Scott, Allen J. 1999. "The US Recorded Music Industry: On the Relations Between Organization, Location, and Creativity in the Cultural Economy." *Environment and Planning A: Economy and Space* 31(11):1965–84.

Sennett, Richard. 1998. *The Corrosion of Character: The Personal Consequences of Work in the New Capitalism*. Norton.

Shade, Leslie R., and Jenna Jacobson. 2015. "Hungry for the Job: Gender, Unpaid Internships, and the Creative Industries." *Sociological Review* 63(1):188–205.

Shandra, Carrie L. 2022. "Internship Participation in the United States by Student and School Characteristics, 1994 to 2017." *Socius* 8:1–4.

Sharone, Ofer. 2013. *Flawed System/Flawed Self: Job Searching and Unemployment Experiences*. University of Chicago Press.

———. 2017. "LinkedIn or LinkedOut? How Social Networking Sites Are Reshaping the Labor Market." *Research in the Sociology of Work* 30:1–31.

Shellenbarger, Sue. 2009. "Do You Want an Internship? It'll Cost You." *Wall Street Journal*, January 28. https://www.wsj.com/articles/SB123310699999022549.

Sheriff, Lucy. 2013. "Alexander McQueen's Unpaid Internship Provokes Angry Students' Letter." *Huffington Post*, January 8. http://www.huffingtonpost.co.uk/2013/07/30/alexander-mcqueen-unpaid-internship_n_3675383.html?ir=UK+Universities+%26+Education.

Siciliano, Michael L. 2021. *Creative Control: The Ambivalence of Work in the Culture Industries*. Columbia University Press.

Siegemund-Broka, Austin. 2013. "Sony, Columbia Records Next in Line for Internship Lawsuit." *Hollywood Reporter*, August 9. https://www.hollywoodreporter.com/business/business-news/sony-columbia-records-next-line-602841/.

———. 2014. "Former Intern Drops Lawsuit Against CBS, David Letterman's Company." *Hollywood Reporter*, September 10. https://www.hollywoodreporter.com/business/business-news/intern-drops-lawsuit-cbs-david-732091/.

Simon, Samantha J. 2024. *Before the Badge: How Academy Training Shapes Police Violence*. New York University Press.

Skaggs, Rachel. 2019a. "Harmonizing Small-Group Cohesion and Status in Creative Collaborations: How Songwriters Facilitate and Manipulate the Cowriting Process." *Social Psychology Quarterly* 82(4):367–85.

———. 2019b. "Socializing Rejection and Failure in Artistic Occupational Communities." *Work and Occupations* 46(2):149–75.

———. 2022. "Trend Accommodation in Heteronomous Fields: How Established Artists Respond to Changing Conventions." *Poetics* 94:101711.

Smith, Vicki. 1997. "New Forms of Work Organizations." *Annual Review of Sociology* 23:315–39.

———. 2001. *Crossing the Great Divide: Worker Risk and Opportunity in the New Economy*. Cornell University Press.

———. 2010. "Enhancing Employability: Human, Cultural, and Social Capital in an Era of Turbulent Unpredictability." *Human Relations* 63(2):279–300.

Smith, Vicki, and Esther B. Neuwirth. 2008. *The Good Temp*. ILR Press/Cornell University Press.

Spangler, Todd. 2021. "Intern Blamed for HBO Max Email Snafu Receives Outpouring of Support Online." *Variety*, June 19. https://variety.com/2021/digital/news/hbo-max-email-snafu-intern-1235000742/.

Spence, Michael. 1973. "Job Market Signaling." *Quarterly Journal of Economics* 87(3):355–74.

Stahl, Matt. 2012. *Unfree Masters: Popular Music and the Politics of Work*. Duke University Press.

Standing, Guy. 2011. *The Precariat: The New Dangerous Class*. Bloomsbury Academic.

Stanton, Kate. 2016. "The Rise of the Middle-Aged Intern." *BBC News*, April 28. https://www.bbc.com/news/business-36129892.

Sterling, Adina D., and Roberto M. Fernandez. 2018. "Once in the Door: Gender, Tryouts, and the Initial Salaries of Managers." *Management Science* 64(11):5444–60.

Sterling, Adina, and Jennifer Merluzzi. 2019. "A Longer Way In: Tryouts as Alternative Hiring Arrangements in Organizations." *Research in Organizational Behavior* 39:100122.

Sternlicht, Alexandra. 2022. "Meet the 28-Year-Old Behind the White House's Decision to Pay Its Interns." *Forbes*, June 4. https://www.forbes.com/sites/alexandrasternlicht/2022/06/03/meet-the-28-year-old-behind-the-white-houses-decision-to-pay-its-interns/.

Stevens, Mitchell L., Elizabeth A. Armstrong, and Richard Arum. 2008. "Sieve, Incubator, Temple, Hub: Empirical and Theoretical Advances in the Sociology of Higher Education." *Annual Review of Sociology* 34:127–51.

Stokes, Allyson. 2017. "Fashioning Gender: The Gendered Organization of Cultural Work." *Social Currents* 4(6): 518–34.

Streib, Jessi. 2023. *The Accidental Equalizer: How Luck Determines Pay After College*. University of Chicago Press.

Stuber, Jenny M. 2011. *Inside the College Gates: How Class and Culture Matter in Higher Education*. Lexington Books.

Sun, Rebecca. 2021. "CAA Revamps Agent Trainee Program with Business, Inclusion Focus (Exclusive)." *Hollywood Reporter*, February 4. https://www.hollywoodreporter.com/business/ business-news/caa-revamps-agent-trainee-program-with-business-inclusion-focus-exclusive-4127698/.

Sweet, Paige L. 2019. "The Sociology of Gaslighting." *American Sociological Review* 84(5):851–75.

Taketa, Kristen. 2014. "At UCLA, Hillary Clinton Condemns Russian Actions in Ukraine." *Daily Bruin*, March 5. https://dailybruin.com/2014/03/05/at-ucla-hillary-clinton-condemns-russian-actions-in-ukraine.

Taylor, Judith, and Kim de Laat. 2013. "Feminist Internships and the Depression of Political Imagination: Implications for Women's Studies." *Feminist Formations* 25(1):84–110.

Taylor, Paul, Kim Parker, Rakesh Kochhar, Richard Fry, Cary Funk, Eileen Patten, and Seth Motel. 2012. "Young, Underemployed and Optimistic: Coming of Age, Slowly, in a Tough Economy." Pew Research Center. http://pewrsr.ch/z3aWPE.

Taylor, Paul, Rick Fry, and Russ Oates. 2014. "The Rising Cost of Not Going to College." Pew Research Center, February 11. http://pewrsr.ch/1eNG64Z.

Thébaud, Sarah, and Catherine J. Taylor. 2021. "The Specter of Motherhood: Culture and the Production of Gendered Career Aspirations in Science and Engineering." *Gender & Society* 35(3):395–421.

The Chronicle of Higher Education/Marketplace. 2012. "The Role of Higher Education in Career Development: Employer Perceptions." http://chronicle.com/items/biz/pdf/Employers%20Survey.pdf.

Tilly, Charles. 1998. *Durable Inequality*. University of California Press.

Titus, Kristen. 2021. "Is the Entry Level Job Going Extinct?" *Quartz*, May 11. https://qz.com/work/200750 o/is-the-entry-level-job-going-extinct.

Tokumitsu, Miya. 2015. *Do What You Love: And Other Lies About Success & Happiness*. Simon and Schuster.

Tomlinson, Michael. 2024. "Conceptualising Transitions from Higher Education to Employment: Navigating Liminal Spaces." *Journal of Youth Studies* 27(8):1079–96.

Torche, Florencia. 2011. "Is a College Degree Still the Great Equalizer? Intergenerational Mobility Across Levels of Schooling in the United States." *American Journal of Sociology* 117(3):763–807.

Trent, John. 2010. "'My Two Masters': Conflict, Contestation, and Identity Construction Within a Teaching Practicum." *Australian Journal of Teacher Education* 35(7):1–14.

Truffaut, François. [1978] 1994. *The Films in My Life*. Translated by L. Mayhew. Da Capo Press.

Tuchman, Gaye. 1973. "Making News by Doing Work: Routinizing the Unexpected." *American Journal of Sociology* 79(1):110–31.

Turner, Victor W. 1967. *The Forest of Symbols: Aspects of Ndembu Ritual*. Cornell University Press.

———. 1969. *The Ritual Process: Structure and Anti-Structure*. Routledge.

US Bureau of Labor Statistics. 2023. *Number of Jobs, Labor Market Experience, Marital Status, and Health for Those Born 1957–1964*. https://www.bls.gov/news.release/nlsoy.nr0.htm.

US Department of Labor, Wage and Hour Division. 2010. *Fact Sheet #71: Internship Programs Under the Fair Labor Standards Act*, April.

Vallas, Steven P., and Angèle Christin. 2018. "Work and Identity in an Era of Precarious Employment: How Workers Respond to 'Personal Branding' Discourse." *Work and Occupations* 45(1):3–37.

van Gennep, Arnold. 1960. *The Rites of Passage*. University of Chicago Press.

Van Maanen, John. 1975. "Police Socialization: A Longitudinal Examination of Job Attitudes in an Urban Police Department." *Administrative Science Quarterly* 20(2):207–28.

———. 1976. "Breaking In: Socialization to Work." In *Handbook of Work, Organization, and Society*, edited by R. Dubin. Rand McNally.

———. 1978. "People Processing: Strategies of Organizational Socialization." *Organizational Dynamics* 7(1):19–36.

———. 1991. "The Smile Factory: Work at Disneyland." In *Reframing Organizational Culture*, edited by P. J. Frost, L. F. Moore, M. R. Louis, C. C. Lundberg, and J. Martin. Sage.

Van Maanen, John, and Edgar H. Schein. 1979. "Towards a Theory of Organizational Socialization." In *Research in Organizational Behavior*, edited by B. M. Staw. JAI Press.

Vande Berg, Michael. 2007. "Intervening in the Learning of US Students Abroad." *Journal of Studies in International Education* 11(3–4):392–99.

Vasel, Kathryn. 2020. "This Is What Internships Look Like in a Remote World." *CNN Business*, July 16. https://www.cnn.com/2020/07/16/success/internship-program-remote-coronavirus/index.html.

Waddoups, C. Jeffrey. 2016. "Did Employers in the United States Back Away from Skills Training During the Early 2000s?" *ILR Review* 69(2):405–34.

Walker, Darren. 2016. "Internships Are Not a Privilege." *New York Times*, July 5. https://www.nytimes.com/2016/07/05/opinion/breaking-a-cycle-that-allows-privilege-to-go-to-privileged.html.

Walling v. Portland Terminal Co., 330 US 148, 152 (1947).

Wanberg, Connie R., Abdifatah A. Ali, and Borbala Csillag. 2020. "Job Seeking: The Process and Experience of Looking for a Job." *Annual Review of Organizational Psychology and Organizational Behavior* 7:315–37.

Warhurst, Chris, and Dennis Nickson. 2001. *Looking Good, Sounding Right: Style Counselling in the New Economy*. The Industrial Society.

Weber, Lauren, and Melissa Korn. 2014. "Where Did All the Entry-Level Jobs Go?" *Wall Street Journal*, August 6. https://www.wsj.com/articles/want-an-entry-level-job-youll-need-lots-of-experience-1407267498.

Weber, Max. [1968] 1978. *Economy and Society: An Outline of Interpretive Sociology*. Translated and edited by G. Roth and C. Wittich. University of California Press.

Weick, Karl E. 1995. *Sensemaking in Organizations*. Sage.

Whyte Jr., William H. 1956. *The Organization Man*. Doubleday Anchor.

Williams, Alex. 2014. "For Interns, All Work and No Payoff." *New York Times*, February 16. https://www.nytimes.com/2014/02/16/fashion/millennials-internships.html.

Williams, Christine L. 2021. *Gaslighted: How the Oil and Gas Industry Shortchanges Women Scientists*. University of California Press.

Williams, Christine L., and Catherine Connell. 2010. "'Looking Good and Sounding Right': Aesthetic Labor and Social Inequality in the Retail Industry." *Work and Occupations* 37(3):349–77.

Williams, Joan. 2000. *Unbending Gender: Why Family and Work Conflict and What to Do about It*. Oxford University Press.

Willis, Paul. 1977. *Learning to Labour: How Working Class Kids Get Working Class Jobs*. Columbia University Press.

Wilson, Eli R. 2022. "Privileging Passion: How the Cultural Logic of Work Perpetuates Social Inequality in the Craft Beer Industry." *Socius* 8:1–12.

Winchester, Daniel, and Kyle D. Green. 2019. "Talking Your Self into It: How and When Accounts Shape Motivation for Action." *Sociological Theory* 37(3): 257–81.

Wohl, Hannah. 2021. *Bound by Creativity: How Contemporary Art Is Created and Judged*. University of Chicago Press.

Wolfgram, Matthew, and Vivien Ahrens. 2022. "'One Internship, Two Internships, Three Internships . . . More!': Exploring the Culture of the Multiple Internship Economy." *Journal of Education and Work* 35(2):139–53.

Wynn, Jonathan R. 2011a. "The Hobo to Doormen: The Characters of Qualitative Analysis, Past and Present." *Ethnography* 12(4):518–42.

———. 2011b. *The Tour Guide: Walking and Talking New York*. University of Chicago Press.

Yamada, David C. 2002. "The Employment Law Rights of Student Interns." *Connecticut Law Review* 35:215–57.

———. 2016. "The Legal and Social Movement Against Unpaid Internships." *Northeastern University Law Journal* 8(2):357–96.

Zafirau, Stephen. 2008. "Reputation Work in Selling Film and Television: Life in the Hollywood Talent Industry." *Qualitative Sociology* 31:99–127.

ACKNOWLEDGMENTS

THE PROJECT from which this book sprung began as my doctoral dissertation, and as such this book is the culmination of my breaking into academia. Since breaking in sometimes occurs over an extensive period and in multiple locales, as was the case for me, at best I only have the space to name a small portion of the people who had a direct impact on this project.

This book would not exist if not for the generosity of the people who gave me their time, shared their stories, allowed me to be part of their world, and at times helped me understand why I needed to write this book.

I am grateful to the friends and mentors I met at the Graduate Center, City University of New York (CUNY), where this project began. From my first day in graduate school, Rich Ocejo and I became immediate friends, routinely exchanging ideas, stories, encouragement, helpful advice, and talking about the arts (music, film, and hockey). It was not immediately clear to me that so many years later we would be doing the same things, but he would also offer in-depth feedback on this book. I also feel very fortunate that my time at CUNY allowed me to meet Jon Wynn, who was writing his dissertation at the time and yet I consider him my first real academic mentor. In the years since, Jon taught me as much about sociology as a discipline and a profession as anyone. While at CUNY, I also benefited from friendships with and critical comments from Jeff London, Colin Jerolmack, Josh Howard, Patrick Inglis, Amy Jones, Benjamin Haber, Michael Crowder, and Ervin Kosta.

As a graduate student, I greatly benefited from my frequent conversations with my dissertation advisor, Paul Attewell. I remain impressed by his ability to combine a remarkable breadth of knowledge, reassuringly calm demeanor, and sustained, careful attention to his students' progress and well-being. Like Paul, Sharon Zukin was among those who saw the early promise of this project and helped me formulate some initial research questions. Her detailed feedback helped shape this book. Bill Kornblum and Mitch Duneier taught me how to do fieldwork and inspired me to read works from the Chicago School tradition. This project came out of an ethnography class with Mitch, and I am grateful that he insisted I continue this research. Throughout my years as a graduate student, I was also fortunate to receive helpful insights from scholars including Stanley Aronowitz, Max Besbris, Sarah Daynes, Tim Dowd, Cynthia Fuchs Epstein, Stuart Ewen, Ashley Mears, and Vicki Smith.

A key turning point for this book, and for my life in general, came when Steven Tepper took a chance on me. Steven hired me as a postdoctoral scholar at Arizona State University's Herberger Institute for Design and the Arts, where I learned much about the education and career patterns of cultural workers. He entrusted me to write a report on internships for the Strategic National Arts Alumni Project (SNAAP), and to design a set of SNAAP survey questions on internships. My time at Arizona State University also allowed me to see higher education from the perspective of the dean's office, allowing me to realize the importance (and promise) of these institutions in the intern economy. During this time, I also gained greatly from conversations with Nathan Martin, who offered feedback on this book, as well as John Parker, Deborah Sussman, Jennifer Janicki, Linda Essig, Greg Esser, Adam Hunt, Derek Brennan, Sarah Hough, and Jen Setlow.

Since arriving at Vanderbilt University, I have benefited from Dan Cornfield's remarkably generous mentorship. Every time we spoke about this book—which probably happened more times than I wish to admit—Dan successfully encouraged me to further deepen and broaden my thinking, always with great patience and kindness. Gillian Gualtieri, one of the smartest people I've ever met, somehow worked as my postdoc during the peak of the pandemic to help me collect and code data; her insights and friendship made this book much better. Also at Vanderbilt, I have learned so much from colleagues who offered insights and support along the way, including Bianca Manago, Holly McCammon, Jake Watson, Laura Carpenter, Rachel Donnelly, Richard Pitt, and Sandy Cherry. I also received superb research assistance from Katie Beekman, who helped me review the literature, offered a close reading of the manuscript, and even helped convince me to keep this book title. In addition, I appreciate the research assistance I received from Megan Robinson, Michael Hendricks, Adam Schoenbachler, Savannah Bastian, and Matthew Tarizzo. Moreover, some of this research was supported by the Curb Center, my other home at Vanderbilt University, and I thank Jay Clayton, Leah Lowe, David Wilson, and Rachel Thompson. During my time at Vanderbilt, this book was also partly supported by an award from Research Grants in the Arts program at the National Endowment for the Arts (Grant# 1891792-38-22).

Many other scholars offered insights that informed the manuscript, notably the members of a book workshop organized by Clayton Childress, including Rachel Skaggs, Angèle Christin, and Vanina Leschziner. I also incorporated feedback from conversations with Matthew Hora, Mary Blair-Loy, Amy Binder, Quan Mai, Vaughn Schmutz, and Joan Meyers.

Thank you to the anonymous reviewers of this book for offering such generous feedback. Also, thank you to Princeton University Press, especially Rachael Levay and Tara Dugan, for shepherding this project along and to Meagan Levinson, for seeing the early promise of this work. The manuscript gained from copyediting by Leah Caldwell and Jennifer Eggerling-Boeck.

I want to thank my friends and family for their encouragement during every step of my academic career. My brothers, Nick and Marc, and my almost-brothers, Anshu Bhargava, Philippe Tremblay, Frederic Babin, and Stephen Billick, helped me stay grounded. My grandparents, from an early age, helped nurture my staunch belief in the value of education. In many ways I owe everything to my parents, Sharon and André, not least because their sense of humor, curiosity, and empathy continually inspire me. A special thank you goes to my wife, Maggie, who moved across the country (twice) to help me break in, and I will forever be grateful for her patience, reassurance, and insights. Lastly, this book is dedicated to our daughter, Simone, whose kindness, creativity, and fierce lust for life propel me every day.

INDEX

A&R (artists and repertoire), 32, 33, 65–66, 74, 119–20, 136, 142, 148, 151, 153
age bias, 135
Alexander McQueen (fashion company), 173
Alger, Horatio, Jr., 104, 108
ambiguity: in breaking-in systems, 6, 12–13, 22–23, 132, 138, 141–42, 148, 164–65, 167–68, 179; in higher education institutions' goals for internships, 13, 26, 167; in internships, 6, 20, 23, 30, 50–63, 65–100, 103, 128, 167, 173, 180, 193n2; in the music industry, 12, 23; in organizational policy and practice goals for internships, 12–13, 26, 50–53; social production of, 30; types of, 23
American Public Media, 8
apprenticeships, 2, 6, 179, 180
Armstrong, Elizabeth, 14
aspirants: age bias faced by, 135; and breaking in, 11, 15–16, 23, 27; competence/commitment of, 27; costs of breaking in borne by, 16; illusionment and disillusionment of, 66, 76, 107; impression management of, 76–77; and mailroom model of training, 104–10, 114–15; in the music industry, 44, 53, 65–66; oversupply of, in the cultural industries, 23–24; personal initiative of, 11, 14, 19, 106; and provisional labor, 15–16; relationship building by, 149; signaling/enacting of competence/commitment by, 133–42; social capital of, 21. *See also* career entry/paths; interns; strategies for success

The Baffler (journal), 106
Bechky, Beth, 121
Becker, Howard, 13–14
Benjamin, Walter, 206n19
Berger, Lauren, 8
bias, in assessment of interns, 134–38, 151. *See also* discrimination
Black, Hugo, 199n3
Black Swan (film), 171–73
blaming the intern, 85, 167, 171, 181, 207n23
breaking in, as a social process: dualistic nature of, 11; individualist perspective contrasted with, 11; myths/scripts underlying, 105; overview of, 11–16; studies of, 68. *See also* breaking-in systems; career entry/paths
breaking-in systems: ambiguity in, 6, 12–13, 22–23, 132, 138, 141–42, 148, 164–65, 167–68, 179; considerations in transforming, 178–81; conventional, 12, 17; inequalities reproduced by, 133, 168; socialization in, 88–90; transformations to conventional, 17–19, 166–69. *See also* breaking in, as a social process; career entry/paths

Brint, Steven, 200n9
Brooklyn College, 137
business/STEM/professional fields: career entry/paths in, 7, 33, 49, 178; internships in, 7, 12–13, 77, 178

career entry/paths: in business/STEM/professional fields, 7, 33, 49, 178; in conventional systems, 17; coordination of work and school regarding, 4, 32, 73–74; in cultural fields, 7, 10; effects of higher education on, 19–20; higher education as preparation for, 20, 24, 31, 33–35, 37–43; internships as barrier to, 8, 10, 195n31; internships linked to success in, 4, 9, 34; internships typically viewed as, 1–2, 7–10, 12–13, 16, 20, 35, 44, 104, 159, 166–67, 206n15; job-search process and, 21–22; Job Seekers and, 73–75; for marginalized groups, 10, 178; oversupply of workers as complicating factor for, 10, 15, 23–24; paid/unpaid internships and, 9, 177–78; personal responsibility for, 11, 14, 18–19, 21, 106–9; transformations to conventional, 17–19, 166–69; work experience required for, 1, 19, 20. *See also* aspirants; breaking in, as a social process; breaking-in systems
CBS (television network), 172
cheap labor, interns as, 31, 51–54, 62, 90, 103, 115, 167, 206n18
Chronicle of Higher Education (news outlet), 8
Clinton, Hillary, 8
clothing, in the workplace, 95–97, 208n32
colleges. *See* higher education institutions
Columbia Records, 24
Combs, Sean (aka Puff Daddy, P. Diddy, Puffy), 66, 112, 114
competence/commitment: employees' perception of interns', 26, 68, 78–88, 92; enacting, 138–42; ideal intern norm and, 133–42; signaling of, 20–22, 133–38
Condé Nast Publications, 10, 175
Cooper, Anderson, 171
Creative Artists Agency, 105
credentials, internships as, 78–80, 83–84
cultural capital: inequalities associated with, 15, 137–38; participation in internships linked to, 49; relationship building and, 150; tactful proactiveness and, 133, 148. *See also* social capital; tactful proactiveness
cultural industries: career pathways in, 7, 10; internship conditions in, 10; linking the educational to the practical in, 36–37; oversupply of workers in, 10, 15, 23–24; precarity in, 10, 25. *See also* music industry

Davis, Tina, 65
Def Jam, 107
Diller, Barry, 105
discrimination, 136, 200n6. *See also* bias
Disney College Program, 170, 216n6, 216n7
Douglas, Mary, 178–79
Drucker, Peter, 19

economic capital: extended investment and, 133; inequalities associated with, 9, 15, 44, 49, 164. *See also* extended investment
educators. *See* higher education institutions
Eisner, Michael, 209n8
employees/employers/supervisors: ambiguity in internship-related goals of, 50–52, 167; attitude toward/treatment of interns by, 2,

4–6, 13–14, 24, 26, 51–52, 67–68, 77–89, 94, 104, 109–16, 134–38, 142–43, 151–59, 180, 205n8; complaints about corporate changes to paid/unpaid internships, 175–77; former interns as, 4–5, 111–14; higher education institutions' relationship with, 29–31, 42–43; higher education institutions' vetting of, 57; and the hiring process, 8, 22; precarity of employees, 12, 18, 24, 77, 94, 104; selecting interns, 52–53, 206n18. *See also* mailroom model of training; organizational policies and practices
Enthusiasts (intern type), 26, 71–73, 77
experiential learning, 13, 28, 33, 37–38, 42, 44, 63, 170, 180
exploitation of interns, 8, 15–16, 59–62, 103, 167, 169–74
extended investment (intern strategy), 27, 132–33, 159–64

Fair Labor Standards Act (1938), 17, 199n3
Faulkner, Robert, 66
first-generation college students, 10, 44, 49, 63, 137, 177
Footman, Alexander, 171–72
Forbes (magazine), 167
Fox Entertainment Group, 172
Fox Searchlight Pictures, 171–72

Geffen, David, 105
gender: division of labor by, 136; inequality or bias, 133, 135, 136, 151, 178, 207n21, 212n7; sexual harassment, 30, 136, 200n6
Génération Précaire, 174
Glaeser, Edward, 9
Glatt, Eric, 170–72
Goffman, Erving, 89, 130, 211n2
Granovetter, Mark, 21

Hamilton, Laura, 14
Handshake (online recruitment platform), 47, 49–50
hazing, 5, 111–12, 114
Henley, Don, 115
hidden curriculum: in higher education, 13–14; in internships, 144, 148, 168; in workplaces, 13–14
higher education institutions: ambiguity in internship-related goals of, 13, 26, 167; career opportunities provided by, 14–15, 35; and career preparation, 20, 24, 31, 33–35, 37–43; complex and competing expectations/demands placed on, 30–31, 33, 37–43, 180, 196n43; criticisms of, 20, 58–63, 116–22, 125; employers' relationships with, 29–31, 42–43; hidden curriculum of, 13–14; inequalities addressed by, 177; inequalities reproduced by, 14–15; intern economy reproduced by, 58–63; internships linked to, 20–21, 28–64; liberal arts mission of, 33, 41, 200n9; marketization of, 201n11; music business programs in, 30, 33, 46, 66, 69–70, 116–23, 179–80, 204n3, 210n17; practical arts programs in, 200n9; return on investment as criterion applied to, 35, 37–41, 48; tuition and the cost of, 20, 30, 37–40; vetting and overseeing internships, 3, 6, 10, 55–58, 173; work transformations' effect on demand for, 19. *See also* internships-for-all policies
hiring process, 8, 22
Hughes, Everett, 17, 211n1

Ibarra, Herminia, 208n2
ideal intern norm, 27, 130, 132–38. *See also* interns: "good"
ideal worker norm, 133–34, 212n7

impression management, 76–77, 151
industry cool, 95–100, 157, 207n29
inequalities: educational system's reproduction of, 14–15; gender-based, 133, 135, 136, 151, 178, 207n21, 212n7; higher education institutions' attempts to address, 177; among interns, 163–64; internships as means of addressing socioeconomic, 45; in the labor market, 133; in the nature and practice of internships, 6, 9, 63, 168, 176–77; paid/unpaid internships and, 177–78; race-based, 133, 135–38, 151, 212n8; recommendations for addressing, 27; reproduced by the breaking-in system, 133, 168; in students' socioeconomic resources, 9, 15, 44, 49, 63, 115, 164
International Coalition for Fair Internships, 174
international students, 177, 216n23
Intern Aware, 174
Intern Labor Rights, 173
interns: abusive treatment of, 7, 10, 30, 109–14; attitude, behavior, and personality of, 95–102, 108, 114–15, 130, 146–48, 155–57; "bad," 82, 85; biases in assessments of, 134–37, 151; blaming, 85, 167, 171, 181, 207n23; as cheap labor, 31, 51–54, 62, 90, 103, 115, 167, 206n18; competence/commitment of, 26, 68, 78–88; coordination of work and school by, 4, 32, 73–74, 125, 161–62; disappointments experienced by, 6, 162–63, 171; economic barriers faced by, 9, 15, 44, 49, 164; employees' attitude toward/treatment of, 2, 4–6, 13–14, 24, 26, 51–52, 67–68, 77–89, 94, 104, 109–16, 134–38, 142–43, 151–59, 180, 205n8; exploitation of, 8, 15–16, 59–62, 103, 167, 169–74; first-generation college students as, 10, 44, 49, 63, 177; "good," 27, 85, 94, 132, 140, 141 (*see also* ideal intern norm); head/lead, 151, 159, 161–64, 175, 214n26; hours worked by, 60–61, 139, 145, 159–62; impression management by, 76–77, 151; inequalities among, 163–64; international students as, 177, 216n23; and knowing one's place or fitting in, 69–70, 89, 134, 146–48, 151, 157, 165; mistakes made by, 70–71, 85–88, 92; names of, 5, 96–97, 111, 150–51; onboarding, 91–94; relationship building by, 27, 76, 132–33, 149–59; responsible for their own education and advancement, 3–4, 14, 27, 45–50, 59–61, 66–67, 74, 79–81, 94, 101–4, 107–9, 122–27, 142–48, 167; rights activism concerning, 173–74; seniority of, 159; shared, 154, 214n30; signaling/enacting of competence/commitment by, 133–42; socialization of, 12, 59–60, 88–100, 130, 146–48, 196n36; stigma attached to, 130, 155, 162, 180, 211n2; suffering of, normalized by hosts, 26, 59, 104, 109–16, 121; types/motivations of, 26, 68–69, 75–77, 85, 100. *See also* aspirants; Enthusiasts; ideal intern norm; internships-for-all policies; Job Seekers; mailroom model of training; provisional labor; strategies for success; Students
The Internship (film), 135
internships and intern economy: ambiguities in, 6, 20, 23, 30, 50–63, 65–100, 103, 128, 167, 173, 180, 193n2; "bad," 58, 62–63; benefits of, 34; in business, STEM, and the professions, 7, 12–13, 77, 178; as career pathway, 1–2, 7–10, 12–13, 16, 20, 35, 44, 104, 159, 166–67, 206n15; concept and purpose of, 1–2; as

credentials, 78–80, 83–84; critiques of, 1–6, 8–9, 169–74; in cultural fields, 7; demand for, 43–46; discontinuation of, 174–77; educational value of, 28–29, 34–37, 53–58, 70, 79, 104, 116–22, 125, 170, 175; expansion of, 2, 7–8, 166–67, 179; exploitation as issue in, 8, 15–16, 59–62, 103; extending, 159–64; guidance provided in, 2–4, 6, 91–93, 101–2; higher education institutions' role in reproducing, 58–63; higher education institutions' vetting of, 55–58; higher education linked to, 20–21, 28–64; inequalities in the nature and practice of, 6, 9, 63, 168, 176–77; music business–related, 30, 46, 56–57, 66, 69–70, 116, 119–22, 204n3; observation as valuable aspect of, 123–27; on-site learning in, 116–27; perks and other intangible benefits in, 72, 97, 205n9; personal branding via choice of, 21; reframing of negative experiences in, 58–63; return-on-investment associated with, 31; social capital accrued through, 21–22; socioeconomic inequalities addressed by, 45; students' finding and arranging their own, 45–50, 66–67; successful outcomes of, 4, 9, 34; typology of, 194n9; variety and diversity of, 6–7, 9, 29–30. *See also* internships-for-all policies; mailroom model of training; paid/unpaid internships; provisional labor

internships-for-all policies: drawbacks of, 62–63, 79, 103; inequalities reproduced by, 63, 168; purpose of, 15, 33–34, 37, 45; socioeconomic factors underlying, 20, 26, 31, 37–38; varieties of intern motivations resulting from, 77

job-search process, 21–22

Job Seekers (intern type), 26, 73–75, 77, 206n15

labor. *See* cheap labor; ideal worker norm; provisional labor; workers

Lawrence, T. E., 89–90

legal issues: paid/unpaid internships, 9–10, 28–29, 54, 171–74, 199n3; sexual harassment and discrimination, 136, 200n6; worker protection, 17

Lewinsky, Monica, 207n23

Lieberson, Goddard, 24

Liles, Kevin, 107–9

liminality, 110, 167, 181, 208n1, 208n2

LinkedIn, 21

mailroom model of training, 103–28; basic principles of, 103, 104–9, 137, 167, 171; employers' reliance on, 14, 26, 59, 103, 167; interns' responses to, 72, 73; interns' responsibility for their own education and advancement in, 103–4, 122–27; normalization of suffering in, 26, 59, 104, 109–16; osmosis pedagogy and, 104, 122–27; real-life examples of, 105, 107–8, 209n6, 209n8; as superior to formal education, 116–22, 125

Making the Band (television show), 112

Marketplace (radio program), 8

Menger, Pierre-Michel, 24

mentors/mentorship: effective, 7, 30, 93, 114, 151, 176, 178, 180; for first-generation students, 177; inadequate, 7, 10, 30, 53, 61; relationship building with, 73, 152–53, 155; vetting of, 57

meritocracy, 9, 15, 109, 134, 167

methodology. *See* research methodology

minimum wage, 17, 28, 170, 171, 199n3, 204n3, 216n7

Moore, David, 13
music business programs, 30, 33, 46, 56–57, 66, 69–70, 116–23, 179–80, 204n3, 210n17
music industry: ambiguity in, 12, 23; gender bias in, 136; goals of, in hosting internships, 51; internships in, 46, 66, 204n3; motivations of interns in, 68–77; norms of conduct in, 95–101, 207n29; perceptions vs. realities of, 80, 82–85; precarity in, 10, 24–25, 74, 117–18; on-site learning vs. formal education in, 116–27; social capital in, 21; as subject/site of research, 6, 11. *See also* A&R; music business programs

names, in the workplace, 5, 96–97, 111, 150–51
National Association of Colleges and Employers, 9
NBCUniversal, 10, 209n8
networking. *See* relationship building; social capital
New York Times (newspaper), 106, 169
New York University (NYU), 69, 117–18, 137, 173
nonstandard work arrangements, 18
NYU. *See* New York University

Obodaru, Otilia, 208n2
Occupy Wall Street, 173
Office Space (film), 110
onboarding, 91–94
optional activities, 145–46
organizational policies and practices, ambiguity in internship-related goals of, 12–13, 26, 50–53. *See also* employees/employers/supervisors; mailroom model of training
osmosis pedagogy, 104, 122–27, 141
overtime pay, 28
Ovitz, Michael, 105

paid/unpaid internships: in business/STEM/professional vs. cultural fields, 7, 178; career outcomes associated with, 9, 177–78; corporate responses to legal and public scrutiny of, 174–77; employer/supervisor complaints about corporate changes to, 175; exploitation as issue in, 8, 59–61, 103, 167, 169–74; frustrations/hardships of unpaid positions, 67, 115, 162–63; inequalities associated with, 177–78; legal issues with, 9–10, 28–29, 54, 171–74, 199n3; public scrutiny of, 171–74; typical salaries of, 216n7. *See also* internships and intern economy
parents of college students: internship support provided by, 3, 15, 44, 49, 80; ROI demands of, 39–41, 48
passion, 12, 67, 70–72, 83, 85, 97, 100, 114, 153, 195n28, 205n9; 206n18. *See also* Enthusiasts; industry cool
Pauley, William, 172–73
Pay Our Interns, 174
perks, 72, 97, 159, 205n9
Perlin, Ross, 169–71, 216n7
personal brands, 21
Philbin, Regis, 209n8
Plaza, Aubrey, 209n8
precarity: in cultural industries, 10, 25; in employment, 12, 18, 24, 77, 94, 104; in internships, 8, 14; in the music industry, 10, 24–25, 74, 117–18; in provisional labor, 15
Presley, Elvis, 24
professional fields. *See* business/STEM/professional fields
provisional labor: companies' use of interns as, 23, 31, 128, 167; defined, 15, 205n11; exploitative nature of, 15–16; Job Seeker interns and, 72, 205n11; mailroom model and, 104, 128; as necessary stage in career pursuit, 16

race: division of labor by, 136; inequality or bias, 133, 135–38, 151, 212n8
RCA, 24
record industry. *See* music industry

relationship building (intern strategy), 27, 76, 132–33, 149–59. *See also* social capital
Rensin, David, 105
research methodology, 11, 183–91
return on investment (ROI): higher education evaluated according to criterion of, 35, 37–41, 48; internships evaluated according to criterion of, 31
Rihanna, 100
rites of passage, 104, 109–11, 115, 127, 164, 169, 208n2, 210n20
ROI. *See* return on investment
Roussel, Violaine, 206n19

Sandberg, Sheryl, 173–74
sexual harassment, 30, 136, 200n6
Smith, Vicki, 22
SNAAP. *See* Strategic National Arts Alumni Project
social capital: career entry/paths dependent on, 21; inequalities associated with, 15; internships as means to accrue, 21–22; internships procured through, 45–46; relationship building and, 21, 133, 150. *See also* cultural capital; relationship building
socialization of interns, 12, 59–60, 88–100, 130, 196n36. *See also* hazing
Solis, Hilda, 28
Standing, Guy, 8
STEM. *See* business/STEM/professional fields
stigma, 130, 155, 162, 180, 211n2
Strategic National Arts Alumni Project (SNAAP), 9, 43, 46, 49, 178, 206n15
strategies for success, 131–65; enacting the ideal intern norm, 27, 130, 132; extended investment, 27, 132–33, 159–64; relationship building, 27, 76, 132–33, 149–59; tactful proactiveness, 27, 132–33, 142–48
Students (intern type), 26, 69–71, 77
study abroad, 180–81
suffering, normalization of interns', 26, 59, 104, 109–16, 121
supervisors. *See* employees/employers/supervisors
symbolic interactionism, 11–12, 166

tactful proactiveness (intern strategy), 27, 132–33, 142–48
teaching practicums, 180
total institutions, 89–90
Turner, Victor, 208n2, 210n20

United Nations, 174
universities. *See* higher education institutions
Unpaid Interns Lawsuit website, 172
US Department of Education, 193n2
US Department of Labor, 28–29, 173, 193n2
US Second Circuit Court of Appeals, 172
US Supreme Court, 28, 199n3

van Gennep, Arnold, 110
Van Maanen, John, 89–90
Vaughn, Vince, 135
vetting, of internship hosts, 55–58
Viacom, 10

Wage and Hour Division (WHD), US Department of Labor, 28–29
Walker, Darren, 9
Warner Music Group, 10, 108
West, Kanye (aka Ye), 99
White House (US), 174
William Morris Agency, 105
Wilson, Owen, 135
workers, legal protections for, 17. *See also* cheap labor; ideal worker norm; provisional labor
Worldwide Pants, 172

Yamada, David, 171
youth and young adults, employment situations of, 194n18